"Greg Haslam offers us sane, biblical wisdom about the prophetic in this vital, long overdue book. This is no inspirational snack, but a gourmet feast to be savoured. For those taking their first faltering steps into the prophetic, as well as the seasoned veterans who might be tempted to think there's nothing more to learn, there are delightful surprises in this warm, practical work. This book is a gift. Don't miss it."

Jeff Lucas, author, speaker and broadcaster

"The best gift is prophecy. Greg Haslam's long experience of the prophetic qualifies him as an excellent guide to this vital ministry."

Dr Michael Eaton, Chris.... , Kenya

"If people ask me, 'Why ...cceed you?', I reply: Read thi ....urself. Greg has dealt with a mc ....crstood subject in modern Christian thin. ... and done so with theological acumen, biblical knowledge and spiritual intelligence. He shows how preaching the Word prophetically keeps the Bible alive and relevant for the 21st century thinker. He takes the reader by the hand and leads them to grasp what many have never even thought about. The Bible was not given to replace the prophetic or supernatural; it was given to correct abuses. Greg will help you to recognize and avoid such abuses in the prophetic world. He will also help you to know the difference between what is peripheral and what is essential, and to stick with the latter. For those who are interested in understanding the prophetic and developing their gift in this area, this book is for you."

R. T. Kendall, Minister, Westminster Chapel (1977-2002)

Greg Haslam is pastor of Westminster Chapel, London. He was previously lead elder at Winchester Family Church. He has written a number of books and is a high-profile speaker at New Wine and other conferences.

MOVING
IN THE
PROPHETIC

A Biblical Guide to
Effective Prophetic Ministry Today

GREG HASLAM

MONARCH
BOOKS

Oxford, UK & Grand Rapids, Michigan, USA

First published in the UK in 2009 by Monarch Books
(a publishing imprint of Lion Hudson plc),
Wilkinson House, Jordan Hill Road, Oxford OX2 8DR
Tel: +44 (0) 1865 302750   Fax: +44 (0) 1865 302757
Email: monarch@lionhudson.com
www.lionhudson.com

ISBN: 978-1-85424-836-7 (UK)
ISBN: 978-0-8254-6175-0 (USA)

Distributed by:
UK: Marston Book Services Ltd, PO Box 269, Abingdon, Oxon OX14 4YN;
USA: Kregel Publications, PO Box 2607, Grand Rapids, Michigan 49501.

British Library Cataloguing Data
A catalogue record for this book is available from the British Library.

Printed and bound in Malta by Gutenberg Press.

DEDICATION

With respect and grateful thanks to God
for a dear friend whom I greatly admire,
Terry Virgo,
leader of the UK-based apostolic church-planting movement
Newfrontiers.
Throughout our long friendship and association, I have valued
enormously your passion for God, fatherly wisdom,
depth of biblical insight, prophetic vision, prayerfulness and
integrity.
I know of no other person who has done so much to foster
and encourage authentic prophetic ministry, especially among
the pastors and churches that you lead –
a truly apostolic and prophetic movement that continues to bless
the nations.

Genesis 12:1–3

Contents

Foreword

One thing I have learned over many years in leadership is this: no church can fulfil its assignment properly without the gift of prophecy. It is simply impossible for us to work out our God-given mission without hearing clearly the Father's voice expressed through dreams, visions, pictures, messages, impressions, Scripture passages and the like. Without the prophetic we will always be restricted to reacting to past crises, rather than proactively building towards future happenings. Much of church life is reactive. But we are also called to be proactive - to access and prepare for the Father's dream for us. If we spend all our time in reactive mode, we end up managing decline. But if we give ourselves to cultivating the prophetic then we find ourselves living on the edge of mission, which is of course where the life of God is to be found. This is the place where we all of God's children are called to live. We were called to be risk takers, not undertakers. The gift of prophecy keeps us planting our feet in the footsteps of the Great Risk Taker, Jesus of Nazareth.

My own life has been dominated by the prophetic. Every major transition I have ever embraced has been the result of receiving prophetic words. Every graduation has been the direct consequence of revelation. My calling to take up the senior leadership role of St Andrew's Church Chorleywood was the result of nearly thirty prophetic words. My current move to lead the Father's House has been the outworking of eighteen months of receiving and weighing prophetic revelation. Everything between these pivotal moments has been governed by prophecy. My life has been and continues to be prophecy-saturated. I simply cannot do without it. No Christian can.

It is for that reason that we are in the debt of my friend Greg Haslam, whose book Moving in the Prophetic is all set to become a seminal introduction to the spiritual gift of prophecy. Of course, many books have already been published on this subject. What is unique about Greg's book is the fact that it comes from a courageous leader in God's church – a man who has practiced and encouraged the prophetic for three decades. His personal experience, as well as his excellent understanding and exposition of the Scriptures, make him unusually qualified to speak with credibility on this subject, and he does so with humour, integrity, and great clarity. Greg is a man of the Word and the Spirit, leading a church committed to the marriage of the Word and the Spirit. His is a voice we can consequently welcome and trust. We would do well to listen to what he teaches and to apply it both individually and corporately.

In the days that lie ahead, we are going to need to see a full restoration of the gift and ministry of prophecy in the Body of Christ. These are critical times for the church, especially in the West. While some are speaking about revival, my own hunch is that there is there is a bigger dream on Abba Father's heart, and this has more to do with Reformation than just revival. I believe that we are living in a season when the Holy Spirit is wooing and urging us to think outside the box and to establish brand new wineskins – new structures and strategies that draw the people of God to break out of current restrictions and infiltrate neighbourhoods and market places with a pioneering and missional creativity. These are not days for "same old, same old" church. These are days for putting the adventure back into the Christian venture. For this to happen we are going to need to see what one Pentecostal Bible scholar (Roger Stronstrad) calls, "The Prophet-hood of All Believers". We are going to need to see everyone in the church developing a God-given prophetic imagination.

If we are to see this Reformation, we must first see a restoration of the prophetic to the church. Conferences are great, and so are training courses and books. But in the final analysis there is no substitute for knowing and hearing the Father's voice, both as we hear it in the timeless pages of God's

Written Word, as well as in the heart-to-heart whispers of prophetic revelation. As the Holy Spirit once impressed upon me, "There isn't a Manual but there is Immanuel".

It's time to lean on the heart of Jesus, like the Beloved Disciple of John 13, and to hear the Shepherd's voice. This is a great book for encouraging both novices and veterans to pursue the "real deal".

Dr Mark Stibbe
Formerly senior leader of St Andrews Church Chorleywood
Founder and Leader of the Father's House
(www.fathershousetrust.com)

Preface

I have been gripped by a growing fascination with prophetic ministry for over twenty-five years now, ever since I first encountered evidently genuine examples of its use and became aware of the beginnings and benefits of it as I personally experienced surprising but undeniable incidences of it.

I am fortunate to have seen many quality and consistently accurate expressions of prophetic gifts in operation in numerous contexts ever since then, as well as being exposed over a long period of time to some of the best practice in relationship to this often controversial ministry due to my involvement with churches and leaders who have sought to be wise and faithful in honouring and deploying this gift as Christ directs in his Word. This has stimulated me to read widely on the subject of prophecy, in the works of many biblically astute and insightful practitioners and writers, as well as to examine carefully the scriptures that deal with this subject. I have also taught numerous seminars on prophecy to many churches and Christian conferences. Some of this material reappears in this book. Increasingly, I came to honour the gift as one of the most edifying and helpful charismata in the Holy Spirit's armoury designed to thoroughly equip God's saints.

My long connection with the UK church movement Newfrontiers has exposed me to some of the most godly prophets and Ephesians 4 ministries in the world. Within this successful and influential mission, I have observed first hand, and on countless occasions, just how powerful authentic prophecy can be when it is anchored to Scripture and submitted to godly authority. I can truly say that my life has been changed, redirected and blessed beyond measure through personal prophecies that have been spoken over me within this association of friends and spiritual comrades.

My pastoral experience of nearly three decades has also underlined not only the enormous blessings that prophecy can convey to our lives at every level but, more importantly, its vital importance in building vibrant and healthy churches. And when it also becomes a regular feature of the preaching ministry of church leaders, then, in my judgement, prophecy truly comes into a new and powerful dimension of its own, as a formidable force for good and for God in many people's lives. In this book I attempt to explain how and why this is the case.

Throughout this work, I have carried an enormous burden to encourage the recovery, practice and developing maturity of the use of the gift of prophecy in the church today. My concern was that the Bible's rich teachings on this matter become better known, understood and implemented – and no longer regularly dismissed, distorted and disregarded. In writing, I bore in mind the whole body of Christ, for I am convinced that prophetic ministry will play a major role in bringing the church to the full unity that Christ prayed for (John 17) and which the Scriptures predict will be the final glorious outcome for the church of the end times (Ephesians 4).

It is my express intention to encourage sceptical Christians to revisit and carefully reconsider this issue, in the hope that they will lay down some of their unjustified prejudices against it. I have also kept in mind the way in which this gift has become sadly neglected, even among Spirit-filled believers who once valued it highly but seem to do so no longer. And I have not been unaware of what is sometimes referred to by critics as the more super-spiritual "lunatic fringe" in charismatic circles (bless them!), who have often unwittingly succeeded in distorting the use of this gift and brought it into widespread disdain and disrepute.

Above all, I desire to help inexperienced and cautious church leaders, and ordinary Christians who are uninformed or nervous about the gift of prophecy, to adopt a more positive outlook. A happy result would be that they are then encouraged to take seriously the apostle Paul's timely exhortation in

1 Corinthians 14:1: "Follow the way of love and eagerly desire spiritual gifts, especially the gift of prophecy." For I am convinced that, if we do this, the result will be a revived church and a wider world that will be awakened once again to take notice of Christ and some of the great things he can accomplish among his people.

Greg Haslam
Westminster Chapel
London

Chapter One

Does God Speak Today?

Prophecy is God's gift to the world and to the church, given to challenge and refine contemporary culture and build up the household of faith.

Yet, whether it is exercised in the church or the world, the gift of prophecy always invites some degree of opposition and controversy. It is one of the most vivid displays of God's presence and power among his people, and since the presence of God can prove to be disturbing and even frightening, many have concluded that prophecy is best forgotten, consigned to the dustbin of history.

Yet we can't avoid the gift of prophecy if we continue to read the Bible. Especially in the New Testament, we read so much about this activity of God in our midst: its importance, how it works, and the honour due to it. Typical of this positive emphasis would be a passage like this:

> ...eagerly desire spiritual gifts, especially the gift of prophecy...everyone who prophesies speaks to men for their strengthening, encouragement and comfort... he who prophesies edifies the church. I would like every one of you to speak in tongues, but I would rather have you prophesy. He who prophesies is greater than one who speaks in tongues, unless he interprets, so that the church may be edified.
>
> 1 Corinthians 14:1–5

In this epistle Paul has already been focusing on the internal life of the church at Corinth, responding to questions his readers had asked about matters of misconduct and malpractice in their corporate life together and about the way the gifts of the Spirit operated. We need to read straight through 1 Corinthians 12–14 to gain a proper understanding of Paul's teaching on this issue. Taking selected verses, or looking only at chapter 13, is not enough. That great chapter on love is the "meat in the sandwich" of all that Paul says here and it indicates that Paul saw charismatic manifestations not in terms of "either love or gifts" but rather "gifts with love" or "gifts without love".

We may be surprised and challenged by the suggestion that it is possible to operate the gifts of the Holy Spirit without the seal of the Spirit's presence – love – upon what we do. Paul warns us that such use of the charismatic gifts is vain and empty.

Yet this does not mean we do better when we aim for love alone, suppressing the activity of the Spirit in the operation of the gifts; for Paul exhorts us to "eagerly desire" the gifts, especially prophecy. We must take Paul seriously as he goes on to discuss how the gift of prophecy is to be used.

A.W. Tozer has been frequently referred to as "that great twentieth-century prophet" and is widely regarded as having been a true prophet to the church, yet during his lifetime he was not esteemed in that way by many. The human tendency is to honour prophets when they are dead and safely in their graves, no longer posing a threat to the way we customarily want things done. Like the teachers of the law and the Pharisees who opposed the ministry of Jesus (Matthew 23:29–32), we build tombs to pay honour to dead prophets even if we were prepared to stone them while they were alive. Tozer is one such prophet, almost universally respected for his words and profound insights now that he has gone.

Tozer once asserted that, "We need to have the gifts of the Holy Spirit restored again to the church, and it is my belief that the one gift we need most now is the gift of Prophecy." Many would agree, seeing prophecy as a desirable gift and one that we most need as a church living in troubled times when, if we are completely honest, our reputation as the church of Jesus Christ has more often been *pathetic* than *prophetic*. Yet the

Spirit of God is faithful and longs to work with us to build a truly effective Christian community in every part of the world. This is why we stand in such need of the authentic gift of prophecy, for it has a crucial role to play in building up the people of God.

Danger – Saints at Work!

Even in churches where prophetic gifts are encouraged and fostered, they are robbed of power if the church leadership lacks confidence and experience to pastor, weigh and discern them appropriately. Much slips by in our churches without accurate weighing, correction, affirmation or admonition; and this is a sign that we are not living the mindful, reflective and discerning lives of true disciples. Sometimes even the plainly ridiculous or dangerous is accepted without question. There is often a high "cringe factor" in many churches, and it is one of the major stumbling blocks that frequently keep both sensible believers and unbelievers away from our meetings. The bizarre things we do and say inevitably turn them off. When this happens, people cease to take us seriously or listen to what we say – and so we dishonour our call to be God's prophetic people in the world. Carelessness makes our words appear ridiculous. From time to time I have come across announcements in church bulletins or notice boards that have made me laugh out loud at their unintentional oddity.

A Baptist church built on a street corner used the windowless wall at the side of the chapel to display "wayside pulpit" posters, but did not take the trouble to reread them. As a result, passersby were treated to such gems as, "Don't let worry kill you – let the church help!". Another read, "Sermon for Sunday: What is hell like?", then, just below that, the apparent answer: "Come in and hear our choir sing"!

An Anglican church, wishing to chivvy the congregation in the direction of more responsible giving, headed a paragraph on stewardship in their newsletter with a phrase from 2 Corinthians 9:7. Careless proofreading sent it to press saying: "God Loves A Cheerful Fiver!" Everyone laughed at the heading, and nobody read the rest!

A notice posted outside an Assemblies of God Pentecostal church in a small town in the south of England boldly advertised their weekly Sunday morning meeting. It read: "Healing service here every Sunday at 10.30 am", then added the alarming words, "You won't get better!" It's a wonder anyone turned up!

Occasionally our errors take us nearer the bone than we intended – as when a Methodist church advertised their forthcoming choir event as a "Sarkey and Moody Evening". Crowds stayed away in their thousands! And one of my favourites was the priceless announcement: "On Wednesday night the Ladies' Liturgy Society will meet, when Mrs Jones will sing 'Put Me in My Little Bed' accompanied by the pastor"! It amused me, but somebody should have spotted that and informed them.

We laugh at these silly mistakes because they are harmless and unimportant, but they are symptomatic of a carelessness that disastrously blunts our prophetic edge. Our message can be effective only when it is supported by a faithful, discerning, honest critique; an ongoing, clear-sighted appraisal. God knows this, and that is why he raises up prophetic voices in his church even to this day, showing us how we can realign ourselves with his revealed will in the Holy Scriptures.

We are all aware that many people, especially prominent Christian leaders, struggle with the very concept of the validity of prophecy today. They have difficulties because God has spoken in his Word, the written Scriptures, and therefore they are troubled by the possibility that God may have direct access to the minds of his children in more immediate and personal ways than reading the Bible alone, through such means as hunches and divine intuitions, intimations or directions, pictures or even words that come directly from the Spirit of God. Such "words" are designed to build up and positively strengthen his church and not to harm it.

Our Speaking God

I myself had serious doubts about the validity of prophetic ministry at one time. What changed my thinking was the reflection that the devil often operates as a speaking agent in the supernatural realm, all too often gaining access to our minds in this way.

Satan is quite capable of putting alien ideas into our heads – unwanted thoughts, unwelcome imagery, dangerous suggestions, accusations, ideas and directions. Some of us see pictures in our imagination; others have had dreams that seem to be demonic in origin. We have sometimes woken up in a cold sweat, trembling with fear because of what has been screened in our imagination and seen by our mind's eye. At other times we hear voices, sometimes even audible voices, suggesting the most horrendous things: "You would be better off dead", "Your life is going nowhere", "You're useless", "Your ministry is over, your influence is finished. You may as well end it all."

It is important to recognize that the devil is a supernatural, speaking agent with access to our minds. But is it really credible to believe that the devil has a total monopoly of airtime on the radio waves of our souls, while God himself – who created all things by his Word, who expressed himself in Jesus as the living Word, who gave us the Bible as his Word of power – is silent when it comes to dealing directly with his people?

Does God have no access to the minds or spirits of his children? Has he no way of conveying pictures or images, words or suggestions, clear directions or specific intimations to them? Is all of this activity the devil's province alone, because God is now decidedly "hands off" when it comes to such activities, having given us a completed canon of Scripture in the Holy Bible? Has God retired from the fray in which the devil is still actively engaged? The logic of this reasoning is totally flawed.

I believe in the full inspiration of the Bible from Genesis to Revelation, and its final authority and total sufficiency for faith and practice, according to the claim of the Scriptures themselves. But I do not believe that when God inspired the last chapter of the book of Revelation, that acted as a kind of suicide note or at least the announcement of his retirement, after which we would never hear from God directly again. This is unthinkable. God has not signed off. He is Immanuel, "God with us", still speaking to us, conveying thoughts, images, promptings and directions to men and women who will listen to him and act as his messengers; and that can include you and me!

In this study, I hope to impart the necessary confidence to every reader to reach out to God for more of the Spirit's encouragement than ever before, coming to terms with our capacity to hear from him concerning people and situations where our words and insights are desperately needed and can become an untold blessing to many. God took Balaam, that mercenary and probably self-appointed prophet, and turned him around. Balaam was a man highly motivated by social status, personal prestige and hefty cash offers – he was actually paid to curse the children of Israel. God supernaturally redirected Balaam, using him to pronounce blessings over God's people rather than curses. If God can use Balaam, surely he can use you and me! Balaam was a man whose character was flawed and whose motives were questionable; but God picked him up and turned his curses into blessings even as they emerged from his lips (see Numbers 22–24).

God also seized hold of the insecure and wayward first monarch of Israel, King Saul. Though a man of decidedly mixed motives and flawed character, Saul was also counted amongst the prophets, at least for a time during the earliest phase of his career, as the Spirit of God came upon him in power (1 Samuel 10:6–7).

It is also worth noting that the pragmatic, politically conniving and power-hungry high priest, Caiaphas, was supernaturally led by God to say on one occasion, "It is better …that one man die for the people than that the whole nation perish" (as justification for the Sanhedrin's planned murder of Jesus). John the apostle comments: "He did not say this on his own, but as high priest that year he prophesied that Jesus would die for the… nation…" (John 11:50–51).

From these examples you can see that God is able to

distribute authentic gifts of a prophetic nature to whomever he wishes, and whenever he likes. And if God frequently did this with such imperfect individuals as the men we have mentioned, how can we fail to have confidence that he is still prepared to bestow the gift of prophecy upon his children in our own day, children who love him, believe him, and want to serve both him and his church with integrity?

The Connection Between the Holy Spirit and Prophecy

The life of the church has seen long periods when prophetic ministry has been hidden and neglected in the mainstream expressions of Christianity. This has usually coincided with times when there has been a drought of the Holy Spirit's presence among the people of God. Prophecy lay unrecognized even in those moments when it has stirred and in those lives who seemed to speak with special power.

It is impossible to institutionalize the charismata of God – the Spirit blows where he wills – and perhaps we should not be surprised that wherever worship is highly ritualized and the faith community becomes the establishment, talk of prophecy fades away.

Yet as we look more closely at the paths in which the faithful have walked, if we look for the byways and field-tracks instead of the high roads of the Christian map books, we discover that God has always spoken among his people. If the synods and the councils and the elders' meetings would not hear him, still his voice was known in out-of-the-way chapels and in prayer meetings held before the main service began, or among ordinary people gathered around the kitchen tables of their homes.

Wherever the Holy Spirit has been welcomed and powerfully operative there has always been a resurgence of the gifts of the Holy Spirit, and particularly the gift of prophecy. In recent times, the wave of Holy Spirit renewal and blessing that has come to the body of Christ all around the world from the mid-1990s onwards was marked by a resurgence and flood of remarkable prophetic activity. This was also true of the birth of the Pentecostal movement in 1904–05, and the charismatic movement that began in the mid-1960s as well.

As these waves of Holy Spirit blessing and activity swept through thousands of churches all around the world, the quality and quantity of prophetic words increased. This is congruent with the prediction of the prophet Joel (Joel 2:28–3:3), affirmed by the apostle Peter on the day of Pentecost, the first day the Spirit was outpoured in fullness upon Christ's new covenant people. Peter cites this ancient prophecy in his address to the potentially hostile Jewish audience before him: "...this is what was spoken by the prophet Joel: 'In the last days, God says, I will pour out my Spirit on all people. Your sons and daughters will prophesy, your young men will see visions, your old men will dream dreams. Even on my servants, both men and women, I will pour out my Spirit in those days, and they will prophesy'" (Acts 2:16–18).

The time-note struck here is important. This is the promise of an outpouring of the Holy Spirit in the "Last Days". Most reputable Bible scholars, though not all, believe that this phrase, the "Last Days", connotes the era between Christ's ascension and his second coming from heaven, his *parousia*. The "Last Days" were not fully played out in the first few decades of the first century AD as the preterist ("past-ist") school of eschatology maintains, declaring that they came to an end with the destruction of Jerusalem and the temple at the hands of the Romans in AD 70.

That event did not complete history, for we are all still here – and not yet fully redeemed residents in the new heaven and earth. Though the Roman invasion and destruction of the temple was important in sealing God's "planned obsolescence" of the priesthood and sacrificial temple worship, it also revealed patterns of God's reaction to the religious autonomy and spiritual deception of wicked men that repeatedly unfold throughout all subsequent history, just as our Lord predicted (Matthew 24–25; Mark 13).

Nor is this phrase the "Last Days" a reference to a short period of time immediately before the end of the world, as futurists would see it, and therefore to be postponed in its fulfilment and significance until the final decades of world history, as though the intervening 2,000 years of church history experienced thus far have been but a parenthesis between two short but significant periods when the "real action" supposedly occurs. A further problem with the futurist understanding of the "Last Days" is that they can only be confidently identified by hindsight – since "no-one knows about that day or hour" when the Son of Man will return (Matthew 24:36). Certainly the predictions, descriptions and criteria for the "end times" in Mark 13 and Matthew 24–25 apply to the times in which we are now living, as they have for the most part to past generations. They seem to describe the whole inter-adventual period from beginning to end.

The "Last Days" have already arrived, according to the New Testament, and we are presently still living within them. Hebrews 1:1–2, for example, tells us that God has spoken to us "…in these last days… by his Son", referring to an era that commenced with the public appearance of Jesus Christ and that has shown no signs of coming to an end even yet. There seems to be a unanimous testimony among the apostles writing in the New Testament that the "Last Days" suddenly erupted in the middle of history, and not at the end of it, as contemporary first-century Jewish eschatology had expected. We now live in the overlap of the "old evil age" dominated by sin and Satan, and the "age to come" that commenced with the first coming of Christ and particularly the great epoch-making, saving events of his cross and resurrection/ascension. In his sermon on the day of Pentecost, Peter proclaimed God's promise (through the prophet Joel) to be fulfilled, so indicating that the Last Days had thus begun. As we are still living in the "Last Days", waiting for the return of the Lord, the promise has surely continued in force for all of the running centuries since then. We have no reason to believe that the promise has in any way been rescinded – "I will pour out my Spirit on all people… and they will prophesy."

Notice also the close connection, in Peter's understanding, between an outpouring of the Holy Spirit and the manifestation of prophetic gifts among God's people. The Spirit inaugurates a new age of revelation, lavish and indiscriminate in its effects upon the people of God. The Holy Spirit is declared to have been poured out on every nation and ethnic group ("all people"), all ages ("young" and "old"), both sexes ("men and women") and regardless of economic status or class (on "servants"). The Holy Spirit is not ageist, sexist, racist or class conscious. Instead, he is an "equal opportunity" empowerer of his people. He breaks down all of the artificial barriers that we might erect in order to limit or monopolize his generosity. There is no elitism in the kingdom of God for, at the moment of Christ's death when the temple veil was torn in two, a way was made open for all people into the Holy of Holies, the very presence of God. At that moment, the prophetic calling to come into God's presence, and receive his Word for this generation, passed from being the spasmodic ministry of a select few to being the regular privilege of all: an every-believer ministry. It follows from this that we should expect to see manifestations of the Spirit's coming in this new way among the whole community of believers everywhere, including the gift of prophecy displayed in diverse forms – such as God-directed speech, dreams, visions, signs and actions, as well as prophetic lifestyles that model God's justice, integrity and love.

In the era of the Old Testament period, the Holy Spirit temporarily anointed select individuals – judges, prophets, priests and kings – to operate in some of these ways. Specific individuals, like Moses and Elijah, were called into God's presence and then sent out to the people with the message of his word and will, but the world was still waiting for the atoning death of Christ to open the way of access to God's mind for all people through intimacy with the presence of God, and the revelatory activity of the Holy Spirit (1 Corinthians 2:16 – "But we have the mind of Christ"), so that all could hear for themselves God's Word for today's world. The Holy Spirit is now available to all as an empowering and permanent presence in the whole body of Christ – equipping men and women, Jew and Gentile, young and old, rich and poor – in such a way that there is now no exclusivity but a fully functioning family to which all may belong.

God's Ultimate Intention

The Old Testament carries hints that this was always God's ultimate plan for the future of his dealings with his chosen people. When the Holy Spirit's powerful presence and anointing was conveyed to certain individuals in the Old Testament, one of the frequent manifestations was prophetic speech. For example, in Numbers 11:16–30 God instructed Moses to bring together the "seventy elders" of Israel, the leaders and officials among the people, in order to assemble them at the Tent of Meeting, which was the God-ordained location for the manifestation of the visible presence of God upon the earth. We might call it his palace or earthly residence, "ground zero", where his glory was especially visible between the golden cherubim on the cover or "mercy seat" of the Ark of the Covenant that was placed in the most holy place of the tabernacle. God then said (verse 17): "I will come down and speak with you there, and I will take of the Spirit that is on you and put the Spirit on them. They will help you carry the burden of the people so that you will not have to carry it alone."

This immense privilege, an extension of the franchise of operating under God's divinely bestowed power, was once the sole prerogative of Moses. God made clear his intention that the anointing, previously at work exclusively in the primary leader among the people, would now be shared out generously among the seventy elders as well – a much wider representation of the people. As a consequence, we're told (verse 24): "So Moses went out and told the people what the Lord had said. He brought together seventy of their elders and had them stand around the Tent. Then the Lord came down in the cloud and spoke with him, and he took of the Spirit that was on him and put the Spirit on the seventy elders. When the Spirit rested on them, they prophesied, but they did not do so again."

25

This, of course, was only a temporary anointing; but the thing to notice in our present study is that it was an anointing explicitly connected with the gift of prophecy.

In Numbers 11:29, two latecomers, Eldad and Medad, who had missed the earlier meeting with Moses and the blessing that accompanied it, were nevertheless also privileged to share in the franchise of God's supernatural empowerment, though Joshua had strongly objected to this. It is recorded that Moses received complaints from Joshua because two belated arrivals had received this gift out of time. He thought they should have forfeited their chance since they were "out of sync" with the remaining number in the seventy. Joshua complained that the gift of prophecy should not have been given to these two individuals – presumably because he thought they didn't deserve it. Moses' reply is intriguing. He says, "Are you jealous for my sake? I wish that all the Lord's people were prophets and that the Lord would put his Spirit on them!" (verse 29). In this way a prophetic leader voiced a prophetic wish concerning a future coming era when all the Lord's people would be able to prophesy.

There is an ancient rabbinical commentary on this passage that notes, "In this world, some men have prophesied, but in the world to come all Israelites will prophesy" (Numbers, Rabba 15:5). This was a clear Jewish eschatological expectation for the Last Days that was finally fulfilled rather earlier than this learned rabbi had anticipated – in the middle, and not at the end, of history. The "world to come" arrived sooner than he and his contemporaries thought. It arrived in the middle of history with the coming of Jesus of Nazareth and his glorious ascension to the right hand of God, after he had made abundant provision for all the Lord's people to become spiritual Israelites, with the result that all the Lord's people would potentially be able to prophesy – Jewish and Gentile believers alike. The kingdom of God, the reign of Christ, though not yet climaxed and consummated, has truly begun.

Is Saul Also Among the Prophets?

Furthermore, as we noted earlier, this surprise extension of privileged access to God's Word was also true of King Saul. After informing Saul that he had been chosen by God to become king (1 Samuel 10:6–7), Samuel told him of an imminent encounter with a procession of unknown prophets that would result in a special encounter with the Spirit of God (verse 6): "The Spirit of the Lord will come upon you in power, and you will prophesy with them; and you will be changed into a different person. Once these signs are fulfilled, do whatever your hand finds to do, for God is with you."

And the result? "As Saul turned to leave Samuel, God changed Saul's heart, and all these signs were fulfilled that day" (verse 9).

Perhaps that's a reference to God's work of spiritual regeneration in human nature; or maybe it simply refers to some temporary reorientation of his life, given Saul's later chequered and wayward personal history. But at the very least, this is the account of a powerful work of the Spirit in Saul's life, for the narrative continues (verses 10–11): "When they arrived at Gibeah, a procession of prophets met him; the Spirit of God came upon him in power, and he joined in their prophesying. When all those who had formerly known him saw him prophesying with the prophets, they asked each other, 'What is this that has happened to the son of Kish? Is Saul also among the prophets?'" They not only saw the strange phenomena that affected Saul's body in a display of unusual physical behaviour, like the dancing of this troop of prophets, they also heard unusually weighty words from his lips. These amounted to an extraordinary change in his life: Saul was doing and saying things he'd never been able to do and say before. He became a prophetic figure, at least for a short time. The Holy Spirit's outpouring had led to the manifestation of the gift of prophecy.

This happened also to the prophet Elisha (2 Kings 2:1–15). We recall the story of Elisha's dogged determination to tail Elijah during the last hours of Elijah's earthly ministry, just before his supernatural transfer to heaven, when Elijah completely bypassed dying and death to be taken physically to heaven in a fiery chariot. We read that Elisha picked up the newly discarded cloak that had fallen from Elijah's shoulders (verse 13), and returned to the banks of the river Jordan they had recently crossed after a miraculous parting of the waters by Elijah. Then Elisha exactly reproduced the miracle Elijah had performed earlier with that very same cloak. He parted the Jordan, enabling a dry crossing to occur. We're told: "The company of the prophets from Jericho, who were watching, said, 'The spirit of Elijah is resting on Elisha.' And they went to meet him and bowed to the ground before him" (verse 15).

This was the launch of an extraordinary, Christ-like, prophetic teaching and miracle ministry that was full of mercy, supernatural signs and straight talk, designed to minister indiscriminately to needy people, irrespective of their dignity or status. Elisha was a bold "type" or forerunner of Christ, with an outstanding prophetic preaching ministry, launched as a direct result of the outpoured Spirit that had moved from Elijah to Elisha upon Elijah's permanent airlift and bodily transfer to heaven. In all of these instances there is clearly a regular connection between the outpouring of the Holy Spirit upon a person, and that person's subsequent ability to prophesy.

New Testament Connections Between the Spirit and Prophecy

We find that this connection between the outpoured Spirit and the gift of prophecy is also the consistent picture throughout the New Testament. At Thessalonica and Corinth, Paul clearly implies the cause and effect relationship between the outpoured Holy Spirit and the manifestation of prophetic gifts in the life of God's people.

We noted 1 Corinthians 14 earlier, but the context of that passage is the discussion of the charismata commencing in 1

Corinthians 12, where Paul speaks of the various manifestations of the Holy Spirit's activity, listing some of the speaking gifts God empowers: words of knowledge, words of wisdom, the ability to speak in unknown tongues, and prophecy. In 1 Thessalonians 5:19–22 Paul makes a terse statement, all the more important because it assumes a situation that was quite normative in the church: "Do not put out the Spirit's fire; do not treat prophecies with contempt. Test everything. Hold on to the good. Avoid every kind of evil".

The Spirit's fire burns within the hearts of believers who have been filled with his presence, so our mutual obligation to one another means that we dare not put out that fire by acting as a kind of spiritual asbestos blanket to smother and extinguish the Spirit's prophetic gifts. Instead, we are to act faithfully in the operation of them in accord with his promptings. The church has for many centuries been adept at putting out the Spirit's fire. We are good at stamping out sparks of revelatory activity on the Spirit's part. There are some who will, without a second thought, throw cold water over even very young Christians hungering for more of God, in the attempt to extinguish any unusual happenings in the church, aiming to quench them at source. Paul's advice to us is pertinent, and we can paraphrase this as: Do not put out the Spirit's fire, because the Spirit's fire brings with it, among many other things, the gift of prophecy, and we dare not despise such prophetic utterances.

Wherever there is a genuine desire to begin operating in the gift of prophecy, we often also find a growing and painful awareness of negative attitudes towards this special gift, to the point where it is denounced as a demonic counterfeit. Sometimes this is argued on theological grounds and, when it is, the critic may need to specifically repent of that sin before he or she will ever be able to move in this gift personally. Christ severely warned his hostile hearers against attributing the Holy Spirit's work to the devil, and spoke of this as blasphemy (Mark 3:22–30). In this connection, to repent is to change one's mind, to admit wrong and line up with reality, to form an alternative opinion that is more accurately realigned with Scripture. It is to come to the place where we gladly recognize prophecy as an invaluable gift from the Lord, and this is vital if you and I are ever going to be free to move in it. I hope that the following chapters will help blow away the cobwebs of any such negative mindsets.

The Acts of the Holy Spirit

The narrative of the book of Acts bristles with prophetic phenomena. Acts is the only inspired church history that we possess, and describes the first three decades or so of the early church's life emanating from the extraordinary events that occurred on the day of Pentecost in Jerusalem. It is important to realize that Acts is not only *descriptive* of remote happenings that occurred 2,000 years ago and 2,000 miles away, at the birth and early infancy of the Christian church; it is also *prescriptive* of what God wants to see happening in contemporary Christian communities around the world today. It is prescriptive of what normative New Testament Christianity should look like, even in the twenty-first century. Furthermore, the phenomena and activities that believers engaged in, recorded in these narrative histories, are not in conflict with anything that we read of in the epistles of Paul and the other apostles in the rest of the New Testament as they expound God's will for his people everywhere. It is misleading to set the epistles of the apostles at odds with the Acts of the Apostles, and then assert that only the former are valid guidebooks for the teaching of normative Christian doctrine and practice, as though Paul's teaching in his letters could somehow be in contradiction with the practice of the churches recorded in Acts.

Instead, the narrative of Acts "fleshes out" all that the apostles taught. Doctrine can indeed be derived from Acts, contrary to the denials often voiced by some teachers, who imagine there must have been some kind of peculiar "goings-on" in Acts that are not endorsed in the body of the New Testament epistles. How could there be a discrepancy between the practice described in the Acts of the Apostles and the instructions given in the epistles by those same apostles? It is a big mistake to fail to see in the book of Acts principles and practices that are still normative for us today, in terms of the operation of apostolic, prophetic, evangelistic, pastoral and didactic ministry – the fivefold anointing of Christ upon his chosen servants spoken of in Ephesians 4:11–13 – as well as in the disclosure of timeless strategies and methods for engaging in mission, church planting, discipleship, church growth and kingdom impact in the secular world.

In twenty-seven out of the twenty-eight chapters in the book of Acts, there are references to, and descriptions of, the revelatory activity of the Holy Spirit, not only through the working of the apostles, but also through evangelists, ordinary believers and unnamed individuals. If this is so, including fairly low-key instances of prophecy of merely local and temporary significance to specific individuals and communities of the time and not duplicated exactly elsewhere, then we can infer from this fact that, at the very least, prophecy was a normative experience of the life of the first-century church, and ought to be the normative experience of the twenty-first century church as well – "Therefore, my brothers, be eager to prophesy… " (1 Corinthians 14:39).

This is the norm. It is subnormal or abnormal to neglect prophetic gifts, for their neglect impoverishes us. We should eagerly covet them. That's why we're told that we bear some responsibility to stir up this gift (1 Timothy 4:14; 2 Timothy 1:6–7). If you have been baptised and filled with the Holy Spirit, then there is an authentic prophetic ability already latent within you that waits to be stoked up and spoken out. So we are compelled to ask about the ethos or climate of every church today: Are you tragically *pathetic* or truly *prophetic* in your corporate willingness to regard highly this gift and cheerfully embrace its operation and power? We really cannot prosper without it. We were never meant to.

The Spirit's Power, Love and Self-Control

In 2 Timothy 1:6–7, Timothy was feeling overwhelmed, intimidated and somewhat demoralized in his difficult ministry, and so the apostle Paul writes to remedy this situation in the life of his apostolic delegate in the very tough situation he was called to lead in the church at Ephesus: "For this reason I remind you to fan into flame the gift of God, which is in you through the laying on of my hands. For God did not give us a spirit of timidity, but a spirit of power, of love and of self-discipline" (2 Timothy 1:6–7).

There are all kinds of spirits that can be operative in the lives of Christians, ranging from the divine, through the soulish, to the demonic. Note how all three sources are operative in the disciples on the notable occasion in Christ's ministry when he asked them a question concerning opinions about his own identity: "Who do people say the Son of Man is?", a question immediately followed by the more demanding inquiry, "Who do *you* say that I am?" This question was particularly provocative to Peter. Human opinions were reported, but Peter made a bold confession of the truth by revelation of the Spirit of God. Yet, when Christ detailed the sufferings of the cross as an inevitable part of his messianic mission, Peter rebuked him. Christ saw behind this the deceit of Satan. Here was a movement of spiritual activity ranging from the fleshly, soulish opinions voiced by the disciples, through divine inspiration of the Holy Spirit, to demonic deception in Peter's mind, all within the space of a few short minutes (see Matthew 16:13–23). Demons can (and will) torment and harass us, seeking to render us ineffective for a while, and all too often through the agency of genuine Christians around us (see 2 Timothy 2:24–26). No wonder Timothy had been harassed and affected by a "spirit of fear" (2 Timothy 1:7). This is a commonplace contagion, one of the many activities of alien demonic spirits who regularly attack us. Timothy was vulnerable to this, since he was prey to natural timidity, which invited a spirit of fear to rob him of effectiveness in his ministry. He needed to perceive that this was an enemy attack, and that God had not given that spirit to him. It was an alien entity and a debilitating presence in his life. Only the Holy Spirit could evict this from him, filling him with new levels of moral authority, fearless love, and immovable level-headedness in every testing situation (2 Timothy 1:7b).

Timothy was, therefore, personally responsible for cultivating the Spirit's work in his life. Because we cannot see the Spirit, he is described in Scripture by a number of powerful images that help us to picture him at work: fire, water, wind, oil and wine. Every one of these images depicts some aspect of the Spirit's powerful operations, but they also imply the responsibility on our part to cooperate with him and receive all that he wishes to do in and through us. We have to fan the flame, or hoist the sails, to experience his activity as fire or wind. We must, at times, deliberately soak in some aspects of the Spirit's work that are like water or oil, so that we "drink" the life-giving draught of his grace and allow him to smear or outpour on us the oil of his authoritative ministry. Sometimes we simply wait and linger around him as serious drinkers and "tipplers" do at a wine bar, and drink of his refreshing presence until we are filled and overflowing – drunk in the Spirit, yet with none of the unhealthy side-effects of an alcohol-induced hangover (Ephesians 5:18–20)! All of these imperatives imply clear personal choices and responsibilities. If we don't respond positively to them, then it will not be surprising if we see little or none of the Holy Spirit's gifts operating among us. The reason is simple: we are quenching and resisting God's Spirit – the very thing we are commanded not to do.

Does God speak today? The answer is surely a resounding "Yes". He addresses us through both his *written* Word and his *proceeding* Word, through both the Scriptures read and preached, and also through the operation of prophecy. The question is: Are we listening?

Chapter Two

Be Eager to Prophesy

The Bible gives us invaluable incentives to explore and mature in the gift of prophecy. We begin our discussion of these with some definitions of what prophecy actually is.

In one of his essays, A.W. Tozer writes, "Prophecy must alarm, arouse, challenge. It's God's present voice to particular people!" Another writer says, "It is the supernatural ability to receive the mind or emotions of God on a given subject, at a given time, by the prompting and revelation of the Holy Spirit." In prophecy God complements the final authority of his written Word in the Scriptures – which are a complete testimony to us and sufficient to instruct us in the understanding of God, the way of salvation, and the lifestyle God wants to empower us to live. It is also a striking fact that, complete as they are, those same Scriptures also urge us to move in the gift of prophecy. To ignore these exhortations is to contradict Scripture, yet some do this in the name of loyalty toward those same Scriptures. True obedience is to acknowledge that God's written Word is to be applied and encountered through God's proceeding Word, by the Spirit's work in our hearts. Infallible revelation in Scripture may be supplemented by existential revelation in our spirits, which is of lesser authority, though not to be dismissed lightly. Preachers know this. Prophets do too. God's eternal revelation in Scripture may become highly personal to us in our everyday present reality and individual circumstances by the revelation of God's "now" Word to our lives.

Scripture exhorts us to prophesy, and Christian prophecy will never be in competition or conflict with Scripture –

though our prophecy is not equal in authority or inspiration to Scripture, it is nevertheless a genuine operation of the Holy Spirit. This gift makes room for God to endorse, apply and underline the final authority of his Word in Scripture, directing its light upon our specific circumstances today. We do not follow the directions and intimations of prophetic words without first weighing their meaning and language to ensure that they are entirely consistent with the teaching of the Bible: that is partly how we recognize a prophecy to be genuine.

Bible teacher and author Dr R.T. Kendall defines prophecy as "immediate revelation from God or knowledge that is beyond natural sense perception". In other words, prophecy discloses things you and I could not know by the use of our own natural powers, things that we could not discern with the five natural senses of touch, taste, sight, smell and hearing or even by diligent investigation and inquiry using our minds alone. Prophecy transcends the operation of our abilities at the level of nature. It is a form of *supernatural* sensing, hearing and seeing. F.F. Bruce, a great 20th-century New Testament scholar and ancient historian, former Rylands professor of biblical exegesis at the University of Manchester and a fine biblical commentator, once said: "Prophetic ministry is the declaration of the the mind of God in the power of the Spirit with a special bearing on the current situation." Solidly Reformed in his theology, and with a Christian Brethren background, Professor Bruce still found room in his thinking for the possibility of extra-biblical communication from God to his people, and so endorsed the validity of prophetic utterances today.

The Bible itself anticipated a coming day when God would not only prepare the way for the possibility of the priesthood of all believers, but also the possibility of the prophethood of all believers. He wanted a company of people capable of hearing and then communicating to others, by both word and actions, something of the mind and heart of God. Old Testament scholar Alec Motyer confirms this when he writes: "Every Christian is potentially a prophet. The pouring out of the Spirit on all flesh carries with it this result, 'and they shall prophesy'."[1] With every fresh outpouring of the Spirit comes a fresh impetus to prophesy.

Bringing Out the Best China

We have probably all come across self-styled prophets, whose eccentric and inaccurate attempts at "prophesying" offended or misled us; but this is exactly the reason why we are commanded to desire the genuine article.

The Greek verb *zeloō* means "to strive for, to be eager for, to be zealous to obtain". It is used in 1 Corinthians 14:1, "Follow the way of love and *eagerly desire* spiritual gifts, especially the gift of prophecy", and this indicates that God does not force his gifts upon his children: they must be willingly sought from him. We must be convinced of their value and zealously reach out to him for them; otherwise we will discount, neglect or even refuse those gifts. Many seek them only occasionally, behaving like nervous housewives who keep their best china tea services packed away, afraid to use them in case they get broken or spoilt. Similarly, in some churches the gifts of the Spirit may come out only on very special occasions, if at all!

The church has often carefully stored all of the gifts of the Spirit like best china in a glass-fronted cupboard, a kind of museum display of past glories, rarely, if ever, taken out and used as they were intended for fear of mishap of one kind or another. As we have seen, this was not how the early church in the book of Acts and subsequent centuries treated the revelatory activity of the Holy Spirit.

Incentives to Seek the Gift of Prophecy

The Bible makes clear that prophecy has a wide range of invaluable functions that will strengthen and equip the ongoing life of the church, and that should surely motivate us to rediscover, welcome and deploy this precious gift.

1. Prophecy exposes us to a vital dimension of Christ's own ministry to his church

In the first three chapters of the letter to the Ephesians, Paul spreads out the broad sweep of God's plan to unite the whole cosmos under one head, Jesus Christ, bringing into being a representative people who will act as the vanguard of his eventual plan to reintegrate all creation in a breathtaking unity that will be modelled and displayed first in his church. In the light of this wonderful reconciliation, which is sourced in God's gift and grace, in the fourth chapter of his epistle (4:7–11), Paul considers the practical responsibilities incumbent on all believers because of their union with Christ, urging us to live lives worthy of our calling. He commences with the issue of the spiritual and visible unity of the church, first addressing the role of the leadership and preaching ministry gifts given by the ascended Christ to empower his church and to bring about visible unity among his people on earth (verse 7): "But to each one of us grace has been given as Christ apportioned it. This is why it says: 'When he ascended on high, he led captives in his train and gave gifts to men.'"

The apostle refers to the fivefold Word-ministries that Christ sends to build, mature and unify his church, the very gifts we frequently see in operation in the advance of the post-ascension of Christ expansion of the early church, and become familiar with in the missional church planting narrative of Acts – apostles, prophets, evangelists, pastors and teachers (verses 11–12): "It was he who gave some to be apostles, some to be prophets, some to be evangelists, and some to be pastors and teachers, to prepare God's people for works of service, so that the body of Christ may be built up until we all reach unity in the faith and in the knowledge of the Son of God and become mature, attaining to the whole measure of the fulness of Christ."

Christ himself is the blueprint for what it means to operate effectively in all five dimensions of Word-ministry – he was *the* apostle (Hebrews 3:1), prophet (Luke 24:19; John 4:19), evangelist (Mark 1:15), pastor (John 10:14) and teacher (Matthew 7:28) of our faith, and included all of these remarkable and distinctive ministry activities in his own person. Yet subsequently, in the post-ascension donation of anointed men listed in Ephesians 4, we are in some way encountering the words, works and wonders of the Lord himself, as his Spirit works through them to extend his kingdom and build his church. There were different gift clusters operating in each of these individuals, so no one man moved totally effectively in all of them. These gifts were all diverse but essential manifestations of Christ's power, often displayed in working teams of church planters and equippers, as they should operate today. Such anointed believers mutually depended upon one another for maximum effect, sharing at least a measure of Christ's own supreme anointing in all five aspects. Their ministries were primarily focused on distinct and different Word-ministry preaching styles and flavours attended by the power of the Holy Spirit, as complementary aspects of Christ's own multi-layered and multi-dimensional Word-and-power ministry to his church from heaven.

I use the fingers of my left hand as a simple mnemonic when I am thinking about these forms of ministry. The index finger is frequently used for pointing – that represents the prophet because the prophet points the way for God's people and is directional, hope-building and future-oriented, able to take us beyond the situation we are locked into and make us ready for what's coming from the future. Prophets bring to the church insight, foresight, hindsight, exhortation and transcendent guidance – powers that are not available through natural abilities alone. They can, however, be accessed by the power of the Spirit in the form of words, visions, impressions and pictures, all to be tested by the final authority of Scripture (1 Corinthians 14:3, 37–38; 1 Thessalonians 5:19–22).

If we then align our fingers together so that the same hand looks like a spearhead, the finger that is most prominent, the middle finger, here represents the evangelist. This is because the evangelist spearheads the church's outreach beyond the faith community, equipping others to do the same, and winning souls for Christ by proclamation and demonstration of the gospel in words, miraculous signs and a holy lifestyle (Mark 16:15–20; Acts 8:4–8).

In my case, on the fourth finger is a prominent wedding ring, the covenant symbol of my commitment to my wife and my desire to live and act consistently and persistently for her total welfare. This finger best represents the pastor. The pastor is someone who is committed to see the body of Christ built up, protected from predators, and properly fed and cared for. Just as a husband and father does with his family, the pastor also desires to see new converts discipled, detoxified and thoroughly grounded in God's scripturally revealed will for their future lives with Christ.

The little finger represents the teacher. Often the pastor/teacher gifts combine in one person, and the structure of the original Greek phrase here in Ephesians makes it unclear whether Paul is speaking of two distinctive ministries or just one. We often encounter leaders whom we would call "pastor-teachers", though these gifts also occur singly: the church's theologian-teachers don't always make good pastors, and some pastors are more exhorters than in-depth teachers and expositors. Thank God that the church is given extremely gifted biblical theologians who are often more at home with their books than with people! This too is a gift from God.

So here we are making a distinction between the pastoral gifting and the gift of being a teacher. The pastor is represented by the fourth finger and the teacher by the little finger. The little finger is sometimes disregarded, but Samurai warriors know that this is the finger which has the strongest grip on the sword. Each finger right up to the index has a progressively weaker gripping strength. Pastors and teachers together have a special influence on people's lives, by their gift and clarity in teaching the Word of God (whether privately or publicly) in the power of the Spirit, cutting through to the heart of things, as keen as a sharpened double-edged blade (Hebrews 4:12). They mature, guide, clean up and protect new converts through their ability to expound Scripture, counsel biblically, patiently instruct and admonish; they lead and feed groups of new converts until they are formed together into healthy, maturing, stable and well-established churches.

Finally, the apostle may be represented by the thumb, which is called the "head finger" in Turkish, the "parent finger" in Japanese, and is depicted in Chinese by a character created from a combination of those for "mother" and "hand". The thumb often works in close collaboration with one or more of the other four digits to grab, grasp, write, pick, count and anchor their overall strength. This is like the apostle working with other gifted ministries described and inferred from the book of Acts and the epistles, for the apostle is a kind of anchor ministry among the rest and has a special role in bringing new faith communities to birth, as we can clearly see in the work of Paul and others in Acts.

The word "apostle" literally means "sent one". It is used in a number of contexts in the New Testament, and only the context can decide its particular meaning in that location. The early church understood that certain individuals were commissioned by the ascended Christ to spread the gospel and found healthy Christian communities to help ensure its preservation and expansion in a geographical locality. In a sense, the apostles in the New Testament had a measure of all of the other gifts/anointings operating in them regularly – for they evangelized, prophesied, pastored and taught. However, the apostles of the ascended Lord were also called to the special tasks of making new converts, planting new churches, and laying the solid foundations of Spirit-filled corporate life together, through ensuring that individuals experienced the full "Peter package" of initiatory experiences spoken of in Acts 2:38–41, and modelled by Paul, for example, in Acts 19:1–7. These included initiatory essentials like repentance, faith, baptism in water, baptism in the Holy Spirit, and being added to the church in meaningful fellowship. The apostles also laid a substantial foundation in essential teaching and doctrine (1 Corinthians 3:10) and then subsequently engaged in longer-term troubleshooting for those young churches as problems arose in congregational life, necessitating decisions and teaching upon matters of controversy and conduct. Thus they helped shape more mature communities of faith, living in the peaceful order of disciplined and holy lives together in Christ (see Acts 15:1–2, 23; 2 Thessalonians 3:6–8; 1 Corinthians 11:14; Titus 1:5, etc.).

The apostle Paul fulfilled this special calling as the first of a new series of apostles of the risen and ascended Christ, but so did many other named individuals in the New Testament who were not one of the original twelve disciples but were nonetheless the apostles of the ascended Lord, and his gifts to the church. Names would include Barnabas, Silas, Timothy, Titus, James the Lord's brother, Julias and Andronicus.

We can also repeat that the apostles frequently worked in partnership with other ministries, just as your thumb works in conjunction with your other fingers to get a varied number of tasks and jobs done. As the thumb is set apart from the other fingers in that it is prehensile and opposable in order to enable it to grasp and work together with the other digits in all kinds of ways – gripping, writing, throwing, picking up small objects and so on, as we mentioned – so in Acts, apostles were set apart to work in varied team ministries with unusual assortments of prophets, evangelists, pastors and teachers depending on the specific occasion and need of the hour. Paul modelled this abundantly and often listed the names of large numbers of men and women who travelled and ministered together with him in apostolic teams as servants to the churches.

These fivefold ministries form the healing, creating, empowering hands of Christ, working together ceaselessly to build the church the way he intended it to be constructed. If some of those fingers are missing – neglected, rejected or ignored in the ongoing work of the church – then the church will not be built as the Lord wants, and may be deficient or severely distorted as a result. Some churches are pastoral but not prophetic (and vice versa); others are evangelistic but never exposed to deep theology and biblical teaching. So churches need exposure to all of these ministries.

We could helpfully summarize the range of Word-ministries in this way: apostles *govern*, prophets *guide*, evangelists *gather*, pastors *guard* and teachers *ground* God's people in the truth. Cumulatively, this is the thrust of Paul's description of their roles here in Ephesians 4. As such, from the moment of

Christ's ascension until his coming again, we should confidently expect to see huge numbers of such gifted individuals emerging to build and equip the church, forming many varied teams among all denominations worldwide. Historically, we have used unbiblical alternative names for them (and often quite misleadingly, since some terms carry unnecessary baggage or controversy with them) and so it would be good to recover the appropriate biblical nomenclature for genuine, Christ-given ministry gifts like these. But whatever titles we use or call them, we must honour Christ's calling upon the lives of these gifted individuals, identify it and receive them appropriately, and then benefit from the effects of their gifting wherever it manifests and whenever they arise. These abilities are not humanly developed but divinely bestowed, so it is imperative that they are gladly and gratefully received by those for whom they are intended. The greatest single step we can take to further the unity and maturity of the church is to recognize, receive and submit to the influence, wisdom and spiritual authority of such trans-local ministries that Christ is giving in the Last Days, right up to the time of his *parousia* or second coming (note the "until" time-note in Ephesians 4:13). Such giftings will foster the effective ministry, emerging unity, spiritual maturity, doctrinal stability and effective mission and growth of Christ's church worldwide until he personally returns to consummate all history (Ephesians 4:12–16).

Authority (Greek: *exousia*) can be defined as permission to command changes in belief and behaviour in people's lives, in line with the will of God. Power (Greek: *dunamis)* is the supernatural ability to cause these changes to happen. Both come from Christ, and both are essential qualities in the discipling process. Without such ministers exercising these special traits, people's lives will remain deficient, disintegrated, diseased and disordered; and without this diversity of ability, the balanced development of the body of Christ is inevitably impaired. Individuals will be improperly spiritually "birthed", and inadequate theological and experiential foundations will be laid in church life. Teachers, when functioning alone, tend to produce passive lovers of doctrine; lone evangelists gather large numbers of spiritual babies who may remain spiritual infants for far too long. Prophets working alone usually forge a handful of fanatical and visionary but off-the-wall enthusiasts, while pastors may cultivate only a flock of well-fed, spiritually bloated, fat, cosy, smugly contented and navel-gazing sheep!

The function of those called to these ministries is not to take centre stage and top billing at Christian conferences and celebrations, or to create a personal following focused upon their own name, person and charisma. They are called to take their place within flexible and interchangeable networks or teams of similarly commissioned servants, for higher ends than their own self-glorification. Exposure to the diversity of Word-and-Spirit ministries, which Jesus gives, brings balance and perspective to the whole faith community as well as to the individuals within it. As Philip Greenslade expresses it:

> Apostles have a fatherly ministry, laying a foundation of life, obedience and doctrine in each place. The prophets, the seers and spokesmen of Christ to His Church, bring vision to believers, giving them a sense of purpose and direction through the living Word. Evangelists proclaim the good news, heal the sick and cast out demons. Pastors rule and care for the sheep, feeding and fattening them for God. Teachers expound in detail the revelation brought by the apostle and prophets applying the whole counsel of God to the lives of believers and making disciples in the process.[2]

Who could argue with the necessity of that?

Prophets are highly significant among these fivefold ministries, and the New Testament tells us that "the testimony of Jesus is the spirit of prophecy" (Revelation 19:10). "The testimony *of* Jesus" is a genitive phrase (a possessive, like saying "Jesus's testimony") and it is not clear whether it's a subjective or objective genitive. Is Jesus the source of that testimony, or is he the object of that testimony? Is Jesus the inspiration and fountainhead of all true prophetic utterances, or is he the one spoken about in the testimony of prophecy?

This is a wise ambiguity on the author's part, because Jesus is actually both. He is both the source of prophetic utterances *and* the glorious focus of their message. Prophecies all come *from* him and point *to* him. They are all meant to bring glory to Christ. If we neglect the gift of prophecy we will fail to discover many aspects of Christ's activity among us, and many facets of his glory, both as individuals and as whole churches or denominations. And the same truth applies to negligence of the rest of the fivefold ministries as well; ignore them and we shall miss out. The absence of any one of these is like sacking the bricklayer, electrician, carpenter, architect or site manager from a building site. Not one should be missing. The project will not go well, or even be properly completed, if any one from this essential workforce is omitted.

The church is built upon the foundation of the apostles and prophets (Ephesians 2:20; Matthew 16:18). This is not just a matter of ancient history dating back to the first century AD, whereby we acknowledge the doctrinal foundation laid down for all time and deposited in the New Testament writings, valid as that perspective is. It refers also to the foundation of living faith, and vital relationship with God, essential in every Christian community and new church plants today. Everything necessary for our salvation came in its perfection and entirety through God's ancient chroniclers, prophets, apostles and evangelists, and was then deposited in Scripture as a permanent basis for life and belief. Part of the teaching of that Holy Word is the ongoing need to establish and develop personal experience of the Holy Spirit's work and activity in new churches and among new converts (see, for example, Acts 10:44–48, 19:1–7; 1 Corinthians 14:5).

As we noted, churches are often founded upon slender and weak footings, their foundations deficient from the very beginning. They were not built upon the apostolic teaching about Christ, his second coming, the grace of God, justification, sanctification, authority and government, team leadership, fellowship, outreach, a full-blown biblical eschatology and the dynamic work of the Holy Spirit. Many churchgoers today have not been taught adequately about such matters as repentance, faith, baptism in water, baptism in the Holy Spirit, what it means to live under Christ's authority and to be added to his church as a living, active, contributing member. They were not properly orientated to the anticipation of our blessed future and filled with expectancy through authentic prophetic ministry that unfolds the wonders of our great eschatological hope vouchsafed for us in the gospel.

These fragile spiritual establishments may have been built principally upon the ministry of a teacher alone, or upon the pastoral foundations of good fellowship and caring mutual love – heart-warming of course, but very inward-looking and parochial in perspective. Sometimes the work was started by an evangelist who soon moved on, leaving a group of new converts with no important dimensions established in their understanding other than the good news of forgiveness and reconciliation to God in the gospel and the need to be spiritually born again, which are essential for the way into Christian life but cannot on their own take the convert through to maturity. Without the ministry of the apostles and prophets to develop and consolidate the life of believers, the church will be shaky, substandard, vulnerable to illicit control or heresy, and incomplete.

All of these ministries are therefore essential. The Ephesians passage suggests that the fivefold ministry gifts are to be exercised in perpetuity and on an ongoing basis: "… to prepare God's people for works of service, so that the body of Christ may be built up until we all reach unity in the faith…" (Ephesians 4:13). These words give us confidence that Christ will steadfastly and persistently provide these ministries until his church reaches unity and maturity in the faith and knowledge of the Son of God, in readiness for his *parousia* – his coming again. These ministries are with us right now. Some are dismissed and dishonoured. Others are yet to be recognized. But one thing is for sure: they are nevertheless there. Christ has seen to that. Isn't it time we also acknowledged them?

Prophets have a vital part to play in this fivefold ministry. Prophets ask awkward questions, unmask and identify dangerous strongholds, point out vulnerable areas, uncover unresolved issues, confront troublesome people, lay the spirit-level of God's standards to our uneven work and bring back the Spirit to dead or dying situations. Prophecy is a powerfully cleansing and creative force in our common life and we ignore or expel it at our peril, for it is part of the ministry of Christ himself.

2. Prophecy conveys vision and purpose to the community of God

All around us, people are longing to discover spiritual meaning and purpose, and find their way into the wider and deeper dimension of reality that is the true context of their lives. In their search, they turn to any experience that seems to offer a chance to crack the shell of mundane, material, grey existence. They experiment with hallucinogenic recreational drugs, with alcohol, and with extreme and bizarre sexual practices, in order to escape a world they don't understand and cannot cope with and to unlock the doors of perception into another world they hope will give meaning to their lives. But these experiments have disappointment and emptiness built into them, for it is the Holy Spirit alone who opens our eyes to see the wonder of true meaning and purpose in life. This is found in discovering the will of God from God himself. He gives men and women the prophetic ability to become "seers". A prophet will always see the reality that lies beyond natural sight and has the gift of opening the possibility of other realities and other worlds to our minds. Prophets tell us what the church is meant to be and what we ourselves can become. They refuse to settle for the *status quo*, a Latin phrase meaning *"the mess we are in"*!

The role of the prophet is vital because it is how we think that makes us what we are. It is new *insight* that changes our minds and lives. Prophets have eyes to see and are there to help us to see those same insights for ourselves. "Do not conform any longer to the pattern of this world, but be transformed by the renewing of your mind. Then you will be able to test and approve what God's will is – his good, pleasing and perfect will" (Romans 12:2).

We depend on the prophetic ministry of the church to pass on to us new insight into God's heart for today's world, to revolutionize, reform, renew, restore and ultimately revive the church. Prophets act like the scouts that accompanied the wagon trains in the Wild West. They travel with us, but frequently ride on ahead of us to scout out fresh pastures and hidden dangers so that we can be prepared for them. "Surely the Sovereign Lord does nothing without revealing his plan to his servants the prophets" (Amos 3:7).

Prophets see regularly what others don't regularly see. Prophets are the eyes and ears of the church (Isaiah 29:10), providing direction and confirming or enhancing vision. They can help us to identify God's call upon our lives, and the mission or purpose for which he placed us on the earth. Prophets can tell us what God is saying above the babble and confusion of human voices, and the raucous, strident clamour we hear so often from our noisy world. We need to listen to the still, small voice of God. We need prophetic ministry.

The British Old Testament scholar, John Goldingay writes, "Prophecy is the gift by which God keeps his church up-to-date, able to understand and live in a changing world." This visionary ministry among the people of God safeguards them against unhappy alliances with shallow and ephemeral spiritual movements, keeping the people of God faithful to their first love for Jesus and his truth (Revelation 2:4; Matthew 6:22).

The prophetic ministry calls us back again and again to the Word of God in the Bible, underlining the magnificence of the gospel, keeping us loyal to its truth, while consistently and credibly living out its worldview. Prophets can help to prevent the church from "bedding down" with the spirit of the age because, as somebody once warned, "If you marry the spirit of the age, you will end up a widow in the next." The "spirit of the age" is always transient and ever-changing. We need to save ourselves for our true husband, Jesus Christ. For this very reason – the fact that the spirit of the age is always changing – those who speak with a prophetic voice are often unpopular, frequently ridiculed and ignored. They are sometimes hated and killed by the world. In the church, the greatest tragedy occurs when prophets have faithfully represented the mind and heart of Christ to his people, only to find themselves vilified and cruelly dismissed.

God's strategy for world history is bigger than anything any of us have yet seen and certainly bigger than our own local church expression or its current temporary phase of development and modest present influence. Even national movements must be challenged to think "outside the box". Prophecy and vision come to the people of God in dynamic ways through prophetic voices and they always take us beyond anything we have yet experienced. God's world purposes are advancing. You and I need to be "clued up" about what God is doing and fully engaged with this and, for that to happen, we need to hear what his prophets are saying. This is not a minor or parochial matter; we are talking about the salvation of the world. It is not a small or unimportant task – everything we are, our future and present wellbeing, depend entirely on this. To get this right, we need all the help God is offering us: and God's prophets are the lifeblood and impulse of his heart, carrying goodness to the body and keeping us both clean and properly energized for God's work.

Sometimes we are so preoccupied by the detail of church politics and the defence of our own point of view that not even God can get a word in edgeways! Prophets are there to help ensure that he does. In Christ's time, even Jerusalem itself had slowly become a bureaucratic religious headquarters, completely devoid of the Spirit. Spiritual decay and political gamesmanship had taken over. What was meant to be a beacon of light for the whole pagan world had become merely a stronghold of irrelevant and legalistic religiosity. Christ's antidote, both then and now, is always to send us prophets (Matthew 23:29–34). Christ sends them to help us all to recover from our diseases and to find our destiny, not simply to help us locate a spare car-parking space at the shopping mall on Saturday afternoon! They come to shake us up and remind us we are not the centre of the universe – God is.

The prophet Amos said, "Surely the Sovereign Lord does nothing without revealing his plan to his servants the prophets"

(Amos 3:7). God wants his people to manifest his vision for the future in the way we build today, but you cannot build the future if you have never looked at the plans or understood the vision. The big picture the New Testament gives us of the coming advance and prosperity of Christ's kingdom, the increase of his government and peace, the mandate to mission which has never been rescinded, and the wonderful Big Story of the Bible as a whole that imparts to us a vast, panoramic view of future world history – all need constant restatement and reiteration in whatever fresh and creative ways that prophetic ministry can commandeer if we are not to lose heart, so that we can be helped to be like the men of Issachar who "...understood the times and knew what Israel should do" (1 Chronicles 12:32). No wonder prophets are often rejected, unwelcome and unpopular. But for these very reasons, they are essential. They exist to tell both the church and the world what neither of them wishes to hear.

We all have a part to play in this prophetic ministry of the people of God. Jesus said: "What I say to you, I say to everyone: 'Watch!'" (Mark 13:37).

3. Prophecy confirms and focuses leadings we have already received from God

There are times when a specific call of God upon a believer's life comes to him or her through prophecy, but it more often confirms the call we have already heard. Jesus said, "My sheep listen to my voice" (John 10:27), and so we do; but we may question our worthiness or suitability for a course of action that God has indicated we should take, or at least exercise a wise caution lest we mistake our own prejudices and enthusiasm for divine opinions. So God speaks to us supernaturally – the prophetic word confirming clearly what we thought we had heard, and enabling us to proceed with peace and confidence.

The apostle Paul was once a rabid, persecuting Pharisee who had obtained letters of permission to arrest believers in a northern city of Syria called Damascus and was actually on his way there with a company of men to persecute and kill Christ's people. He never got there. Instead of Paul arresting Christ's people, Christ arrested him. Without warning Paul was struck violently from his horse by an encounter with the living Christ and totally blinded by the dazzling sight of him. Then, in that encounter, the risen Lord spoke directly to him, calling him to be an apostle.

Years later, in his testimony to King Agrippa recorded in Acts 26, Paul summarized the elements of this call that the narrative of Acts 9 misses out. It tells us what the apostle knew from day one of his Christian life, in that the Lord Jesus said to him:

> I have appeared to you to appoint you as a servant and as a witness of what you have seen of me and what I will show you. I will rescue you from your own people and from the Gentiles. I am sending you to them to open their eyes and turn them from darkness to light, and from the power of Satan to God, so that they may receive forgiveness of sins and a place among those who are sanctified by faith in me.
>
> Acts 26:16–18

It took a period of at least ten years from that encounter for Paul to be properly launched on that apostolic ministry. All kinds of things happened in that decade. He retreated into the deserts of Arabia, reviewing and reappraising his former theology and worldview from the bottom up, then developed his extraordinary teaching and preaching ministry and helped to build a significant and wonderfully integrated church in Antioch, made up of former mutually hostile Jews and Gentiles – a marvellous demonstration of the apostolic gospel. Here, Paul heard from God about his long-term future again and again.

By the time the major confirmatory event recorded in Acts 13:1–4 occurred, he had already spent many years at Antioch under Barnabas' supervision and encouragement, helping to build a large Christian community there, when a leaders' meeting of prophets and apostles was suddenly interrupted by a world-changing prophetic utterance as the Holy Spirit said, "Set apart for me Barnabas and Saul for the work to which I have called them" (Acts 13:1–2). Here was the striking confirmation Paul needed that his call to international missionary work, heard many years beforehand, was genuine and that his years of preparation and training were now over. He was to launch that apostolic church-planting ministry in totally virgin territory. It was this unusual combination of both the prophetic and the teaching gifts of the Holy Spirit in Antioch's leaders that facilitated this supernatural communication from heaven, ensuring clear guidance about the imminent future for Paul and Barnabas. This demonstrates the difference between the prophetic ministry and the ministries of preaching and teaching. Prophecy is distinct from them both, though it often accompanies those ministries. This was a direct call from the Holy Spirit to confirm God's plan for Paul's life.

Later on, in Acts 21:10–14, a prophet called Agabus foretold the troubles that Paul was to face in Jerusalem:

> After we had been there a number of days, a prophet named Agabus came down from Judea. Coming over to us, he took Paul's belt, tied his own hands and feet with it and said, "The Holy Spirit says, 'In this way the Jews of Jerusalem will bind the owner of this belt and will hand him over to the Gentiles.'" When we heard this, we and the people there pleaded with Paul not to go up to Jerusalem. Then Paul answered, "Why are you weeping and breaking my heart? I am ready not only to be bound, but also to die in Jerusalem for the name of the Lord Jesus." When he would not be dissuaded, we gave up and said, "The Lord's will be done."

The clear inference drawn from the prophet's words by Paul's friends was that he shouldn't go to Jerusalem at all and that he would be advised to avoid the city altogether if such hostility and maltreatment awaited him there. Paul's own interpretation was different: What a confirmation! I knew I was meant to go to Jerusalem and the Holy Spirit has told me that those sufferings await me there, and that is why I must go no matter what happens (see verses 13–14).

The prophecy was clear, but those who heard it did not agree on how to act upon it. The crucial factor here was that Paul, for whom the prophecy was intended, recognized the warning as a confirmation of a previous leading he had already received. Prophecy is invaluable in sealing and confirming the whisper of God's Word in our hearts in this way.

We can thank God for those who are capable of both sensitive and selective listening on behalf of other people. Sensitive, because they can internally amplify the volume and hear God's voice above the cacophony and noise of many clamouring and contradictory voices seeking our attention. And selective, because they know what is most important in what the Lord is saying to benefit individual lives at particular times. Parents with a newborn baby are regularly awoken by every murmur and snuffle of their child, but after two or three months they become more discerning. They are able to know when that child is really in need, and awaken at those times alone. They become hardened to the wrong kind of crying. The most important things in our Christian experience coincide with what God wants to say to us, and prophetic people often hear these things on our behalf and communicate them to us. As we cultivate this ability to hear from him, we will be strengthened in the confidence and authority that will steady his children who are going through periods of doubt, discouragement, uncertainty and fear.

I can personally vouch for the value and importance of such prophetic confirmations, since I have benefitted from them many times, especially in connection with my move to Westminster Chapel in London. From the first arrival of Dr R.T. Kendall's personal letter asking me to begin to consider the possibility of coming to pastor Westminster Chapel upon his retirement from that work in February 2002, I began to hear prophetic words from many individuals clearly confirming that this was God's will, phenomena that continued for a whole year until I had something like forty to fifty clear prophetic words during that period. Some of them were totally stunning in their detail and accuracy. Some clearly indicated that I would be moving to London, describing the route I would take up the M3 motorway to get there, and the specific places I would pass on the way. Others described the reactions of friends around me, and sometimes the opposition this call would trigger. I was even shown an old sepia brown photograph of the interior of a building that looked exactly like the auditorium in Westminster Chapel, and the prophet then pointed to this picture (which happened to be of a crowded building in New York in the 1950s), and then announced that this was the kind of place and ultimately the fruitful ministry that God had in mind for me in the work to which he was sending me. This happened one year before I was finally called to move, and it came through people who knew nothing about the private contact and correspondence I had with Westminster Chapel. Prophecy can be astonishingly accurate.

God must have known I needed this, because he ensured that I received abundant confirmations of his will, more than I had ever received in my life! Personal experience may well vouch for the reality of this kind of thing in your own walk with God. God has probably spoken specifically to you about such detailed things and confirmed his will through various prophetic voices. Prophecy needs other methods of divine guidance to accompany it like God's providence, the Holy Scriptures, the wise counsel of friends, the peace of God and so on, but what a wonderful gift prophecy is for us in this matter, assisting us to confirm and become clearer in discerning God's will when it is characterized by such astonishing accuracy.

4. Prophecy prepares and fortifies us for things coming from the future in both the world and the church

God is able to prepare us for the imminent or long-distant future so that we may be ready to meet it in very practical ways. However, let me warn you that there are counterfeit sources of deceptive information operative in this sphere: futurologists, mediums, psychics and fortunetellers. Futurologists closely observe sociological, economic and other present trends or tell-tale signs in society today, then make plausible predictions for the benefit of manufacturing industries, planners and businesspeople, so that they may prepare and position themselves for the future. Sometimes they are right and sometimes they are wrong. When they are wrong you have simply paid them a lot of money for nothing. Genuine prophecy is not like this, nor does it resemble the fortunetelling or predictions of Nostradamus, Jeane Dixon, Mystic Meg or Russell Grant, which could be wildly ambivalent or misleading.

Prophets are not operating simply to satisfy our personal curiosity about the future. They are there as midwives to help bring God's future into the present and to show us the way to align our lives to the new thing God is bringing to birth. The Word of God through his prophets is not like the advice of "get rich quick" schemes or tips on "how to succeed in business without really trying". God wants us to become a people who know what the church is meant to be in preparation for challenging days ahead, ready and equipped to meet the needs of the hour. He shines the light of truth, exposing the corruption of present practice at times when we are in danger of getting lost and need to return to more disciplined and faithful lives, and he shows us the future in order to convey hope to us. Somebody once complained in a wry tone to me about prophetic people, saying, "You know, the irritating thing about prophets is that they just go around building everybody's hopes up!", as if that was a bad thing to do. I replied, "*Exactly.* That's their job description!" This is so vital. We *need* to have our hopes built up. And by God's grace, when this is done accurately in the Spirit, we are not given a false optimism but included in God's future plans as his confidants and friends (John 15:14).

Think of the exiles who, under the liberating leadership of Zerubbabel and Jeshua, courageously returned to a devastated land from their long captivity in Babylon, to rebuild the burned-out ruins of God's temple, long since destroyed and abandoned in Jerusalem.

> Now Haggai the prophet and Zechariah the prophet,
> a descendant of Iddo, prophesied to the Jews in Judah
> and Jerusalem in the name of the God of Israel, who
> was over them. Then Zerubbabel son of Shealtiel and
> Jeshua son of Jozadak set to work to rebuild the house
> of God in Jerusalem. And the prophets of God were
> with them, helping them.
>
> Ezra 5:1–2

No doubt these prophets had been given, along with the rest of the volunteers, all of the tools, weapons and architect's blueprints they needed to complete the task of restoring properly authorized worship of God in this hostile environment. But the best help the prophets of God could give their colleagues and fellow-labourers was to regularly convey and report bulletins of God's mind and heart towards his people, imparting his divine perspective and motivating them with major incentives to see this difficult project through to completion.

Reading the prophecy of Haggai, you will notice that its two short chapters are full of promises and reassurances of safety and protection, as well as challenges not to lose heart and give up. All of this confirmed the vital conviction received from God: "I am with you!" (Haggai 1:13). The narrative in Ezra 6:14–15 tells us specifically about the positive outcome of this ministry: "So the elders of the Jews continued to build and prosper under the preaching of Haggai the prophet and Zechariah, a descendant of Iddo. They finished building the temple according to the command of the God of Israel and the decrees of Cyrus, Darius and Artaxerxes, kings of Persia."

Important things like kingdom-building projects are encouraged towards completion when there are prophets around, because with their help we are constantly reminded that we really heard from God, even if the going is tough and the money hasn't all come in as yet!

As we read the books of Zechariah and Haggai, we notice that these two prophets were entirely different in style from one another. Zechariah had a colourful, poetic and vivid imagination, placing before the builders a number of images and prophetic visions to keep their imagination awake to the secret sources of spiritual power available to them (Zechariah 4) and also the world-transforming influence of that completed temple in the future (Zechariah 8). Haggai's style was much more prosaic and to the point. Even so, how encouraged the people must have felt when they heard Haggai succinctly declare, "The glory of this present house will be greater than the glory of the former house... And in this place I will grant peace" (Haggai 2:9). We need to hear promises like this when we're involved in a project where our lives could be in jeopardy or the project seems impossible to complete. These are some of the ways prophets orientate us to the future, bringing God's tomorrow into our today, so that we can learn to live in its light.

In 1993, in the church I previously pastored for many years, I went through a testing time in the latter part of that year. We had an influx of people converted from a New Age "traveller" background and, because they were rooted in rebellious, anti-authority, strongly independent and individualistic attitudes, they were among the most difficult people we had encountered for a long time in teaching, discipling and nurturing them as new Christians in the Lord. We would experience unnecessary conflicts and run-ins over a number of issues. Though they clearly loved both me and my fellow church leaders as father figures, they reacted negatively to some aspects of that fathering role, and I sometimes had to exercise the discipline they had never experienced in their lives before as I challenged or rebuked their behaviour. By the end of that year I felt that I had simply had enough of all of them, after their subversive behaviour had nearly split the church, undermining the confidence and trust in their leaders of the rest of our young people. There were other difficulties accumulating in the church as well, the familiar turbulence so common at such times of spiritual warfare.

In sheer desperation I called on the Lord for more help and wisdom, saying, "Lord, what we need is another wave of your Holy Spirit to come to us and refresh us!"

In the early spring of 1994 we began a season of special

evening prayer meetings, praying that God would come and visit this church in grace once again. From the very first night of what would become many weeks of almost nightly prayer, we began to hear remarkable prophecies delivered by those in attendance at the meetings, and all to the same effect – Jesus was coming back to his church with armfuls of gifts; but this time it wouldn't be the gifts that would most occupy us, but the Giver himself. We received pictures of incoming tides and waves splashing up a beach, allowing formerly stranded or beached boats, left high and dry in the mud, to become buoyant and able to move in their natural element once again. We saw vivid pictures of powerful cleansing and empowerment, great healings, tremendous advance; images of rains ending our drought, powerful trade winds propelling our lives in new directions and changing them for the better forever – all clear predictions that the Holy Spirit was coming to do some mighty works among us. And two months later he did! In the mid-1990s, a well-reported and widespread move of the Holy Spirit swept and caught up thousands of churches and tens of thousands of believers. In the very first week that this news was shared with the leaders of the Newfrontiers church network we were part of, our church was to experience this also. We had nearly four years of the most astonishing blessing, favour, healing and transformation as a result, and some of the most powerful encounters with God I have ever personally experienced as a pastor.

The main point here is that God told us this would happen. When it came, people started dropping sideways off their seats under the power of God, shaking and falling on their faces on the floor under God's power, laughing with joy in some cases or crying with deep emotion in others, as formerly hidden hurts began to be uncovered so that God could heal them. Over that time we saw the Lord accomplish spectacular transformations in people's lives that we had never encountered before. But we weren't fazed at all by the unusual ways in which he operated, because he had told us it was going to happen!

The Lord had said, "I am going to send my Spirit among you, operating in new and unforeseen ways, along with new spiritual manifestations and spiritual gifts. His empowering will come to my people throughout this season, and the long-term effects will be for the expansion of my kingdom through you, so don't be alarmed. It's me."

Sometimes we really need to know "It's me", don't we? God can come to his people in ways we have never experienced before and fail to recognize even though such happenings are often recorded in the Bible. A friend expressed it to me like this: "God often offends our minds in order to expose our hearts." Prophetic foretelling is God in grace providing for his people's needs and reticence to acknowledge his answers, reassuring us by preparing us for a previously unforeseen future. This equips us to keep walking in peace and trust, despite any negative criticism or unhelpful misinterpretations of God's activity, or manmade obstructions to it. We become receptive to God, full of faith and responsive to what he is saying and doing.

Old Testament scholar Alec Motyer said, "The task of the Old Testament prophets was to address the present in the light of the future." And Philip Greenslade observes, "The prophet is quick to detect movements of the Holy Spirit and to stir the church to respond."

Is your church quick to detect movements of the Holy Spirit? Do you at least have key individuals in the church who are? God help us if we haven't. It is so easy to succumb to the danger of resisting the Holy Spirit when he comes in new and surprising ways, even when we can observe such unusual visitations already recorded in the Bible. For some reason we erroneously conclude they are not for today. Mostly, we are wrong about that.

Those praying and longing for revival, sadly, may be among the very first to refuse to recognize it when it comes – sometimes even denouncing it as work of the devil. Tragically, conservative Christians, past and present, have often responded like this to genuine spiritual renewal and awakening, missing what the Lord is doing because he comes in ways we didn't expect, saying unfamiliar things we've never heard and doing things we never thought we'd see. People who have prayed so hard for God to touch and speak to us may lack the necessary discernment to recognize the movement of the Holy Spirit they have prayed for when finally it comes. But prophecy orientates us towards God's future surprises so that we are more prepared to own it and less inclined to dismiss it, and therefore ready to receive the Lord and not miss out on his special grace for us "in the day of God's power".

5. Prophecy strengthens, encourages and comforts the body of believers

The opening verses of 1 Corinthians 14, discussed at the beginning of this chapter, include Paul's concise definition of the purpose of prophecy: "…everyone who prophesies speaks to men for their strengthening, encouragement and comfort" (1 Corinthians 14:3). There are five verbs used in 1 Corinthians 14 in connection with prophetic gifting and ministry:

a) Prophecy "builds up" (verse 3; Greek: oikodomeō)

This creates the image of a house-build. If the church is a dwelling in which God lives by his Holy Spirit (Ephesians 2:21–22) and if the church is also the "pillar of truth" (1 Timothy 3:15), then God will not be content with a shoddy, poorly constructed "house", any more than you or I would feel happily at home in a dilapidated, dirty or ruined building. God wants his house, the church community, built the way he designed it – the way it *must* be if he is to feel at home among his people; that's why the gift of prophecy is important. It helps to ensure that both individual lives and the corporate gatherings of our churches are built according to the very best designs drawn from the Architect's blueprints and assembled with the very best materials available. On brand new housing developments in the UK there is often a "Show Home" already completed by the contractors, fully furnished, fitted out and decorated. All appliances, soft furnishings and lighting are installed, making the whole house "picture perfect". Usually, this is the first house the prospective buyer encounters on the corner of the entrance road to the unfinished building site. It will have a prominent sign: "Show Home", to enable every viewer to imagine vividly what the incomplete neighbouring properties will look like when they are finished. People would not be persuaded to buy one of those under construction, with its bare foundations, rain-puddled, muddy garden, and only the bare beginnings of unfinished brick walls, until they had seen how the finished house would look.

In the very same way, local churches can become God's "show homes" in the Holy Spirit, though still under construction. The unfinished building contains wonderful evidence that God is powerfully at work there, and prophecy offers a vision of what God is ultimately aiming to accomplish among his redeemed saints. Christ is saying to us, "I want my church back, please, and I do not want it built any longer by fleshly, self-directed ministry and human ability. I want it built according to the Architect's blueprints recorded in Scripture."

As visitors walk into church on Sunday morning, seeing the joy on everybody's faces, experiencing God's dynamic work of healing and transformation, catching the vision of a people unafraid to move in the prophetic, they will be moved to respond, "Wow, this is amazing! I never knew that church could be like this. How do I join? Where do I sign up? When can I move in?"

Only God's Holy Spirit can guide, empower and direct us to accomplish this, enabling churches everywhere to become part of God's "Ideal Homes Exhibition" – glimpses of a future shaped by grace. Prophecy helps us to build things right. It restores the "Wow-factor" to church life. We are living out our prophetic calling when we inhabit by faith, in our daily lives and worship gatherings, the joy, love and peace of Christ's coming kingdom.

b) Prophecy "exhorts" (verse 3; Greek: parakaleō)

This verb means "to come alongside and summon to a change of action, to a different outlook, a new mood" or "to impart courage". Prophecy calls us nearer God than we were before, enabling us to hear his counsel and be stirred out of apathy, compromise and inertia. As we move in the prophetic, the Holy Spirit hauls us out of the mire when we stand knee-deep in the raw sewage of sin. It's a wonderful experience to have someone come alongside you and say, "God sent me to rescue you. I know the way out. The Lord has told me what you need to do to escape this mess." This gift can save a lot of time in the counselling rooms where the *paraklesis* of the Holy Spirit is most urgently needed.

c) Prophecy "encourages" (verse 3; Greek: paramythia)

This word denotes the God-given ability to draw close to someone with words of tenderness when they are grieving, confused or hurt. Such prophecy calms fear, bringing profound peace. Someone may be going through a tough time, facing a personal struggle, journeying alongside a loved one who is dying, afraid of an awaited medical diagnosis; then the word comes to a person with no natural awareness of these difficulties: "The Lord has put on my mind to tell you, 'Don't be afraid; I am with you, and I will never leave you.'" One of our church members was suddenly struck with a terrible pain in her abdomen and hospitalized within the hour. When I went to see her she was writhing with agony on her bed; but during the drive there I had asked the Lord if he had anything to say to this woman. He put a verse from John's gospel into my mind (John 11:4), so that I was able to stand at her bedside saying, "I believe the Lord has told me to tell you this sickness will not end in death, but is for the glory of God. I think the Lord is going to heal you, and heal you very quickly." Her illness was eventually diagnosed as an acute attack of pancreatitis, a potentially fatal disease. But against all the usual medical expectations, she quickly recovered and came home from the hospital in just five days. I had not heard of pancreatitis before and didn't know how dangerous it can be, until three years later when I too was afflicted with it after a trip to India, suffering for six months from its effects, drawing very close to death several times. The doctors were astonished that I survived at all and, years later, my niece went to train as a nurse in that same hospital and my case was still referred to in training lectures as "a miracle" even then. At the time of my illness, I was similarly upheld and encouraged in my struggle for life by the most encouraging prophecies from both friends and strangers, who assured me of my future healing and miraculous recovery. All of these prophecies proved true; we both lived – my friend and me – *hallelujah!* These were clear examples of the power of prophecy to encourage a believer, strengthening the inner being, promoting healing and hope. In such dire health crises, death can come early when hope is lost. Prophecy can literally save lives. God is good; he built up our hopes and ultimately kept his word.

d) Prophecy "convinces" (verses 24–25; Greek: enlenketai)

Paul says, "If an unbeliever or someone who does not understand comes in while everybody is prophesying, he will be *convinced* by all that he is a sinner and will be judged by all, and the secrets of his heart will be laid bare. So he will fall down and worship God, exclaiming, 'God is really among you!'" (1 Corinthians 14:24–25). The verb "convinced" here in verse 24 carries the idea of marshalled evidence bringing conviction of sin and the only appropriate verdict. This is a vital part of personal evangelism and the public preaching of the gospel, as the living God shows us specific things about our hearers, often in detail, bringing to light their special need of encounter with him. Those who have attended services may often say to the preacher, "How did you know that? Where did you find out about me? Who told you about me?" The explanation is that God knows this person and brings these things to mind as we prepare or speak, so they will understand the depth of his love for them and that he knows and cares about even the details of their lives. The Holy Spirit may prompt us to say things we never anticipated, so they're suddenly intruding into the address as we stand up to speak, and this can have remarkable effects on those listening. The apostle Peter, in Acts 5:1–11, saw some hidden but deadly secrets operative in the lives of a deceitful, ambitious couple – Ananias and Sapphira – who were eager to impress their faith community and faked their pledge for the church offering in order to gain some kudos. God supernaturally disclosed their lies to Peter, who pronounced a prophetic judgement on each of them for their duplicity, with shocking, sudden and devastatingly deadly effects. The result was that "great fear seized the whole church and all who heard about these events" (verse 11). Prophecy brings the clean fear of God to people.

Some years ago my friend Jeff Lucas, a very gifted British Bible teacher, told me about an unusual incident at the Pioneer church in Chichester, West Sussex, when they launched their young people into a programme of street evangelism and door-to-door witnessing with the bold intention of using the gifts of the Holy Spirit for the benefit of unbelievers. A young girl of around 17 years of age was sent out with a companion and knocked on a neighbourhood door. There was no answer, so she rang the doorbell. Eventually, a big-bellied, burly and rough-speaking man came to the door. She was very small, around 4 feet 8 inches, and he was over 6 feet. He stood there eating a cake. "Yeah, what do you want?" he asked.

She replied, "I've come to talk to you about Jesus."

"I'm not interested in Jesus," he retorted. "I'm not remotely religious, I don't even believe there's a God. He doesn't exist." Then he threw out a challenge, "Go on, prove to me that there is a God."

She stood there in a nervous silence for a few moments, praying, "Lord, give me something to say to this man." Then she said, "God just told me that you're a thief!"

He replied angrily and in great shock, "How *dare* you come to my doorstep and tell me I'm a *thief*, when I've never met you in my life! Who do you think you are?" Then he added cynically, "What is it I'm supposed to be stealing?"

The young girl went white with fright and said under her breath, "Lord, please tell me something else about him!" Within a moment she dared to add a specific detail to her previous statement: "Do you know anything about pub signs

– those painted boards that hang on posts outside inns and restaurants?"

Now it was his turn to feel nervous, as he responded: "Er… what do you mean?"

She replied, "I don't know what I mean, but God just told me something about pub signs." Then after a further pause as clarity came to her, she suddenly said, "You steal pub signs, don't you?"

God had shown her this man's secret hobby. He would regularly drive around the Sussex countryside in the middle of the night, long after closing time, with tools and a ladder, quietly removing the picturesque wooden signs suspended outside pubs, then mounting them on the walls of his stairs and landing, and even in his living room. He was really fazed by this revelation from a complete stranger.

He bluffed, challenging the girl: "Anybody who knows me knows I collect pub signs. No, you'll have to do better than that!" With that, his wife appeared in the hallway behind him, saying, "Bert, what's going on?" He replied, "It's this little girl from the church around the corner, and she's trying to convince me there's a God, but she's not doing very well. Ha! Ha!"

So the girl added one more thing the Lord told her, "Does the name *Dorothy* mean anything to you?" He went completely red with embarrassment from his collar upwards and, seeing this, his wife looked quizzically at her husband – because her name wasn't Dorothy! She said, "Bert, what's wrong?" He could hardly get out of that situation fast enough!

I wish I could tell you I knew he had been converted, but I can tell you this story is absolutely true. God is capable of revealing the secrets of people's hearts. Prophecy can bring the fear of God to people. It can bring conviction of sin, and sometimes leads to their spiritual conversion. At the very least, they know God is real!

We once had two women drive from Northampton one Sunday morning to be at our meeting in Winchester. This was in a school hall, because we were erecting a new church building on the site of our old one. Only one of these women was Christian, but her non-Christian friend had said to her: "I've got to go to a church I've heard about in Winchester next Sunday. I don't know why, but I've just got to visit that place. Can we go together?" So they got up very early that morning and drove to Winchester – a journey of a hundred miles! They had trouble finding the school where we met and arrived late, just as I started to preach. The usher found them the only seats left – on the front row, right in front of me! As I spoke I could see that both women were unusually attentive, even riveted to what was being said, occasionally whispering to one another during the message.

As they listened, tears began to roll down their cheeks and, when I gave the invitation to respond to the gospel at the end of the service, one of the women, the unbeliever who had urged her Christian friend to accompany her that morning, suddenly dropped on her knees on the wooden parquet floor of that school hall and wept copiously, face-down on the ground, soaking the floor until a pool of tears had collected in front of her.

I learned from her friend, who called me some days later, that this was a "divine appointment": everything I said in that sermon spoke directly to her companion, who became a Christian that morning. Apparently, I had even recounted conversations they had shared in the preceding weeks and months. Now she knew there was a God who loved her, knew her and had called to come and meet him for herself. Wouldn't you like to see that happen regularly, or even occasionally, in your church? It can. The Holy Spirit will be there convicting unbelievers of his reality and the truth of the gospel that he has ready as his gift for them; if only someone will pass on the message.

Christ had many notable experiences of this very kind. The woman of Samaria heard Jesus gently expose the emptiness of her inner life and recount his discernment of her many sexual partners. She responded, "Sir, I can see you are a prophet" (John 4:19) and later told her friends, "Come, see a man who told me everything I ever did" (John 4:29). This encounter changed her life, bringing her to faith in Jesus as the Messiah.

We can see similar effects today, because the same Holy Spirit accompanies us prophetically in the task of evangelism.

e) Prophecy "instructs" (verse 31; Greek: manthanō)

This verb means "to learn knowledge that will affect one's manner of life". Some kinds of knowledge do no more than fill our heads with information that wasn't there before, but real learning is transformative knowledge that brings about change in our characters and lifestyle. Paul says, "For you can all prophesy in turn so that everyone may be *instructed* and encouraged." Prophecy touches all areas of our inner life, not just the intellect: it informs the mind, but it also moves the emotions and influences the will. It conveys experiential knowledge of God's presence, compassion, love and intimate understanding of our human condition. As such, the effects of prophecy are always entirely positive. It never leaves people feeling confused, degraded or condemned. It frequently exposes and convicts of sin, but never without offering hope, giving directions that enable us to escape sin's binding effects upon us. It is the word of a God who forgives and sets people free. Even when they have done the most terrible things, the compassion of God radiates through the use of his gifts and, when the church is moving in the prophetic, people should never feel intimidated, put down, or crushed under an oppressive sense of their inferiority.

As we have seen so far then, prophecy builds up, stirs up, cheers up and cuts up our consciences so that we can feel "genned up" concerning God's heart and plans for our lives, situations and corporate life together. But there is more.

6. Prophecy carries tremendously persuasive evidence of the reality and love of God

When Jesus passed through Samaria (John 4:4ff), he was entering quasi-Gentile territory that most Jews bypassed because of its pagan associations and the syncretistic beliefs of its people. Jesus felt compelled to cross merely human barriers and go into this area, so long populated by foreigners who had adopted elements of the Jewish faith but were not true to the whole of Scripture. The Jews, who avoided Samaritans, must have found it profoundly shocking that Jesus actually approached these outcasts. You will recall that he sat down to rest at a well, engaging a Samaritan (shocking) in deep conversation, and also recall that this Samaritan was a woman (even more shocking). And not just any woman, but a woman of bad reputation, plummeting downwards in a spiral of self-destructive sensuality. But the Son of Man came to seek and save those who are lost, and as Jesus conversed with this woman, he teased out her longing and thirst for spiritual realities – simultaneously exposing her great ignorance concerning them.

As Christ began to touch some of her deepest, unsatisfied aspirations, he suddenly sprang a surprise request, asking her to go and fetch her husband. Maybe she went pink with embarrassment, but she nevertheless admitted honestly that she was not married. Then he told her in a single sentence, "The fact is, you have had five husbands, and the man you now have is not your husband" (verse 17–18). Her immediate response was, "Sir, I can see that you are a prophet" (verse 19). She recognized what many Christians today fail to acknowledge: this utterance was a manifestation of the gift of prophecy. It is often, in my view, a mistake to describe such a disclosure of hidden information as a "word of knowledge". I think that particular designation, used by Paul in I Corinthians 12:8, actually relates to the teaching gifts of the Holy Spirit, referring to the ability to teach and communicate in the power of the Spirit divinely revealed truth found in the Scriptures, in such a way that they sink with transformative effects into the minds of those who hear us.

By contrast, when we receive supernatural information about a person that we could not have known naturally, the correct terminology for that is "prophecy". It is the very essence of a prophetic word. We "know in our knower" something we did not know before. Jesus prophesies to the Samaritan woman about her private life, with the outcome that not only is she converted but, on the strength of her testimony, her whole village also. Her excited reaction, voiced to her neighbours, was "He told me everything I ever did!" (John 4:39). Christ had told her only one specific detail of her life, but sometimes that one thing is everything. It tells you all about the person. The Lord shows pinpoint precision accuracy in his utterances, knowing exactly what we are wrestling with. He told the rich young ruler, "If you want to be perfect, go, sell your possessions and give to the poor, and you will have treasure in heaven. Then come, follow me." The immediate effect of this is also recounted: "When the young man heard this, he went away sad, because he had great wealth" (Matthew 19:21–22). Sometimes there is just one major issue holding us back, and Christ knows exactly what that issue is. He tells us "everything [we] ever did" because he identifies the major stronghold in our lives, as he did with the Samaritan woman.

The account of the duplicity of Ananias and Sapphira, referenced earlier, is an example of the way the Holy Spirit unerringly finds the heart of a situation. They were practising deceit at a tender and vulnerable time in the early church's history and God was not about to allow such blatant hypocrisy to corrupt his church so early on in her mission. Lessons learned now would be formative and, since hypocrisy is a deadly blight that threatens the health of any and every faith community, a salutary lesson was needed. So the Holy Spirit enabled the apostle Peter to expose Ananias and Sapphira for their deceitfulness in lying to God and, one after the other, they were both suddenly struck dead. Great fear came upon the whole church, which once again displayed tremendous evidential and persuasive proof of God's holiness, immanence and power among believers and unbelievers alike.

Another relevant incident is the encounter of Paul with the slave girl at Philippi who followed the apostle and his companions, boldly announcing the truth, "These men are servants of the Most High God, who are telling you the way to be saved" (Acts 16:17). We might have expected him to welcome the publicity, but Paul knew instinctively, by the Holy Spirit's discernment, that the inspiration of her proclamation was an unclean spirit of divination, a serpent-like counterfeit "python" spirit of witchcraft constituting merely psychic and demonic knowledge – not authentic revelation from the Holy Spirit. So he turned in anger – upon the evil spirit, not the girl herself – saying, "In the name of Jesus Christ I command you to come out of her!" (Acts 16:18). Her fortunetelling ability was completely lost from that moment onwards. It had gone. One result of this was that the citizens of Philippi knew that there was a unique servant of God present among them, a somewhat dangerous and powerful servant of God who could threaten the welfare of their local spiritualist folk religion and its hitherto impressive practitioners. This was so dangerous to the local economy that Paul had to be imprisoned; but even in close confinement Paul could not be stopped.

One leading Anglican bishop once asked, "How is it that wherever the apostle Paul went there was either a riot or a revival, but wherever I go they simply serve cucumber sandwiches and tea?" One answer may be that it is because the prophetic dimension, so vividly apparent in Paul's ministry, is not consistently and powerfully present in the lives of many of our bishops, vicars and pastors; for wherever this prophetic gift is present and active, the powers of darkness will be thoroughly shaken and stirred!

The Holy Spirit is able to bring great fear and a sense of the reality of God to people who were hitherto oblivious to his presence. Prophecy grabs people's attention in irresistible ways as the prophetic enables God's servants to "read people's mail" – hearing their very thoughts and disclosing some of their deepest secrets as God's Spirit engages with their souls. We don't need to act as God's "bounty hunter" in this, personally pursuing the person for whom this prophetic word is intended; God will find them even as we speak and they will come to us (as the women from Northampton travelled all the way to Winchester). They will have heard themselves described in detail through an agent who knew little or nothing about them previously. Yet this fear that comes upon people, and the exposure they experience, will not be destructive to their welfare. "The fear of the Lord is pure", says the psalmist (Psalm 19:9); and the experience brings a sense of cleansing, relief, light and joy.

Some years ago, a young man walked into the church I pastored in Winchester. He was hard and cynical in appearance and sat chewing gum throughout the worship time. His sister had recently been converted and was now a member of the church, and he had come to visit her for the weekend, deciding to attend church that Sunday night simply out of curiosity. As worship began, I received a strong impression of a particular young man in the crowded building. I didn't know for sure if the young man in my mind was actually in our gathering, but the mental picture formed so strongly and persistently, throughout the worship time, that I eventually stood up and began to describe him. I recounted his private life, what he was doing at weekends, how he was spending his money, his occupation, and the specific ways he thought about life. The young man heard this, recognized himself and was so cut to the heart he came forward at the invitation concluding the message, falling on his knees to give his life to Christ.

A close friend and work colleague, to whom he later told this story, was so amazed that someone could reveal secrets like that in a church meeting that he also travelled 40 miles to church the following Sunday with our new convert, to see what was happening in this unusual church – and he was converted too! That's why this gift is so beautiful: it finds people exactly where they are and helps to reveal the reality and love of God to those who do not as yet even know they are hungry and searching.

7. Prophecy restores an accurate view of self – it enables people to see themselves as God sees them

Most of us are not particularly secure in our identities as men or women of God, or at ease with the way God made us and the gifts he has bestowed upon us. We often carry some kind of "chip on the shoulder", as well as hidden wounds that inhibit us from loving God and other people, preventing us from moving confidently in the abilities the Lord has given us. We are all damaged people. There have been many harmful things done to us, and nasty words spoken over us. Our self-perception has been distorted by negative words and cruel curses uttered by school teachers, parents and other influential people who have put us down. I once heard of a man who couldn't bear to watch a live rugby match because, every time the team members went into a scrum, he thought they were all talking about him!

How do you react when you look through old family photograph albums, showing the pictures to visitors, relatives or friends? Do you turn the page over quickly when there is a photograph of you on it? Is this in order that everyone is forced to move on quickly because you don't like the way you look, either then or now, and you don't like people seeing you in your swimming costume/reading glasses/dated fashions or strange hairstyle?

There are many ways we can manifest this lack of confidence and negative view of ourselves and that is why we can no longer rely on the wrong and often deliberately distorted information that has been fed to us about our identity. Not all of it is accurate and some of it is from the devil. We have to begin to hear from God about his perception of us and the good things he has planned for us, as well as the special abilities or gifts of the Holy Spirit that he has equipped us with, and the unique calling he has placed upon each of our lives.

An aeroplane flying in fog is a very dangerous plane unless the pilot has the appropriate electronic instruments on the panel and he knows how to read them. There have been a number of fatal accidents involving two-seater aircraft where the pilot has suddenly been caught in low cloud without instruments, or does not possess the ability to read the instruments he has. When an aeroplane in flight encounters fog, the pilot has no way of accurately assessing exactly what that plane is doing by his senses alone. Vertigo begins to distort the perceptions of his brain. The pilot doesn't know whether the plane is tipping from the horizontal to the right or to the left, or whether or not it is slowly descending. He can't tell if he is flying straight by sight alone in those clouds and he's not even sure if the plane is still at the same height, flying horizontally, climbing skywards or diving dangerously towards the ground. But if he has the appropriate instruments, they will tell him objectively all of the information he needs to know – the pitch, the turn, the height – and even though the information may conflict with the sense-perception he would instinctively trust (implying that his instruments are totally wrong!), he has to rely on the objective information from the instrument panel and not his senses if he is to save both his own life and his passenger's.

We too need to shun dangerous and misleading subjectivism. Instead, we must rely on the objective truths God himself sees and speaks about us in his Word. The angel of the Lord appeared to Gideon as he was in hiding, secretly threshing what little remained of his grain harvest that year in a hole in the ground, knowing that Midianite marauders might at any moment arrive without announcement to steal it and ransack the rest of the countryside in search of plunder. Nervously squatting in a wine press, Gideon was burning with anger, frustration and fear, and desperately longing to see circumstances turn around for his people. The angel said, "The Lord is with you, mighty warrior" (Judges 6:12). That's not the most obvious description of a desperate man hiding in terror in a pit, trying to avoid enemy invasion in the form of Midianite raiders! But perhaps God could see more in Gideon than anybody else could. Maybe God could see that though Gideon was beleaguered and afraid, he still had something of a fighting spirit about him: "But sir... if the Lord is with us, why has all this happened to us? Where are all his wonders that our fathers told us about when they said, 'Did not the Lord bring us up out of Egypt?' But now the Lord has abandoned us and put us into the hand of Midian" (Judges 6:13).

You can almost feel his inner turmoil and internal debate with God, and the way his spirit had been aroused by recent cruel events and enemy aggression. This man's fighting spirit was just waiting for its chance. So God begins his encounter with Gideon by addressing that very characteristic within him, hailing him as "...thou mighty man of valour!" (KJV). God has spoken to him and neither he nor his nation will ever be the same again.

This is one reason why the overwhelming majority of prophetic words are simply statements of the obvious under the power of the Holy Spirit, though that may not be so apparent to the person bringing the prophecy or to the hearer for whom it is intended. The wonder does not reside in God telling us something original and hitherto unknown, but in shining a light on something that is either new to us or that we have let slip and desperately need to hear affirmed at this moment. God tells us things we ought to have known, but have forgotten – that he loves us, that he is for us, that he is our Father, that we are his children, that he has a plan for our lives, that we are precious in his sight, that he has gifted us, that we are important to his kingdom purposes. We can get all that from the Bible any time we care to read it, but it has to come in a revelatory way to our hearts if we are really to believe and receive it.

People have no idea of their worth or value to God or to others, often because they have been fed lies for most of their lives by negative people or by the devil. They nurse deep wounds of rejection, anxiety and negative reactions. God can bring physical, emotional and spiritual healing to such individuals with a simple prophetic word spoken in the power of the Holy Spirit. There is nothing more likely to be the agent of this than the preached word, carrying a prophetic edge because the preacher is capable of hearing from God for the people. Thus God speaks prophetically into their hearts, in order to touch upon their deepest needs and reorientate their lives in purpose, peace and joy.

The Bible says, "Do not conform any longer to the pattern of this world, but be transformed by the renewing of your mind" (Romans 12:2). And note, it does not say "the *removing* of your mind" but "the *renewing* of your mind", which means that our minds are important and need to be changed if we are to be healed. Any old and inaccurate data is wiped from the hard drive and replaced with completely new programming, installed through the progressive reading of Scripture and through the prophetic voice of God speaking to us again and again, so that we begin to perceive and think differently. We change our minds about God, about the world, about Jesus, about the church and about ourselves. Our minds are progressively renewed. They are now marinaded in truth instead of the lies we used to believe, and hence our lives are completely transformed. Prophecy therefore lines us up with the truth: reality as God defines it to be.

The late Bible teacher Arthur Wallis once voiced a striking insight with regard to the more distant future. He said, "It is my conviction that recognizing apostles and prophets and letting them function, will yet prove the most important restoration breakthrough of our time." Since he wrote this, the emergence of the ministries of both apostles and prophets has triggered enormous controversy in the body of Christ from the 1970s onwards, right up to this present day. In step with an increasing recognition of the validity of the prophetic, we must also learn to recognize the validity of apostolic ministry; for the truth is that we need both.

Terry Virgo once summarized his personal perspective upon the vital necessity of prophetic ministry in the building of healthy churches: "Many a congregation contains good people but they are not sufficiently exposed to the prophetic ministry and so fail to be excited by God's ultimate purpose. A church that is exposed to prophetic ministry will become uncompromising in its commitment to obey God's revealed will, whatever the implications of that obedience may be."

Is your church, and are you personally, uncompromising in your commitment to obey God's will in this matter and willing to respond to all that he does by his Spirit to restore the gift of prophecy in your life together? This is a good indicator of the health and spiritual condition of your church. Prophetic people help to restore divine health to a church. They are able to hear what Christ himself would say to his people and are prepared to report it accurately to us, whether this is well received or not. We need that kind of truth-telling. Therefore, "be eager to prophesy".

What a wonderful, positive force is the gift of prophecy: building up the people of God, convincing people to repent of sin and flooding their hearts with the knowledge of God's love for them; strengthening and encouraging the faithful when they are demoralized, weary or afraid; and releasing among the believers the sheer delight and exuberance of God's Spirit, reigniting the fire we so easily lose.

My aim is to dispel any lingering theological reservations about this gift, to enable you to see its biblical validity and its indispensable necessity in blessing our lives, and to stir a new eagerness to try for yourself this amazing, empowering every-believer gift. It is for everyone; the gift will not be yours any more than it is mine – it is the Holy Spirit's gift, and God gives his Spirit to everyone who turns to him and asks. If you have received the Spirit of God into your heart, then already the gift of prophecy is there – but perhaps you just haven't unwrapped it yet.

Chapter Three

Prophetic Watchmen in the Church

The Old Testament prophets were often called "watchmen". We are familiar with the term "watchmen" in contemporary society, as people commissioned to guard industrial complexes, public buildings, even the perimeter fences of army base camps – any place vulnerable to trespass or encroaching danger. In the ancient world, watchmen were summoned to guard whole cities and had an important role to play in relaying advance notice of the arrival of visitors and messengers, as well as hostile armies. The watchmen took positions of prominence on city walls and high towers, to expand their visual horizon and detect any approach from even great distances. They also watched over the safety of the city during the vulnerable hours of the night.

In the body of Christ today, there are many self-appointed "watchmen" who exercise what they describe as a "Last Days discernment ministry". They see their role as discerning spirits and doctrinal errors – sounding the alarm when they identify what they believe to be hidden dangers. I prefer to call many of these individuals "watchdogs" rather than watchmen because, like a dog on guard that lacks discernment to distinguish friend from foe, they are often unnecessarily alarmist, "barking" at anything that moves and reacting loudly to anything unfamiliar to them, seeing inherent threats in phenomena they do not know or understand.

This is really the opposite of discernment. The watchman discerns the activity of the Holy Spirit in genuine ministry, wisely searching the Scriptures to weigh the substance of new phenomena or an unfamiliar approach. The watchdog simply sounds the alarm, announcing, "It's of the devil!" or demanding, "Where's that in the Bible?", every time God does something new. This can be destructive, because it inhibits one of the central purposes of the Holy Spirit's gifts – that of strengthening and building up the body. The watchdog barks and the flock panic and scatter; the household of faith, frightened and disturbed, begins to distrust the healing and transforming work of God among the people.

The true watchman, called of God to protect and build up the household of faith, is actually not looking for trouble but looking for the movement of the Holy Spirit. The detection of enemy activity is a secondary function of his role. The watchman's eyes are fixed upon God, and it is as we are attentive to the Holy Spirit's whisper in our hearts that we pick up the still, small voice of truth and insight alerting us to the danger of anything false, shoddy or sinful that may be threatening the wellbeing of the believing community or the individual soul. Then the watchman's task is to announce the warning that has come not from personal prejudices and an oversensitive habit of suspicion, but from God who looks not on outward "seeming" but on the heart.

Individuals in Danger

There was a man I knew some years ago who had been very prominent in the church's life, very influential and much loved. Suddenly his zeal cooled, he became erratic in his attendance at meetings and, though his wife didn't say much, I knew that she was distressed. I had numerous contacts with him and spoke to him about my concerns, but every time he deflected my enquiry, suggesting that the problem was me, or that the church was in the wrong because we weren't approaching this or that matter correctly, or the worship wasn't satisfactory and the preaching was no longer meeting his needs. Eventually things went really quiet and we saw nothing of him for many weeks, until one wintry February morning I happened to meet him in town, asked him how he was, and we stood and chatted for a while about general matters. Then, with a jolt, as we were talking, a really shocking idea occurred to me, intruding suddenly and insistently into my mind. When God speaks, he relies on us to trust him despite embarrassment or fear of looking foolish or causing offence. Knowing this, and believing that my unexpected, persistent thought might be the voice of the Holy Spirit, I looked him straight in the eyes and said, "You know, I've been concerned about you for a long time. I want to ask you a pointed question. Are you having an affair?"

My friend immediately stepped backwards in shock and coloured with embarrassment. His head and eyes went down and he then lifted his gaze and looked straight at me and replied, "Yes".

I asked, "How long has it been going on?"

"Months," he replied.

It is often the case that some unacknowledged moral issue is the root of the problem when a believer begins to find fault with different aspects of church life and ministry and to raise objections to miraculous accounts and hard sayings in the Bible. So it was in this instance.

I thank God that I am able to tell you, that man actually repented. The morning I met him in town, he had been on the verge of leaving his wife that very day for the other woman. He had first met her at a business conference held in a hotel and they had chatted in the lobby. Later that same evening she arrived at his hotel room door, dressed only in a bath robe which she opened as he unlocked the door. She stood completely naked before him and that, as they say, was it. Now, many months later, at this crucial moment when he stood on the brink of throwing away everything dear and valuable in his life, God made a divine appointment with him, alerting his watchman to bear the prophetic word that cut straight to his heart and saved his marriage, then saved his Christian walk and finally restored him to service in the body of Christ. The watchman waits for God's Word; and God sees and knows the hearts of his people, knows every detail of this world that is the creation of his love.

Dangerous Individuals

On another occasion I had a dream. It occurred at the end of December 1988, at the approach of the New Year. I was awakened in the deepest hours of the night by vivid images that kept coming in rapid succession to my mind, concerning two individuals.

The first man in my dream had recently started visiting the church, effusively friendly, gathering people round himself, slyly undermining their trust and confidence in the pastoral oversight and ongoing ministry of the church, and slandering the eldership team.

Then rapidly succeeding this sequence of events I saw another suave, smooth individual ingratiating himself with the attractive single women in our church, of which we had many. I realized that these women were in danger from a predatory fake who would come in and try to rob them of their purity and seduce them.

Amazingly, just as the dream indicated, in January two new individuals turned up at our church, one of them within a week of New Year. The first was an elderly man with a long white beard and white hair. He looked like Charlton Heston as Moses in the movie *The Ten Commandments*. In fact, we were nicknaming him "Moses" within two or three weeks of his arrival. He would seat himself on the balcony and, in the middle of the worship, he would exclaim, "Thus sayeth the Lord!", and then prophesy in a pretentious style, in words that couldn't be called wrong exactly, but sounded hollow and ostentatious. Though he said nothing actually false, I felt nonetheless, "I'm not sure about this man, at all. He's not a church member anywhere, I haven't even met him yet, and he's speaking authoritatively to the church, when we haven't welcomed his ministry and I don't even know his name!" He returned three or four times after that until, one Sunday, while I was preaching elsewhere, my fellow elder had to confront him. My colleague told me later, "He came and prophesied at the microphone this morning, whilst you were away preaching, and I was really troubled by him. So I quizzed him. He was offended."

I replied, "Next time he does it, I'm going to speak with him myself." He did so one week later. He had already been holding conversations with numbers of individuals around the church but after he prophesied I asked him, "Which church do you belong to?"

He said, "I don't belong to any church. I am a gift to the whole body."

I responded, "Then you aren't accountable to anybody. That being the case, you can't prophesy here until we are confident that your heart is good toward us. Because you are not under pastoral authority anywhere, and certainly not under mine, I cannot receive anything you have to say while you remain aloof and accountable to no one in this way. I am not going to allow you to talk to the church until we know who you are and why you have come here."

A real prophet would have asked how to join us and would have shown humility and accountability to the God-given pastoral oversight of that church, proving willing to be tested by it – but not this man. That was the last we saw of him.

Simultaneously, another man – younger than "Moses" – also arrived at the church and began to attend meetings regularly. He was charm itself. He was affable and outgoing, participating weekly in the cell group that he joined. He even cried during the messages! He often came forward to seek prayer ministry and told us he was repenting of many things. I eventually found out that he was married to one woman while living with another. He refused to return to his wife and, while he was with us, had become very, very friendly with a number of attractive young women in the church.

So I called him in to speak with me, saying, "You are welcome to stay in this church because there is a good chance you will be cleaned up and sorted out if you truly repent, but these are my conditions: you are to cease hugging all the young women in the church and you are to keep a discreet distance from them until we are satisfied that you have repented of the misconduct that is causing our concern." I also added, "I don't want you to be alone with any of them outside of our meetings either and I don't want you giving them lifts in your car or asking for lifts from them. I want you to be accountable to me for your contact in these areas."

That was the last I heard of him as well, except that he told everybody that I was a really savage pastor, aggressive and unreasonable in my attitudes and approach to ministry! We cannot prevent the possibility of being slandered by such individuals, but I am so glad I stopped that man from doing any further harm in the life of the church.

Do you recall how this all came about? This was a dream that came from God, and woke me from my sleep with such an urgent sense of its significance that it put me on the alert as one of God's watchmen. Had I relied on my own wisdom and perception, I might have felt ashamed at my uneasiness and sense of disquiet towards those men – but so vivid a dream gave me the forewarning I needed. God watches over his people.

Dangerous Situations

Joseph, husband of Mary, into whose care and protection God entrusted Jesus, was warned in the same way about Herod's plans to kill the infant Christ. He was directed by the messenger in his dream to seek refuge in Egypt until the murderous and infanticidal king was dead (Matthew 2:19–22). This is an example of God's prophetic "now word" operating as a warning alarm designed to avert danger for his people.

Sometimes the Spirit warns us of adverse circumstances as well as dangerous people. The book of Acts records,

> During this time some prophets came down from Jerusalem to Antioch. One of them, named Agabus,

stood up and through the Spirit predicted that a severe famine would spread over the entire Roman world. (This happened during the reign of Claudius.) The disciples, each according to his ability, decided to provide help for the brothers living in Judea. This they did, sending their gift to the elders by Barnabas and Saul.

Acts 11:27–30

Adversity comes to us all and, indeed, is a necessary aspect of our character development, teaching us humility and gratitude, strength and patience, and reliance on God. But God does not abandon us to adversity. He equips us to pass through times of trouble with our peace of mind and joy of heart intact: "Blessed are those whose strength is in you, who have set their hearts on pilgrimage. As they pass through the Valley of Baca, they make it a place of springs" (Psalm 84: 5–6).

God provides springs of grace for his people passing through periods of struggle and challenge, but we are expected to avail ourselves of the gifting of the Holy Spirit in order both to get through hard times in good shape and to develop a workmanlike faith in God's provision. The prophet Agabus was aware that sometimes that provision comes through God's people and their generous giving. Prophecy is as practical a part of that provision as the launch of a famine relief fund (Acts 11:29–30)!

Dangers to the Church

Occasionally, prophets warn us of inherent weaknesses threatening the life of the local church. Prophecy is for communities as well as for individuals and can address whole churches concerning damaging tendencies within their corporate life. We see an example of this in the prophetic words Jesus sent to the seven churches via the apostle John in Revelation 2 and 3. Each of the churches was addressed very specifically, and the Spirit of Christ unmasked their situations by way of both commendation and condemnation, as well as offering them consolation. If the Lord had anything against them, a prophetic word would make this clear. Fascinatingly, the ascended Lord addressed "the angel of the church". Some people read this as a title for the messenger or senior pastor of the church, among the eldership team. Others suggest it refers to a guardian angel, for angels are present when the church gathers and are aware of what we do and even the fashions and hairstyles we wear (1 Corinthians 11:10)! They are guardians of our welfare.

Again, some suggest this phrase signifies something more abstract and is a reference to an invisible power, a "group personality" or the corporate spirit or style of the church, arising from the common life of that church and revealing its unique make-up, feel and personality. This is very persuasive or, at least, worthy of serious consideration. When the Lord spoke to the angel of the church at Ephesus, he rebuked their abandonment of their "first love". At Pergamum he unmasked the occultism and immorality tolerated within their midst. When he spoke to Thyatira it was the operation of a Jezebelic spirit that was exposed, a controlling and manipulative demonic presence working in this case through a woman, who was self-promoting and anti-male, anti-authority and sexually amoral. She was controlling the church and silencing God's prophets. The Jezebel spirit, in all its historic and demonic manifestations, hates the prophetic. Just as the historic Queen Jezebel of Israel, the wife of Ahab in the ninth century BC, wanted Elijah's death, so there is a false, religious spirit that hates prophetic ministry and the prophetic voice of God whenever it is genuinely operative in the church today. It would squash and kill it like a fly if it could, so that the way might be cleared for "Jezebel" to rule the roost, unopposed and unhindered. Francis Frangipane writes, "When we speak of a Jezebelic spirit or Jezebel we are actually identifying the source in our culture of excessive sensuality, unbridled witchcraft and hatred of male authority."[3]

There may be churches that you are aware of, perhaps even your own, where there are strong, controlling powers working subversively and destructively. It could be within the church diaconate, or a prominent and strong family, or through an individual who is quenching the spirit and criticizing every move of the Lord designed to foster spiritual renewal. Such individuals are often found denouncing the worship or opposing the pastor's preaching where it encourages and promotes essential changes that the Holy Spirit deems necessary. It's wonderful when the prophetic ministry unmasks this undermining antagonism, identifies it for what it is, enables us to confront it, and eventually rids the church of it altogether.

The Laodicean church was challenged in this way. Behind many superficial appearances of wellbeing and competence, it was lukewarm; marred by a tepid, smug spirituality of prosperity, self-sufficiency and success. I wonder how many churches marked by that same Laodicean spirit the Lord would see in our towns and cities – "lukewarm – neither hot nor cold" – a spiritual temperature that makes Jesus want to vomit (Revelation 3:16). So Christ speaks the word that alone can stir them up, counselling them to buy from him riches for their poverty, authentic attire to cover their pitiful nakedness, and salve to anoint their eyes so they can see (see Revelation 3:18).

The Lord strengthens his church in these ways by revealing and identifying areas of weakness, rebellion and disobedience, syncretism with false religion and dangerous hidden tendencies that will lead in the end to unfaithfulness. How precious to us is the gift of prophecy that can reveal, heal and refresh our walk with the living God.

Dramatic Prophetic Actions

Sometimes the prophet can best express the heart of God to the people by a message acted out rather than delivered in words.

Matthew's gospel tells the story of Christ's memorable and dramatic cursing of a leafy fig tree adjacent to the holy city of Jerusalem (21:18–19). It is an intentionally prophetic action, like a living parable, warning of coming judgement on hypocritical lives that are abundantly showy but bear no spiritual fruit. Jesus points out the fig tree, takes his disciples up to it, and they watch as he peels back its branches and searches among the promising leaves for its lush, sweet fruit. Finding nothing, he prophetically curses it. Within hours it dries out and withers from the ground upwards.

Even today, prophetic ministry may "search and destroy" in just the same way on occasion. Prophets can penetrate beyond the misleading façade of outward appearances in the search for genuine fruit in the churches. Like the Lord himself, they can expose the fact that there is "nothing but leaves". Unless there is repentance, the consequences may prove to be disastrous.

Truly Prophetic Preaching and Teaching

If you are called by God to a preaching ministry, opening the Scriptures to the understanding of the household of faith, then pray for this dimension to be present in your own ministry and in the lives of other pastors and preachers you know. Ordinary preaching can become extraordinary when this dimension is present. It has been said that some Roman Catholics tend to believe in a Trinity of Father, Son and Holy Virgin; that some Protestants (particularly High Anglicans) believe in the Trinity of Father, Son and Holy Sacraments; and that the Evangelicals believe in a Trinity of Father, Son and Holy Scriptures. But of course, the real Trinity is Father, Son and Holy Spirit, and the missing dimension in our Christian experience is all too often the forgotten third person of the Trinity, the Holy Spirit, who becomes conspicuously present and manifest among God's people when the prophetic dimension has been restored to the Church's life and ministry, particularly within the regular activity of preaching. It is possible to make the Bible our god, and yet to become stone deaf to the voice of the God of the Bible.

The Word of God is there for us in the Bible, and yet merely working systematically through the texts in regular exposition may not be enough (though sometimes even then God surprises us). A mere series of Bible studies is not enough. There must be a powerful anticipation that God can and will speak to us; and therefore an expectancy and a resolve on the part of the preacher to be open to the gift of prophecy as a regular and major component of all good preaching. It is said that preachers need the heart of a child, the mind of a scholar, and the hide of a buffalo! This is especially true when the prophetic element is present in their ministries. If a preacher has been able to keep out of trouble until now, wait until the Holy Spirit's gift of prophecy erupts within his life and ministry!

C.H. Spurgeon, the great 19th-century Baptist preacher, was remarkably open to the prophetic dimension, constantly seeking God for the specific text for each Sunday morning and evening, often rejecting as many as twenty to thirty sermon outlines that he had prepared for each service until the right text gripped him. The prophetic regularly invaded his messages. In his autobiography, *The Full Harvest*, there are many examples of the way this prophetic dimension was manifested at the Metropolitan Tabernacle in London. For example, he tells of a woman who objected to her husband attending the Tabernacle week after week to hear Spurgeon preach, until eventually her curiosity overcame her and she felt she had to find out what it was that drew him back every time. Anxious not to be identified, she mingled among the crowds gathering there, covering her usual long dress with a nondescript coat, adding a shawl, and a veil over the whole ensemble. She climbed the heights and found the obscurity of the auditorium's third gallery to ensure she would be hidden completely out of sight. Her husband was somewhere in the auditorium, but so were 6,000 other people, and she was secure in the knowledge that there was no chance of him or the preacher seeing or recognizing her. Or so she thought.

Spurgeon reports that he found out from her that she

was very late in reaching the building, so the preacher was already announcing his text at the precise moment she entered. It so happened that the first words to be sounded in her ears were strikingly appropriate to her case, especially as she later declared that Spurgeon pointed directly to her in the upper gallery as he said, "Come in, thou wife of Jeroboam, why feignest thou thyself to be another? for I am sent to thee with heavy tidings."

Not the most common of preaching texts (1 Kings 14:6 KJV)!

This striking coincidence might have been dismissed had it not been followed by words that made an even deeper impression in the course of the sermon:

> While thus speaking about the occasional hearer, an idea haunts my mind that I have been drawing somebody's portrait in here tonight. I think there are some here who have had their character and conduct sketched out quite accurately enough for them to know who is meant. Do remember that if the description fits you, it is meant for you, and if you yourself have been described don't look about among your neighbours and say "I think this is somebody else", rather, let it be like you take it home to yourself and God will send it into the centre of your conscience so that you cannot get rid of it.

When she got home, abandoning her attempts at concealment, the woman challenged her husband: "Who told Mr Spurgeon that I would be there tonight in disguise?" Of course, her husband hadn't known she would be there, let alone Mr Spurgeon and, as a result, she came to the Lord through that supernatural identification in the meeting.

On another occasion, at the Exeter Hall at the Monday evening prayer meeting on 31 July of that year, in the course of the service Spurgeon pointed to someone seated in the gallery, saying, "Young man, those gloves you are wearing have not been paid for; you have stolen them from your employer." At the close of the service the young man in question, looking very pale and frightened, approached and waited to speak with Spurgeon, begging for a private interview. On being admitted, he placed a pair of kid gloves on the table, saying tearfully, "This is the first time I've ever robbed anyone and I'll never do it again; you won't expose me, will you, sir? It would kill my mother if she knew I was a thief." Spurgeon concluded that the man was probably saved that Monday evening from committing any further crimes for the rest of his life. It is no exaggeration to conclude that unless such occurrences happen regularly in our pulpit messages and preaching, we are probably not preaching at all!

The gift of prophecy makes preachers bold and uncompromising. On the day of Pentecost when he stood up to explain the phenomena associated with the coming of the Holy Spirit, Peter had already been turned from being a *slave* of public opinion to become a *shaper* of public opinion. He was no longer a man who timidly followed trends, but one who fearlessly began to set the trends in the Jerusalem of his day. In the words of Martin Luther King Jr: "There was a time when the church was very powerful. It was during that period when the early Christians rejoiced when they were deemed worthy to suffer for what they believed. In those days the church was not merely a thermometer that recorded the ideas and principles of popular opinion; it was a thermostat that transformed the mores of society."[4]

Peter's Pentecost sermon illustrates the way flashes of prophetic insight enrich preaching with fresh discoveries of the rich content and application of Scripture. On this occasion he boldly proclaims that "God has made this Jesus, whom you crucified, both Lord and Christ" (Acts 2:36). The Holy Spirit gives us the courage and discernment to look men and women in the eyes and tell them the truth directly, identifying and freeing them from what specifically binds and diminishes them, seeing and affirming their faithfulness, lifting them up when they've faltered or fallen. Preaching with that kind of cutting-edge sharpness and accuracy most frequently wins souls to Christ, for they have heard his voice in the voice of the preacher.

This quality of prophetic accuracy enables us to illustrate and apply the Word of God with wonderful precision. I have seen people laugh out loud in congregations I have visited as a guest preacher because, in the course of the sermon, while illustrating a point about relationships in the church, I unknowingly reported the very conversations that took place at the church members' meeting the previous Wednesday night, in this way shining God's searchlight on trivial incidents that reveal underlying attitudes – such as the often pointless or disproportionately heated discussions we have over which particular soap bars should be placed in the ladies' toilets, or what colour to paint the passage to the kitchen. This unmasks so accurately the spirit of argumentativeness in the church that it loses its power and the people are released to laugh at themselves!

Prophetic preaching thus brings elements of the startling and unexpected to our hearers. If you don't appreciate being surprised and shocked, then don't appoint a prophetic preacher to your pulpit, because they will regularly amaze, electrify and even at times outrage their audiences. Prophetic preaching turns the *logos* word of God (i.e. the written and infallible Word of God) into the *rhema* word of God (the living, speaking "now word" of God) which cuts straight to the heart. When Paul writes to Timothy about what is sometimes translated as "rightly dividing the word of truth" (2 Timothy 2:15), he uses a word that describes someone who can cut a direct path across rough ground to get straight to the chosen destination – rather like the way the ancient Romans characteristically built their roads, in fact. The expositor is someone who not only allows Scripture to say exactly what it's meant to say at that point, but also allows the sharp edges of the *rhema* word of God to do its work as well, emerging from the *logos* word of God to pierce the hearers' hearts like a "double-edged" sword. "For the word of God is living and active. Sharper than any double-edged sword, it penetrates even to dividing soul and spirit, joints and marrow; it judges the thoughts and attitudes of the heart" (Hebrews 4:12).

When the writer of Hebrews uses this metaphor, interestingly the word translated "double-edged" is not merely an allusion to the sword-like, penetrative power of the Word of God that Paul alludes to in Ephesians 6:17, it is the special use of the Greek adjective *distomon* which means, literally, "double-mouthed". This is an unusual word. One explanation for this could be that there are two voices speaking in such an activity as speaking God's Word. First, God's "mouth" speaks into the mind of the preacher; then the preacher uses his mouth to convey accurately what God has put into his mind. The first Word is God's, and his voice is sharp, but it is the addition of the preacher's voice that makes it "double-edged". As such, wielded like the Roman soldier's formidable weapon, the short, stabbing sword known as the *gladius* (Latin) or *macairos* (Greek), the Word of God penetrates the hearer's inner life and becomes an act of divine surgery on every part of his or her humanity – body, soul and spirit. When we are privileged to sit under anointed preaching like this, we can know most certainly that we have heard from the Lord. This is truly "cutting-edge" preaching, for *logos* words become *rhema* words to our ears. We shall revisit this distinction later.

Peter Lord (pastor, author and lecturer) says he frequently travels hundreds of miles and pays lots of money to attend pastors' conferences in order to hear a truth or a word from the Lord, which his wife would have told him for free if he'd just stayed at home and listened to her! There are perhaps no others better placed to speak prophetically into our lives than our spouses. My wife can at times speak God's words so exactly into my life that it is painful. I find myself squirming as she uncovers unerringly some character issue I need to deal with in my life and have been avoiding. It isn't that she is being critical; I have no one who is more prophetically encouraging than my wife when I need lifting up, but the Holy Spirit's voice is heard in the intimate spaces between those who have yielded their lives to him. Such prophetic sensitivity should be highly prized in all speaking and preaching – especially in that most testing of all discipleship environments, your own home. In the powerful words of Howard Hendricks: "If your Christianity doesn't work at home, it doesn't work at all. Don't export it."

Whether in church, at work or at home; whether engaged

in close study of a portion of Scripture or standing back to gain an overview of the whole journey of faith, the prophetic dimension enables us to see holistically. It presents the big picture of what the Lord is doing in contemporary society, both in our own neighbourhood and nation, and in his world as a whole, and allows us to set that in the context of the whole broad sweep of salvation history reaching back into centuries long gone. It enables us to see the wood for the trees. Prophetic people spend time with God, deepening their understanding of the human–divine covenant relationship that unfolds in the Scriptures as a whole. They immerse themselves in the themes and vision of the Old Testament prophets, reaching back into the sacred past, so that they can become burningly relevant in the present.

Three Kinds of Preaching

So we could put it like this: There are three kinds of preaching you will have been exposed to in your life. First, there is preaching which travels from the preacher's voice box to your eardrums and doesn't penetrate any more deeply than that. Second, there is preaching that journeys from the preacher's head to your head, so that whatever information is stored away there gets conveyed more or less intact to your head also. But, third, the best kind of preaching you have heard happens when the living Word arcs like lightning from the preacher's heart to your heart, enabling you to see, feel and act on the very things the preacher has seen, felt and acted upon, because we have both heard from God together. Isn't it obvious that we need more of that kind of prophetic preaching in the church today?

The 16th-century Swiss reformer John Calvin said, "Prophesying does not consist in the simple or bare interpretation of Scripture, but also includes the knowledge for making it apply to the needs of the hour, and that can only be obtained by revelation and the special influence of God." Exactly.

Prophecy Lifts Every Believer into the Possibility of Becoming a Voice and Not Merely an Echo

Joseph the Hebrew slave, a jailbird for many years of his life because of a false accusation of adultery with his master's wife, was suddenly promoted from the dungeon to the cabinet office as prime minister of Egypt. Why? The answer is: *the gift of prophecy*. Within moments of taking a wash, a shave and a change of clothing upon his sudden and surprising release from prison, he was standing in the presence of the king. He was enabled by God to interpret dreams and was invited to tell Pharaoh not only the content and meaning of the king's frightening nightmares and dreams, but also what needed to be done in the light of those disturbing prophetic communications from God. Those dreams, and above all the prophetic interpretation of them, saved not only Egypt from famine and disaster – they saved the neighbouring nations as well. It wasn't that Pharaoh had a man here who read *The Egyptian Times* on a daily basis and made some astute political observations. Joseph was a man who heard from the Holy Spirit on a daily basis. He didn't just listen to the many pundits lamenting the state of the nation; he wasn't lulled into a false sense of security when bountiful harvests came, thinking present abundance would keep Egypt at the top of the economic heap indefinitely. Joseph heard from the Holy Spirit: he was ready for the bumper crop and he knew that beyond present temporary prosperity, disaster was also looming for that land.

How we need individuals like Joseph in our national life, resolved not merely to echo what others are saying, but to act as a voice for God himself in regard to the social and political scene, so that men and women come to know truth they can rely upon and wisdom that is causative because it comes from God, instead of endless commentary that changes nothing. We need individuals with the courage to tell both the church and the world what both of them are refusing to hear, not from any desire to make trouble but because they have spent time in the presence of the living God. Where are messengers of this kind? We need voices that simply cannot be ignored, cannot be silenced and cannot be permanently denied, because they simply speak for God – and when we hear what they have to say, we all know it.

When the queen of Sheba came to visit Solomon to test his renowned wisdom with hard questions, she concluded, "...not even half was told me". It was God's gift of prophetic wisdom that made the nation of Israel the envy of the world (1 Kings 3:5–28; 4:29–34; 10:1–13).

When the Hebrew statesman Daniel grew up among the exiles in Babylon along with his fellow companions, he too was enabled by God to become an interpreter of dreams and to speak to kings in such a way that brought favour on his own life and the lives of his people, helping to bring about their preservation and subsequent rescue and return, due to the knowledge and fear of God he brought to the middle-eastern despots who held them prisoners of war (Daniel 1 – 6).

In the same way, Jesus himself stood before the powerful but vacillating Roman governor Pontius Pilate. Jesus was not intimidated by his judge, though his own life hung in the balance upon the outcome of this interrogation. Christ remained poised and in complete control when he responded to Pilate's questioning, saying, "... for this I came into the world, to testify to the truth... You would have no power over me if it were not given to you from above" (John 18:37, 19:11). We are not looking here at a frightened wretch, a subdued Galilean artisan and preacher grovelling before the capricious figure of corrupt Roman authority, a man with enough prestige to pronounce a sudden death sentence upon the Lord. No. Christ is unmoved. He rests in God. He knows that God is the one who is ultimately in charge here. And so Christ's words bear the weight of a deeper authority, hallmarked by direct, forthright prophetic truth: the authority of the holy Servant of God whose faith and stature expose the ephemeral and arrogant political power systems of Rome that have been duped into believing "there is no God but Caesar".

Pilate was no prophet. He had no idea what he was walking into that day (he should have had the humility to listen to his wife, as Peter Lord decided to, for on this occasion Pilate's wife Claudia was prophetic – see Matthew 27:19!). Of course, Pilate asked the cynical question, "What is truth?", but, sadly, he never waited for the answer and had no insight to recognize that truth was staring him in the face as Christ stood there in silence before him. He had in fact already met the answer in Christ's fearless silence. Judgement will come, and in that day Pilate will never be able to say he didn't know the truth, or that nobody told him, because in his brief exchange with Christ he had the chance to meet with ultimate reality in a way not granted to many. The way, the truth and the life stood in Pilate's presence, and Pilate washed his hands of him. The Word of God made flesh was now in dialogue with him, and Pilate missed his chance to let that voice shape both his life and his eternal future.

It was really the prophetic ministry of Christ that confronted Pilate's relativism, scepticism and syncretism. And Christ did so with capital "T" Truth, truth that cuts through to the very heart of things and tolerates no nonsense. For with all his sophistication and cynicism, Pilate was obviously not free in the same sense that his prisoner Jesus was free. Trapped by political expediency, the pressure of moral imperatives, and the necessity to exercise the full status of his office if he was to avoid further offence to the Jews and possible riots, everything was in the balance for him as he decided what do about Jesus. Truth was a Person, and that Person was now standing directly in front of him. He was left with only two alternative reactions to that Truth incarnate that stood before him – capitulation to it, or denial and escape from it. He chose the latter. Yet, the prophetic Word that was also the Logos himself had left Pilate without excuse. It always does.

Similarly, in the account of Paul's voyage as a prisoner to Rome, recorded in Acts 27, we read that Paul knew prophetically that some men would abandon ship during the height of the storm that eventually wrecked their vessel, and he told them that unless everyone stayed in the boat, their lives could not be saved. Humanly speaking, who was going to believe a landlubber, a weaselly little academic who knew absolutely zero about sailing or handling a boat in a storm? Unless, of course, God was speaking through him. By the witness of the Holy Spirit everybody knew this was the voice of the Lord, and everybody did exactly what Paul said; and in spite of the incredible danger that ensued, even to the point of having to throw the cargo overboard, they obeyed Paul's prophetic instructions. They stayed with the ship as directed, and their lives were saved – every single one of them, just as Paul had promised.

It would be advantageous to have someone like that around in a nation's defence department, or the capital's police headquarters, in the local fire brigade or even your company's head office, wouldn't it? It would be great to know that there was someone on the board of directors who was able to hear from God about the welfare of the company. It would be reassuring to know that there was someone like that on the eldership team of the church, who would know when potential shipwreck was looming and know exactly what to say in those circumstances to help save the church from disaster. God is prepared to raise up such voices. And he still continues to do so. How can we dismiss this precious and powerful gift as irrelevant?

This is the very dimension we need in much of our speaking. Philip Greenslade admirably summarizes the importance of this prophetic dimension:

> Without the prophet the church becomes a spiritless organisation in which even apostolic work hardens into a new form of religious bureaucracy. Without the prophetic thrust, the teaching ministry perpetuates cycles of timeless truth but is deaf to what the Spirit is saying now to the churches… Without a prophetic voice challenging God's people to lay down their lives for the world, pastoral nurture can easily degenerate into self-serving group welfare or an inward and unbiblical withdrawal. Evangelism too, desperately needs to hear the prophet if its methods are to be as godly as its message and if it is to avoid giving stereotyped answers to questions people are not asking.[5]

We have already noted with some dismay that there is an entrenched and widespread theological position in the evangelical church today that, along with the other miracle and sign gifts of the Holy Spirit, declares that prophecy died out at the end of the first century AD, along with the first apostles. On these grounds, prophecy and the other charismata of the Holy Spirit are repudiated as redundant and, therefore, safely ignored in the church's life. Any claim to move in those gifts is deemed to be some form of demonic counterfeit and deception. But as I have tried to argue so far, both personal experience and the authoritative teaching of the Scriptures themselves combine to lead us to a fresh realization that the work of the Holy Spirit is still alive and active in the modern world. If we neglect his gifts, the life of the church diminishes in power and effective witness, its health deteriorates to the point where many secular critics begin to predict its demise and death, our walk of faith and personal holiness as Christians stagnates, and the world Christ came to save is left without the spiritual authority and authenticity that could awake it from its ignorance, calling it to the freedom and joy of repentance.

Over forty years ago, as the charismatic movement was beginning to make its impact upon nearly all of the mainstream denominations, prophecy in particular was regarded as one of the most controversial and unsettling of all the Holy Spirit's gifts. Robert Brow, an American theologian, tried to set this gift within a broader perspective. He wrote, "It is not just a question of a little word of building up and a few consoling thoughts. The building-up is lifting men and women out of the humdrum into the great movement of God in history and the *paraclesis* is the application of the Holy Spirit, the Paraclete Himself, to shake a man to the very core and stand him on his feet again to do exploits for God."[6]

We need the witness of the prophetic. We need to see a new generation of believers arise who know how to hear from God and who will faithfully pass on what he has conveyed to them. We now turn to the Bible to discover for ourselves how this can be done.

In the meantime, perhaps we can appreciate more fully now some of the reasons why the apostle Paul made the following exhortation the starting point of his discussion about prophecy and tongues. This verse would also make a good starting point for us, as we open the map that will guide us on our prophetic journey: "Follow the way of love and eagerly desire spiritual gifts, especially the gift of prophecy" (1 Corinthians 14:1).

Chapter Four

Pursuing the "Real Deal"

Perhaps you have had the experience of visiting London's Oxford Street or a major city-centre shopping mall, where you have gazed at some of the designer displays but never made a single purchase, or even entered the shops. You just looked through the windows. Some stores are so chic and expensive that the management doesn't stoop to supplying price tickets for the articles arrayed in the storefront – if you have to ask the price, this is not the shop for you! You can look, you can dream, but that's all. You can never afford to be more than a window-shopper.

What a shame and a sad waste it is that so many Christians are nothing more than window-shoppers in their approach to the Bible.

We stand on the outside looking in, staring in wonder at what happened to others 2,000 years ago and 2,000 miles away, wistfully beholding the birth and expansion of the early church that looks so different from what we have at home. Convinced we could never go in and get some of this for ourselves, assuming it's way beyond anything that's meant for the likes of us, we gaze through the window at the way things might have been, never realizing it is for ordinary people like us to take back to our churches and workplaces, to share with our neighbours and our families, and – this has to be the most amazing thing of all – it is entirely, absolutely, unconditionally, no-strings-attached free: Jesus bought it for us; he has already paid the price.

It can be hard to grasp this – hard to understand it and hard to believe it. But when it comes to the Word of God in the Bible, it's important to realize we don't have to fully understand everything in order to experience or benefit from it. In fact, sometimes those with the simplest faith and the least understanding enter more fully into God's provision for our needs than those with a comprehensive theological knowledge behind them.

When I became a Christian at the age of fourteen, I did not fully understand God's plan of salvation and, frankly, I still don't even now, though I've learned so much about God's grace in the last forty years. But back at the beginning, when I knew very little, I still knew enough to trust in the saving death and resurrection of Christ and enter into the power of his salvation. Similarly, I freely confess that I don't understand very much about electricity but I don't intend to stay in the dark until I can deliver a lecture on how electrical products function. I have no idea how to put a television set together. But I don't have to wait until I do, to demonstrate that the one in my living room works very well.

I find the digital computer technology I'm using to write with at this very moment to be something of a mystery and a wonder to my mind, along with all that accompanies it in the magical world that we call cyberspace; but I do know how to send emails to my friends, and my profound ignorance of the inner workings of the electronics involved won't stop me from doing this regularly. You don't have to understand everything in order to participate in it and enjoy it. You just need to know enough to get started.

When it comes to prophetic ministry, you can see this in the Bible, when Jesus sends out his disciples on a mission tour of signs and wonders, driving out demons, healing the sick and announcing the kingdom. When they return, they have a request to make of him: "Lord, teach us to pray" (Luke 11:1). In some parts of the church, we have spent decades and generations preparing ourselves in prayer for something that never gets around to beginning. These travelling companions of Jesus didn't wait until they were fully trained, prepared, practised and knowledgeable. Instead, he sent them, they went, and it worked. We all have to start somewhere.

We have already seen several reasons why prophecy should be eagerly desired and developed in our lives, but there are still some more important things to say about it if we are to move in it more confidently. It may be helpful to delineate a profile of what prophecy is – and is not – so that we can be sure we are pursuing the genuine article, the "real deal".

What Prophesy is Not

Prophecy is a phenomenon that results directly from the access the Holy Spirit has to our minds, whereby he can create pictures in our imagination, and supernatural dreams while we are asleep. He can put words, ideas or scriptures into our heads with such force that we know that there is something weighty and unforgettable going on, something that carries with it the responsibility to pass on and relay what the Holy Spirit has communicated.

I received a telephone call from a lady in her seventies, who had been told she might obtain some help from our church. She explained that during the last four or five years she had been absolutely tormented by voices in her head and sometimes violent assaults on her body, along with the choking feeling of being strangled by invisible hands. She was so bound now by the oppression of these demonic powers that she was unable to make any journey or even leave her house; she could no longer conduct a normal life at all. As I was speaking to her on the phone, I did not receive the impression that this woman was unbalanced or insane, but rather that she was a sober, intelligent woman who had somehow come under a demonic assault on her mind. Even as we were talking, she told me there was a voice in her head arguing with everything I said. When I mentioned Jesus Christ, the voice said, "I don't like him!" When I told this spirit of its future judgement, it said, "I know, I know. I don't like you talking about that."

Though such experiences are bizarre, and uncommon in the lives of most people, there is general acceptance, both within and beyond the church community, that these unsettling supernatural manifestations are both powerful and real. Now, it's a strange thing that we are prepared to believe evil spirits have access to our minds in these sinister and oppressive ways, and that they are very persistent and personal in this activity, but at the same time believe God must remain silent because he has given us a complete canon of Scripture in the Bible and no longer deals directly with his children. A moment's thought would tell us that this position neither tallies with Scripture nor personal experience – nor is it convincing as a piece of reasoned logic. If unwelcome spiritual entities can manipulate us, inhabit us and speak through us, then surely God who made and loves us, in whom we live and move and have our being, is not muzzled and bound, limited to communicating through the channel of the written Word alone. Far from it. God has many ways of speaking to us, and one of those ways is prophecy.

Precisely because we can claim God speaks to us and through us in this way, it is important to be clear in our thinking concerning this remarkable gift. Woolly thinking and lack of definition tend towards corruption and make us gullible and vulnerable to manipulation. We must be clear about what prophecy is.

It is said that the pope, on seeing Michelangelo's amazing statue of David, asked the sculptor how he accomplished such a wonderful creation. The artist replied, "It's simple. I just cut away everything that didn't look like David." Wisely guided by Michelangelo's approach, let's begin by excising from our minds all that prophecy is not. We begin then with the negatives.

1. Prophecy is not preaching

Though all of the best preaching includes a prophetic element, the New Testament letters of Paul use an entirely different vocabulary to describe the activity of preaching from that used to describe prophecy. Preaching and teaching consist of the interpretation, exposition and application of Scripture. Prophecy is an entirely different gift. Yet in the older Reformed traditions, including those of the sixteenth century continental and English church reformers and their seventeenth century successors the Puritans, as well as many who adhere to their legacy, the term "prophesying" is used loosely to describe what happens when the Bible is expounded for an hour or so on Sunday mornings by those gifted as teachers and preachers to perform this task. This is not a totally inaccurate use of the biblical terminology, for very often the gift of prophecy operates within Spirit-anointed preaching, but such preaching should not be equated with prophecy. Preaching and teaching are the explication and application of Scripture, but prophecy also has the element of immediate, existential, revelatory activity present within it as God shows the speaker, in the act of preaching, something directly relevant and important to his hearers that may not have been derived at all from his study, research and exegesis of the biblical text earlier. Nevertheless, it is something that is true, relevant and of immediate concern to the life of the congregation or the people who are within earshot of it, even if it does not involve the direct exposition of Scripture.

Teaching is one of the listed and required qualifications for elders and leaders of the church, according to 1 Timothy 3. But Paul never makes the ability to prophesy a qualification for the elders of the church, either in that list or in the one found in Titus 1. It's a different kind of gifting. Prophecy is important for all believers to receive and practise, but teaching is a different qualification and an essential for church leaders, if only on a one-to-one and face-to-face level with individuals in need. We should also note that Paul encourages women to prophesy in mixed gatherings of men and women in 1 Corinthians 11:5 and 14:27–33, with one proviso – that their heads are covered (a feminine hairstyle, hat or veil have been some of the suggested meanings here – we'll revisit this later) as a token of their submission to male headship, the headship of both their husbands, if they are married, and also the male leaders of the church to which they belong.

But Paul never encourages women to teach the Bible in mixed gatherings of men and women together in the church and, in fact, overtly deters then from doing so in mixed settings where men are present. This would carry the risk that such women teachers would assert a personal authority over men through the exposition of God's Word (see 1 Timothy 2:12–15). Now that's a very curious distinction in Paul's thinking. But it underlines the validity of distinguishing prophecy from teaching. Prophecy is not the same as preaching, for it is a more direct revelatory communication through a man or woman to those needing to hear a personal word from God. The authority contained in such a word lies in the Spirit-given content of it, not in the personal authority of the particular speaker.

2. Prophecy is not mischievous public rebuke

Prophecy is open to abuse. It can be abused when people attempt to shame a church or expose individuals to ridicule, tactlessly divulging hidden things that bring public embarrassment to others in an unnecessary and unedifying way. Prophecy is not a form of "kiss and tell" where someone has obtained intimate knowledge of a person from sharing their privacy, only to go public with secrets from their lives, as celebrity ex-lovers sell their stories to the tabloid newspapers. Prophecy is not like that. It is a very positive gift. Even when it convicts individuals of sin it nearly always shows them the way out (with the possible exception of Ananias and Sapphira, but even they had space to own up and repent) and points the way forward. It was never designed to simply rebuke a person without offering them hope. Prophecy is not an excuse to "get something off your chest". We can disguise some of our emotional responses to people in an apparently spiritual way, but to do so would be an abuse of the prophetic ministry.

Perhaps you've heard people in public prayer meetings ostensibly praying to God when, in reality, they are sharing "loaded" information with the church, telling us what they personally think needs to happen in this place under the pseudo-spiritual guise of addressing the Almighty. It is possible to abuse the gift of prophecy in much the same way, by venting pet peeves or grudges against individuals under the cover of prophecy in a form of public griping and whining about things we've discovered that offend us, and doing this in the name of the Holy Spirit so that we personally cannot be blamed for our complaints. Prophecy never functions like this. In fact, prophecy does not work, at all, on the basis of what we already know about situations and people by natural observation. Prophecy deals with some form of supernatural, existential, lower case "r" revelation (as opposed to the plenary inspiration and infallible capital "R" Revelation that went into the Bible) disclosed by the Spirit of God directly to us for an outcome of positive change. This may involve change in the life of an individual, a faith community or a nation, sometimes because they have strayed and God is now calling them back to himself, sometimes because they are faithful but need encouragement and new direction.

3. Prophecy is not equivalent to Holy Scripture

The Old Testament prophets spoke and wrote words of absolute divine authority. They would frequently preface their message with the words "Thus says the Lord", wanting their hearers to know that they were operating under the full inspiration of the Holy Spirit to such a degree that this rendered their words completely infallible and beyond question. Many of these oracles and utterances were recorded in writing, carefully preserved, and eventually deposited in the canon of Holy Scripture, becoming authoritative in the lives of the people of God, not only for their own time but for all time. The same degree of authority and inspiration continued in the lives of the apostles and others who wrote the books of the New Testament under the Spirit's direction and superintendence, all of whom either taught infallibly on occasion in the congregational life of the new churches, or became agents in the task of writing Scripture, conveying God-given truths in God-given words (see 1 Corinthians 2:6–13).

It is important to declare that the inspiration that lies behind the gift of prophecy today is more of a mixed phenomenon, not sharing the infallibility of the Old Testament prophets and New Testament apostles (and of other writers like Mark, Luke, the unknown writer of Hebrews, and Jude the Lord's brother, who are not explicitly named as apostles) as they experienced God's revelation and inspiration to write Scripture. Scripture is now a completed canon. It does not need to be extended or supplemented by the writings or utterances of men and women, as if it were open-ended or in some way lacking. We dare not add to the material contained in the Bible. Indeed the book of Revelation, which closes and completes the Bible, includes an explicit warning against adding to its contents, on pain of deadly plagues and exclusion from the paradise to come (Revelation 22:18–19). We are not authorised to add to Scripture in prophecy, but only to minister its truth and requirements through thoughts and pictures that God brings to mind. Our expression of these intimations comes in merely human words, not verbal inspirations such as we find everywhere in the Bible, but they are still significant and weighty words if the Spirit is genuinely behind them. Yet even with this proviso, even while we frankly confess that the prophetic ministry within the church does not carry the same degree of inspiration as the prophetic and apostolic words of the Scriptures, nonetheless we still want to maintain that today's gift of prophecy is the precious bearer of authentic, relevant and helpful communication from God.

According to 2 Timothy 3:16, the Holy Scriptures are "God-breathed" (i.e. breathed out by God; Greek: *theopneustos*), so that Scripture in its entirety is equivalent to God's own spoken Word itself, his *ipsissima verba,* the precise and literal words of God. Therefore, what Scripture says, God says.

The Holy Spirit's activity in conveying prophecy to people today is "inspired" only in a looser and less authoritative sense than within the Bible. The Holy Spirit still breathes into his servants to convey knowledge, information, ideas and truth, but these must always be tested by the higher authority of the content of Scripture. This resembles what happens to preachers speaking in the pulpit. God is at work in their minds and hearts to communicate powerful thoughts and inspired ideas, but we would never regard our pastor's sermons as infallible wisdom that shares the same level of inspiration as Scripture (indeed my sons often joke that "Dad is preaching now, he's not telling the truth" when I mess up the details in an illustration and inadvertently tell factual errors!).

Paul's and Peter's words went into the Bible, but our preaching and prophecy come out of it. We merely apply the word, and are under the word, because the degree of accuracy present in the operation of the Sprit in both preaching and prophesying is of an entirely different order from his work in producing Holy Scripture, even if preaching and prophecy today are unquestionably inspirational to both recipients and hearers. Because prophecy is inspired in this lesser sense, it will inspire others in turn – it puts a "breath" or "second wind" of hope and encouragement into them, while still remaining a fallible phenomenon that we must treat with a care and reserve that we do not bring to the Bible itself.

What Prophesy Is

1. Prophecy is often an agent of healing in the body of Christ

Paul affirms the truth that, "There are different kinds of gifts, but the same Spirit" (1 Corinthians 12:4). The Spirit inspires the operation of these manifold gifts and manifestations of his presence among us, so we can be sure that they will have positive and transforming effects. In discussing prophecy, Paul writes, "Two or three prophets should speak, and the others should weigh carefully what is said. And if a revelation comes to someone who is sitting down, the first speaker should stop" (1 Corinthians 14:29–30).

There was a dynamic operating in the meetings of the early Christian community whereby the Holy Spirit could convey words and ideas to individual believers in ways they never planned or prepared, for the edification of the whole faith community. These inspirations came spontaneously, and Paul's instructions give us an indication of how abundant manifestation of the gifts can be managed in a way that allows worship to proceed in order and peace, instead of degenerating into an exciting but confusing babble.

The proper management of abundant public contributions has hardly been a big problem for the church more recently, since spiritual gifts are so rarely encouraged in many churches. But it must be given some thought if we are to move once again in this area of the manifestation of public spiritual gifts. It is often more discreet and wise if major or controversial prophetic words can be weighed beforehand, rather than after they have been shared publicly. The Holy Spirit is just as capable of inspiring the prophetic in advance of a meeting as he is of inspiring it during a meeting. Meetings can be both orderly and edifying when, just as the preacher prepares his inspired word in advance, so also the prophets and healers and speakers in tongues listen carefully to God in advance of a meeting, submitting notice to their leaders that God wants to use them in a particular way when the church gathers. This way the leaders will know if the prophecy accords with Scripture and can be brought to the people, because they will have had time to check: they will know if it is well for those who speak in tongues to proceed, because God will have prepared others to interpret. But the truly spontaneous must not be hindered either.

We are not used to including the gifts of the Spirit in our preparation because all too frequently we are not used to them at all. But Spirit-given inspiration is not something that hits you without warning like epilepsy, an imperative kind of spiritual "fitting" that is completely beyond our control. The household of God can be both orderly and inspired: it's all in the preparation of our hearts and minds in advance, as well as through making ourselves available to God in the moment.

On many occasions I have seen this exciting phenomenon whereby God gives specific advance notice of his willingness to act among his people in a particular meeting, whether that be in words to be shared or signs and wonders such as miraculous healing. I took a sabbatical leave from my regular pastoral ministry in 1995, planning to meet with some American pastors whom I knew and visit the five growing city churches they led in San Antonio, Texas; Columbia, Missouri; Paducah, Kentucky; Evanston, Illinois; and Hampton, Virginia. Just before I left England, I attended a pastors' conference where my very close friend Bernard Thompson leaned over to me to say, "You're going to America next week. I keep getting this name persistently to mind – 'Jim'. I believe God wants you to pray for 'Jim' and see him healed, when you get to the USA." He had no more information to convey than that, but I took this very seriously as he has an excellent record for accuracy in the prophetic realm. So when I came to America, in every city where I gathered with church leaders in ministers' meetings, or more generally with their people in congregational life, I would ask if there was a "Jim" present. And believe it or not, though on some occasions there were hundreds of people present, I never met a "Jim" anywhere, and certainly not a sick one!

My fourth trip was to Evanston, a small university town north of Chicago. At the end of a wonderful week there with a Vineyard church and some of its staff, just before I was to move on to Hampton, Virginia, I met late that Sunday evening with the pastor Steve Nicholson and a number of young men he discipled. We met at his home for a time of prayer, conversation and worship late into the night. Quite early on, I asked if any of them was called "Jim", and the reply was "No". Time passed. At about midnight when some had already left, suddenly the door opened and two young men walked in. It was a warm spring evening and they were dressed in running gear, shorts and brightly coloured T-shirts. As they walked in, I heard Steve Nicholson say, "Hi, Jim". I immediately exclaimed, "*Jim!* That's the first Jim I've met in three weeks!"

Yet this particular "Jim" looked the picture of health. He looked as if he should have been on the cover of a sports magazine, rippling with muscles, and ultra fit. And so, rather nervously I said, "Jim, this sounds strange, but I must ask anyway. You haven't got any health problems at the moment, have you?"

Jim looked at Steve, and Steve looked at him, then a wry grin came over their faces. "Well, yes, as a matter of fact I have serious health problems", came the surprising reply.

It was explained to me that Jim had been on a forty-day fast twice already that year, which had resulted in a strange and debilitating effect upon his body. He was totally without energy and could no longer run at all now, though he was the national champion for his college. Indeed, not only could he no longer run, but he could only get out of bed for a couple of hours each day before he had to go back to sleep again.

I said, "I know this sounds strange, but an English pastor told me I would meet a guy called Jim in the USA, and that I was meant to pray for him. I know I'm 4,000 miles away from England, but I believe God sent me to heal you.' I felt somewhat impertinent in adding, "So, I would just like to pray for you", knowing he had been prayed for many times by these believing friends of his, yet for six weeks he had been incapacitated. It was 12.15 am. I said, "Just stand there", and I simply touched him on the forehead, announcing, "Be healed, in Jesus name." At that very moment it was as though he was hit by a lightning bolt. His feet left the ground and he fell backwards in an arc onto the sofa, bounced upwards on its well-upholstered springs and crashed onto the floor, where he lay like a dead man for over two hours.

I had to leave the meeting before he came round, but a week or two later I heard from Steve Nicholson, who told me, "Wonderful news! Jim didn't get off the floor until about 2.00 am, but he was totally healed in that time. He has fully recovered and is now running again like a champion! He is completely well and he's had no recurrence of the problem." And that was still the case three years later when I last spoke to Steve. Jim was doing fine.

God sends forth his Word to heal people (Psalm 107:20) and it is quite astonishing when he does so. You cannot forget incidents like that. Another time, I visited Bernard Thompson's own church and preached for him. That morning, I had had a number of words and impressions in my mind concerning conditions that God wanted to heal and, eventually, I dared to announce them in order to see if they were right. I said, "There's a young girl here with painful verrucas on her feet. She is finding difficulty even walking because of the pain."

Right in front of me, seated on the first row, a girl in her mid-teens instantly shot her hand up and said, "That's me! That's me!" She had tried every treatment available, but her condition had lasted for well over a year, and the soles of her feet were riddled with verrucas. I didn't ask her to remove her shoes, but said, "I think God is indicating that he wants to heal you, so we'll pray." I laid hands on both of her feet and prayed, "Lord, we convey your healing power in the Name of Jesus. May the Holy Spirit clean this contagion out of her feet and deal with these verrucas."

I then continued praying with the people who had responded to other calls. At the end of the meeting the girl was waiting eagerly to get my attention and said, "Immediately after you prayed for me, I went out to the toilets at the back of the church because I was so excited that I wanted to see what God had done! I took both of my shoes and socks off. You will never believe it, those verrucas have dropped off my feet and there is perfectly clean skin there now. I've been healed!" Prophecy massively helps and encourages the people of God in that it targets specific individuals for special healings and enables us to hear from God in advance, so that we can plan and make space in our meetings for what he wants to do in our midst.

2. Prophecy is the conveyance of God's penetrating power to his people

There is a divine energy operating within prophecy to achieve what God wants to achieve. If the tiniest post office in a small country village can bear a letter that may wreck or bless a nation, then the simplest life can relay blessings that may rock a continent for God. We are to believe in the possibility that God may use us in this way. Hebrews 4:12 tells us, "The word of God is living and active. Sharper than any double-edged sword, it penetrates even to dividing soul and spirit, joints and marrow; it judges the thoughts and attitudes of the heart."

This is a graphic illustration of the power of God's Word when it is goes forth with the inspiration of the Holy Spirit.

It cuts precisely, and often very deeply, like a surgeon's scalpel or sword, as we noted earlier. God knows where to cut, what to cut and when to cut. The prophetic word has the power to penetrate people's hearts more deeply than any merely human words. A single sentence can change a person's life forever. It can even affect whole churches in this way.

3. Prophecy convicts of sin because it tells us the truth and demolishes deception

As we prophesy, we begin to see beyond appearances to discern the reality as God sees it. We glimpsed something of that earlier, as we read of visitors present in our meetings who will hear the secrets of their hearts disclosed, and come under conviction: "But if an unbeliever or someone who does not understand comes in while everybody is prophesying, he will be convinced by all that he is a sinner and will be judged by all, and the secrets of his heart will be laid bare" (1 Corinthians 14:24–25).

A gardener may turn over a stone in a field on a warm day, and the sunlight suddenly penetrates the darkness, exposing everything once covered under the rock. All kinds of formerly hidden creeping and crawling things are seen immediately in that moment. They scatter in every direction. Similarly, men and women do not realize their sinfulness until they hear prophetically from God. Creatures of darkness are brought into the light.

A little girl, who regularly went to church with her father, used to look up and read the Ten Commandments mounted on framed wooden boards to either side of the altar. They were all listed: having no other gods, not worshipping graven images, not taking the Lord's name in vain, honouring the Sabbath Day and so on. One morning as she sat reading them, she nudged her dad and whispered, "Dad, I don't like reading those things; they just put bad ideas into your head, don't they?" Under the influence of the Holy Spirit, the Ten Commandments were provoking a consciousness of sin in this little girl's life, triggering and exposing her fallen nature in the same way Paul the apostle describes in Romans 7:7–11. Prophetic ministry can do this also. It brings human sinfulness into the light. Men and women may choose to live in darkness all of their lives until, under accurate prophecy, they come blinking into the light like creeping, crawling creatures that have been hidden under a rock. They are transformed as aspects of their lives, suddenly exposed by the Spirit's light, are faced up to, confessed and properly dealt with by his power.

4. Prophecy dismantles even the hardest resistance to God

Jeremiah 23:29 endorses this. "Is not my word like fire," declares the Lord, "and like a hammer that breaks a rock in pieces?"

We need to see more of this dimension in our preaching and teaching of the Bible, so that our words will carry the authority, weight and spiritual force needed to set people free. When the prophetic is at work, people are changed. Prophecy melts people and breaks their shells of cynicism and unforgiving attitudes. Where they are trapped inside ossified habits of thinking and behaving, it cracks them wide open to God's saving grace and to his forgiveness. Prophecy smashes hardened resistance to his truth. It demolishes wrong-headed thinking and false ideological strongholds. It exposes the empty claims of counterfeit spiritualities and false religion. It exposes cultists and occultists to a power greater and purer than anything they have personally experienced before, and points them to the clean power of Christ.

5. Prophecy effects radical and lasting change

The prophetic changes the lives of individuals and church communities, and can affect whole neighbourhoods and even nations: "So is my word that goes out from my mouth: It will not return to me empty, but will accomplish what I desire and achieve the purpose for which I sent it" (Isaiah 55:11).

We noted some of these effects in our discussion of the fivefold ministries listed in Ephesians 4:11ff. Without prophetic ministry operating within a church, one fifth of Jesus' word ministry to his church is missing. The five ministries of "apostles, prophets, evangelists, pastors and teachers" are all necessary to build churches the way God designed them to be. They are foundational in any living church to this day. They will make-over whole churches into the shape God had in mind, from the inside out. Among them, this vital ministry of the prophet – the voice of Christ speaking through his chosen servants – shakes the attitudes and preconceptions of the household of faith until all complacency falls away and only what is truly of God may remain (Hebrews 12:25–29). Is your life in need of a good shaking so that some contraband goods and destructive toxins can be separated out from your life? Sometimes when God visits the lives of individuals in this way the prophetic word is so powerful and active that it shakes loose and scatters all the stale, stolen, poisonous rubbish that blocks and chokes up the airways in the house of the human soul. Sometimes God shakes the church when his Spirit comes down in the power of prophecy that is incisive, honest and fiery, and it shakes the people free of sinful strongholds like unforgiveness, longstanding feuds, controlling individuals or occultic activities like spiritualism and Freemasonry.

Do you sense that something or someone has been a menace to the freedom of the Spirit that the Lord wants to bring to a particular church? The prophetic can often identify root issues and dangerous people, then courageously work towards their nullification or eradication. This shaking of the Spirit exposes root issues that are at work in corrupting the faithful; it shakes loose the strangleholds of bullying and manipulation that suppress the freedom and growth of the community.

6. Prophecy reveals Jesus Christ to us

As the book of Revelation affirms, "The testimony of Jesus is the spirit of prophecy" (Revelation 19:10). Therefore one of the regular and certain results of prophecy is that people's eyes will be opened to see Christ again and glimpse more of his glory. Of course, the work of evangelists, apostles, pastors and teachers all do that very same thing, but there is a special "seeing" of the Lord that prophetic people can lead us to experience as well. This is what the apostle John does so graphically in recounting his vision of the ascended Christ to us in Revelation 1. Prophecy stirs and encourages others to prophesy, and John in his turn is here taking his cue from the prophet Daniel in Persia some six centuries beforehand, who saw "a man dressed in linen, with a belt of the finest gold round his waist" (Daniel 10:5), a vision that left him prostrate and half-dead at the feet of this figure (verse 9). We all need such a sight of Christ from time to time, living as we do in an increasingly secularized atmosphere that is so heavy with the earth-bound and reductionist political and materialistic agendas of humanity, and woefully lightweight in its awareness of the transcendence of God.

With the same cynicism that blinds people of our own day until revelation comes to them, Christ's jaded contemporaries who saw him in the flesh and experienced his ministry scoffed, "Can anything good come out of Nazareth?" Yet the truth is that *everything* good that has come to the world since then has come out of Nazareth, because in Christ all the fullness of the Godhead dwells in bodily form. Believers and unbelievers alike stand in desperate need of a greater revelation of Christ in his greatness and power. This will be what converts the secularist, Buddhist, Hindu and Muslim worlds, but first it must convert the Christian world. A powerful factor in achieving this will occur when the prophetic dimension is present in our preaching and speaking. It will then reveal Jesus.

7. Prophecy builds the church with the very best materials of living stones

Ephesians 4:12–13 tells us that, along with other ministries of God's Word, prophets exist "to prepare God's people for works of service, so that the Body of Christ may be built up until we all reach unity in the faith and in the knowledge of the Son of God and become mature, attaining to the whole measure of the fulness of Christ". So the gift of prophecy is one of the tools God uses to cement and build our lives together with others. How precious is this depth and stability in the life of the Christian today, when so much around us is changing and feels unreliable. So many Christians find it hard to settle, trying one church after another, sometimes slavishly following a favourite preacher and filling notebooks with his words, but never finding a spiritual home. They end up disappointed, because God's Word must be written in our hearts, not just in our notepads, and it has to lead to commitment, lifestyle change and contributing membership that ministers to the welfare of the body of Christ.

I have seen this consolidation and encouragement for myself. Over a period of nearly thirty years I have pastored two churches where prophetic ministry has been increasingly honoured until it became a central component of the church's common life. These congregations are becoming strong and loving communities with heart, as the prophetic ministry plays its part in building up, maturing and stabilizing the church family.

The Spirit of God settles the solitary in families. John Wesley said, "There is no such thing as a solitary Christian." As the great early Church Father expressed it, "Unless we come to experience the Church as our Mother, we will never fully experience God as our Father." Prodigals and orphans can now come home, and the wanderers need to become rooted in stable Christian communities where they can experience true family, where the cancers of sin, independence, autonomy and rebellion can at last be eradicated from their lives. This would prove to be a truly prophetic breakthrough for some.

Chapter Five

Hearing the Voice of God

The gift of prophecy has not always been well received. Because it is powerfully supernatural, it sometimes spooks and alarms people. It very often disturbs the status quo. When the prophet Amos faithfully executed his call to be a prophet to the decayed and decadent nation of northern Israel in the eighth century BC, even the religious authorities and their most prominent representative resented God's prophet.

Amaziah, the priest at the sanctuary at Bethel, the unauthorized rival centre of worship in the divided northern kingdom, made no attempt to disguise his contempt for God's prophet and the content of Amos' messages. He raged and blustered through a range of contemptuous denouncements in his eagerness to rid the land of the unwanted voice of God speaking through this somewhat uncouth prophet from the south (Amos 7:10–17). These hostile responses included cynicism and wilful misrepresentation of the message (verses 10–11), denial of Amos' call and credentials as God's messenger, including ridicule of his person (verse 12a), and all in a wicked scheme to discredit the prophet's character, finally concluding with a bold attempt to evict the prophet from his spiritual territory altogether (verses 12b–13).

An honest assessment of the unfolding centuries of church history since the ascension of Christ would indicate that the reaction of prominent church leaders and their congregations to the prophetic ministry has often differed very little from that of Amaziah the priest. For long stretches of our mission and ministry, much of the church of Jesus Christ has acted like a "non-prophet organization"! The gift of prophecy has been ignored or neglected. When prophetic figures have arisen they have been treated with contempt, hostility and suspicion, with the outcome that the gift of prophecy has frequently been forced to the margins of church life and deemed totally irrelevant. That's why it has been worthwhile for us to spend time discovering the many features of New Testament prophecy which indicate the value of this gift of prophecy in the church today. In summary, we have noticed two things:

1. The gift of prophecy was a fairly normative experience in the New Testament church

We've noted that the book of Acts records revelatory activity of the Holy Spirit in twenty-seven of its twenty-eight chapters. Specific examples include Agabus' prediction of a famine (Acts 11:27–28) and his warning to Paul of coming danger in Jerusalem (Acts 21:9ff). Prophets and teachers were used to indicate the timing and launch of a special mission for Saul and Barnabas (Acts 13:1–2). Also typical of the kind of functions carried out by prophets was the subsequent follow-up ministry of prophets such as Judas and Silas amid the churches previously planted by these two apostles (Acts 15:32). Note also the way in which Philip's sensitivity to the voice of the Holy Spirit was inherited by all four of the evangelist's daughters, since they all prophesied as well as their father (Acts 21:8–9). Similarly, prophetic gifts featured prominently in the ordination and equipping of prominent second-generation church leaders like Timothy (1 Timothy 1:18; 4:14).

2. The gift of prophecy is not infallible like the writings of the Old Testament prophets or the apostles of the New Testament

We had reason to point this out in chapter 4, but it is worth underlining this fact again here. Paul says explicitly that "we prophesy in part" (1 Corinthians 13:9), where the Greek term *ek merous* means "partially" or "imperfectly". We shouldn't be surprised by this. In the Old Testament, prophecy was a verbally inspired phenomenon for the most part. There may well have been a lesser gifting that operated in the schools of the prophets and among a wide range of unknown and anonymous prophets whose utterances and writings never made it into the canon of Scripture, but we are not explicitly told that this was the case. We know that the Old Testament prophets were taken very seriously and were relied upon absolutely to hear and deliver the authentic Word of the Lord. This is why spurious prophecy was such a grave offence. Deuteronomy 13:1–5 and 18:20–22 speak about the required punishment of stoning for those who prophesy falsely, a fate deserved because they did so in the name of other gods and because their wild predictions resulted in failure. So the Old Testament prophets were expected to speak the very words of God under an extraordinary degree of inspiration and in complete loyalty to Yahweh. To disobey the prophets was to disobey God himself.

However, it is very clear that the prophetic climate of the New Testament is not quite the same. Here the gift is often less accurate but more widely distributed among ordinary believers as well as their leaders. We are allowed to reserve judgement about the accuracy of a prophecy until a proper assessment has been made, and we are never told to kill false or inaccurate prophets, even if they serve other gods as they often did in the ancient Greco-Roman world. Instead, we are allowed to be cautious about receiving prophetic words and urged to test and weigh them (1 Thessalonians 5:19–20; 1 Corinthians 14:29).

We shouldn't be surprised, therefore, when a prophetic ministry today displays occasional mistakes while remaining a valid ministry of the Holy Spirit. We readily accept that this is true in connection with all kinds of New Testament ministries. We don't expect a pastor to be infallible in his teaching. We test what he says in the light of the Scriptures. We know that pastors sometimes inadvertently say the wrong things, and their Bible teaching may be inaccurate on some issues, but we don't stone them as a result. The same is true of evangelists. They may plan events that have clearly been arranged outside the will of God and, in some of their preaching, flights of fancy and exaggeration occasionally occur when they are operating in the flesh and promoting their own self-importance – a phenomenon sometimes known as "evangelastics"!

It is also an obvious fact that those engaged in other ministries, such as overseas missions, deliverance ministries and healing, may err, sometimes badly. Those who operate in healing gifts don't succeed all of the time and it is not always clear to us why some healing includes miraculous physical results when in other cases the work of God brings spiritual benefits but not a full physical cure. In all these instances we should not dismiss a person's ministry, whether pastoral, evangelistic, teaching or divine healing, simply because of a few mistakes or because our expectations are disappointed by failure. All ministries sometimes fail, including that of prophets. We recognize that most of these giftings operate only "in part", partly because of the provisional nature of the arrival of God's kingdom – it is already here but not yet fully consummated, so we live continually within the tension between the "already" and the "not yet", the tasters of "kingdom come", and the disappointments of "kingdom now". This is no less true in connection with the operation of the gift of prophecy. Our accuracy, sensitivity, consistency and degree of anointing for the task are all somewhat inconsistent and fairly unpredictable, but the Bible urges us to keep on doing this anyway. Hence, the need to weigh New Testament era prophecies properly.

"Test All Things"

Because of the inherent imperfection of our prophetic ministry, an essential aspect of it, without which it is risky and incomplete, is the weighing and testing of all prophetic utterances. Not only must the people who feel called to prophesy be known to the leadership of the church, but the content of what they have to say must be sifted and held up to the light of God's Word in Scripture. We are sorting out what is nourishing and useful from what is simply incidental and irrelevant, even harmful, as a fisherman might sort out and weigh his catch, throwing the inedible back into the sea.

During the Old Testament era, from Elijah to Malachi, Isaiah's prophecies or Amos' oracles were not weighed and sifted to the same degree, but nevertheless some judgement had to be made. These prophets were heavy with God's glory and God's presence, even to the point of absolute accuracy, and to a degree we simply cannot expect of all prophetic ministry today. Anyone who resisted their lofty utterances risked being flattened by them. After the death of Jesus, when God tore the temple veil in two, opening the way into his presence for all believers everywhere, the ministry of prophecy passed from being the responsibility of a few tried and trusted individuals to become the calling of the whole people of God – "I will pour out my Spirit on all people." Therefore, since prophecy is now an every-believer ministry, it is the individual utterance rather than the individual prophet that must be accredited. And so Paul writes in 1 Corinthians 14:36–38, and elsewhere, about the necessity to test all things. If prophecy today equalled the authority of the written Scriptures then Paul would never have told believers not to despise prophecy, as he did in 1 Thessalonians 5:19–20. The temptation to despise it is precisely because its authority is less than that of the Scriptures themselves. Testing implies that prophecy contains a mixture of some things which are useful, and some which are less constructive and better left unsaid. Thankfully, in my experience, prophecy is more often helpful and edifying than not. Especially where people are maturing in the gifts of the Spirit and following New Testament guidelines in exercising them, prophecy is nearly always a very powerful, beneficial and trustworthy gift.

In a previous chapter, I referred to the slightly inaccurate but nevertheless helpful prophecy of Agabus to Paul, warning him of trouble ahead (Acts 21:10–11), which was interpreted as a deterrent from God stopping Paul from completing his intended journey to Jerusalem. Paul would have none of this. Was Agabus therefore totally wrong? Maybe he was mistaken in some of the minor details of his interpretation and application, but the substance of what he had seen was very accurate indeed. This shows us clearly both the value and power of the prophetic ministry and its imperfect quality even in the era of the New Testament and under the fullness of the activity of the Holy Spirit. On that occasion Paul said, "I am ready not only to be bound, but also to die in Jerusalem for the name of the Lord Jesus", and he would not be dissuaded from his chosen course, so they gave up trying to persuade him and said, "The Lord's will be done." Paul felt free to disregard the interpretation of this prophecy given by trusted servants of the Lord. He trusted what he had heard from God in his own spirit more than he relied on the prophetic interpretation of his brothers in Christ. Whether he was right or wrong, this endorses our observation that there is only a relative – not absolute – value to New Testament prophecy. It is inspired, but it is more rarely infallible or inerrant.

Paul knew that his apostolic authority took precedence over prophecy, even in the Corinthian church where the charismata were in regular, high-profile operation. In the lengthy discussion of prophecy in 1 Corinthians 14, it is apparent that disputes about his own influence, and about his right to speak into the life of communities in the manner he did, were contributing to the many tensions in the life of the church, especially when the extent of Paul's authority was being questioned by false apostles who were trying to steal his sheep. One of the most delicate issues was the debate over the relationship and interplay between men and women in their distinctive role relationships, especially in the matter of the exercise of spiritual authority in the weighing of prophecy and other contributions in the meetings. Paul gave his advice on this (1 Corinthians 14:33–35) and, knowing that this counsel would prove problematic to some of his critics, especially to those who considered themselves more "spiritual" than their founding apostle, he wrote: "Did the word of God originate with you? Or are you the only people it has reached? If anybody thinks he is a prophet or spiritually gifted, let him acknowledge that what I am writing to you is the Lord's command. If he ignores this, he himself will be ignored" (1 Corinthians 14:36–38).

Paul firmly positions prophetic gifting, no matter how mature, developed or accurate it might be in the church at Corinth, decidedly under his own apostolic authority and accountable to it. Since his writings as an apostle were eventually accepted into the canon of Holy Scripture, they bore even at the time of writing the added stature of biblical authority. Now, as then, the safest place for any prophetic gifting to be positioned is under that same trustworthy apostolic and scriptural authority.

All present-day words of the Lord must be tested in terms of their total harmony with the eternal Word of the Lord – neither adding to it, nor subtracting from it, and certainly not deviating from the overall content, thrust, truth, ethics and central emphases of Scripture. The written Word of Scripture always takes precedence over the spoken words of prophecy. Scripture and prophecy are two different things. As Arthur Wallis has said, "God never intended prophecy to replace Scripture."

Moving in the Prophetic

We turn now to the issue of receiving prophetic revelation or hearing the voice of God – getting started in the prophetic ministry. My intention is to be very practical about this, in order to help make this gift as accessible as possible to all of God's people and to encourage their regular use of it. I want first of all to offer some guidelines for the operation of all spiritual gifts, before directly addressing the gift of prophecy itself.

1. Spiritual gifts are, generally speaking, given to those who desire them

It's no wonder that prophetic gifting has for so long been such an insignificant feature of the life of the church. It is simply because we have not desired those gifts. It was the so-called charismatic movement, spreading across all the mainstream denominations from the mid-1960s onwards, that reawakened an interest in the gifts of the Spirit on a much wider scale. That movement in the 1960s, and every successive wave of the Holy Spirit since then, stirred up again and again the desire to move in the prophetic.

You and I, as parents or guardians, don't foist unwanted gifts or favours on children who don't appreciate them and who would not be grateful if forced to accept them. If we detect that our generosity won't be welcomed, we spend our time and money on other things. Similarly, God doesn't foist his gifts upon his children where they are neither desired nor welcome. Therefore, "be eager to prophesy".

2. Gifts are not a reward for good behaviour

That's true of presents we receive from friends or family. It is also true of the Holy Spirit's gifts, including words of knowledge (i.e. the teaching ability), words of wisdom in counselling, healing gifts and miracles – these are not rewards for good behaviour. The gifts of the Spirit cannot be considered as merit badges or grounds for personal pride or boasting. Receiving any or all of the Spirit's gifts is a summons to humility and wonder. We obtain by grace what we can never really deserve. So Paul asks, "For who makes you different from anyone else? What do you have that you did not receive? And if you did receive it, why do you boast as though you did not?" (1 Corinthians 4:7).

These are gifts in the normal sense that they are deemed to be freely given to us, and in the further sense that they are not talents or attributes inherent to us, but they belong to the Holy Spirit who has loaned them to us. One day they will all cease (1 Corinthians 13:8–13). We have no grounds to boast of something that is not in any case our own. Even as we acknowledge that the Holy Spirit's gifts are not a reward for good behaviour, we must also emphasize that there should be a visible connection with our character and behaviour, and especially in their summons to humility! We have obtained by grace what we could never have deserved.

3. Gifts are not necessarily an indicator of spiritual maturity

We sometimes confuse flamboyance and power in ministry with Christian maturity, putting people on a pedestal because of their outstanding gifts. We take note of talented musicians, singer-songwriters and worship leaders, making celebrities of them and setting them up as public performers, often long before their character has matured sufficiently to match their gifting. This may explain the tensions that arise sometimes between worship teams/worship leaders and the pastoral team who lead the church and anchor its meetings. Worship leaders sometimes struggle with the authority of church leaders over the conduct of a congregational service on Sunday morning. This is mostly a character issue, usually occurring when the gift has outstripped progress in godly character.

Likewise, we sometimes put an eloquent, insightful and theologically acute young preacher in a pulpit or on large public platforms, often before he is quite ready for this. It may only foster the budding preacher's pride. He risks the danger of becoming inflated with a sense of his own self-importance as he receives praise and appreciation, and it goes to his head as he makes disdainful comparisons of himself with others. This vulnerability can also jeopardize the gift of prophecy. People can rapidly develop a fairly mature prophetic gifting, but if their character doesn't match this progress in talent, we must be careful that their gifting is used cautiously and not given a sudden high profile. Watching and imitating what Jesus does is always good practice; and Jesus went out of his way to resist advertisement of his powers. Again and again he requested that those he healed tell no one. Often we see him looking for the lonely and quiet places. He was not eager to advertise himself as Israel's Messiah, not directly anyway, and he offered the information about his true identity only to a chosen few. In the way of Christ there is a principle of lowliness, hiddenness and humility. And surprisingly to us, hiddenness often lasts far longer than disclosure. Sometimes God takes us "off the radar" of the celebrity-seeking Christian scene until we can handle it and demonstrate that we can serve God faithfully and refuse to promote our own self-importance.

4. Gifts flow through human personalities and reflect that reality

We ought not to try to stereotype prophetic styles. The prophets God uses vary, in keeping with the created diversity of humanity. God does not make clones of us when we become Christians; there is a peculiar interplay between the gift and operation of the Holy Spirit and the personality of the individual through whom he works. Everyone is unique and that's as it should be. God does not want mere "drainpipes": bland, manufactured conduits channelling the flow of his Spirit. There is a belief that as long as the "water" is flowing, it doesn't matter through whom it flows just as long as it gets to its destination. In fact, it is often implicitly believed that the function of a good drainpipe is that the water will be conveyed to its recipients without any trace of contact with the pipeline at all. But this is not how prophecy or any other ministry works.

In this case, the channel of God's blessing is the God-shaped humanity of the prophet, whose own style and life experience will colour the manner in which the content of prophecy is delivered. Prophecy, like preaching, is truth coming through human personality. It will flow in harmony with who you are, and it will inevitably have aspects of you, yourself, present and mingled with it. This is indisputably the case with all of the true preachers we have ever heard, and we accept that, but it extends to the other speaking gifts of the Spirit as well. When you prophesy, listen to God but be yourself, and don't try to imitate other people. Be authentically who you are. As a fine black preacher once colourfully and memorably expressed this, when teaching a preaching class to a group of "wannabe" trainee preachers, "Be who you is, because if you ain't who you is, you is who you ain't!"

125

5. Gifts need time to develop and mature

Prophetic gifts do not usually come full-grown, though they occasionally appear to do so, as we have just noted. You can often see a great gift of prophecy operating within an immature, even childish person, but gifts still take time to develop fully. Our early steps are often similar in their operation to a toddler learning to walk. There are more slips and falls than steady, confident progress. There is often much stumbling and nervous hesitancy, and that's fine. Nevertheless, we can still grow in the gift of prophecy and in sensitivity to the Holy Spirit's voice. We can grow in discernment of his operations and in the depth, weight, accuracy, authority and quality of the prophetic communications that God gives us.

Be diligent in seeking from God the gift of prophecy. It's not for the casual. It's not for the apathetic and the lazy. It's for those who are going to give themselves wholeheartedly to developing a ministry for the Lord. So these are some general guidelines about the use of spiritual gifts.

Fully Acknowledging the Place and Importance of Scripture

If prophecy is a servant of God and of his inscripturated Word, so that it is under the authority of the Bible and meant to be coloured in its content by the truth of Scripture, then it follows that the prophetic individual must have a correct attitude to the Bible if he or she is to be any use whatsoever to the church of Jesus Christ.

This means that we have a perpetual obligation to get to know the Word of God very well indeed, to become familiar with it in its entirety – indeed, to be marinaded in it. Your aim should be to read the Bible carefully in its entirety and on a regular basis. I once bought a secondhand theological book in an antiquarian bookshop. The book dated from around 1860 and was a thick volume of about 600 pages. As I opened the cloth-bound cover, I noticed a hole on the front page that looked like somebody had drilled it with a fine drill bit. As I began to flick through the pages, I noticed that this hole went all the way through from the front to the back of the book and had even drilled into the back hard cover of the book which was marked by a shallow burrowing of random twists and turns. This was obviously caused by the munching and tracings of the same bookworm that had eaten its way through the whole book. That bookworm had gone through that book from page 1 to page 600, cover to cover! It struck me that it would be a very good thing if more believers did the same thing with the Bible – devoured it from cover to cover!

Those who have read the Scriptures through from Genesis to Revelation, from beginning to end, and done so repeatedly, can expect to become familiar with God's Big Story both in its details and as a whole and at the same time will have soaked their minds in the vital truths of Scripture. This safely anchors prophetic ministry to divine revelation, helping to channel aright the flow of prophetic gifting. It safeguards our minds from error and enriches the content of our utterances.

It is particularly helpful, in developing prophetic ministry, to become familiar with the biblical prophets, with the content and style of their prophesying, so that we see God and the world as they did, understanding burdens that often overwhelmed them as they saw the activities of the people of God and the behaviour of surrounding nations.

As we read we also become aware of the guidelines and teaching that Scripture imparts, related to the gift of prophecy. These principles have been given to us to safeguard our spiritual health and wellbeing. It is a dangerous thing to become manipulative and controlling in the use of the gift of prophecy. It is a dangerous thing for the church to treat this gift with such respect and even awe that we never stop to question the accuracy or content of what a prophetic individual has said to us. This is why the Bible gives us clear guidelines about the testing and weighing of prophetic utterances and instructions on how to flow in this gift. Familiarize yourself with this advice.

We have also a responsibility to memorize, meditate upon and study the content of Scripture, respecting its supreme authority as the infallible voice of God. This says loudly and clearly to our hearers that we honour and elevate the Word of God in their own lives and want to see it honoured in the church's life also.

The primary means of hearing God's word in the life of the church, for instruction and guidance, is the regular preaching and teaching of the Bible and the daily private reading of it by every individual Christian. Prophecy supports and underscores that centrality of the Scriptures in our lives; it complements but never supplants it.

This practice will also add weight to our prophecies. If you are under authority, you can also exercise authority. The individual who is submitted to Scripture will know an increased authority in the use of prophetic gifts. The converse is also true. This is why we should pay little or no notice to maverick prophets who have no roots in the local church, little respect for church leaders, and who sit loose to the authority of Scripture. No one oversees and pastors them, and there is no accountability to other ministries in the Lord – they just do their own thing. Anyone who refuses to submit cheerfully to authority, and also to become cheerfully accountable to it, is like a loose cannon on an old wooden warship. It is not properly anchored by the required ropes, tracks and pulleys, nor held in the right place and pointing in the right direction at the gun port. It's not tied down and it's not facing the real enemy. It could just as easily swing around and put a cannonball through the crew or the masts and side of the ship. "Loose cannons" are dangerous. And so is freelance prophetic ministry. It must be under authority – the authority of the Bible and the authority of other experienced leaders in the church.

Personal Preparation for Prophetic Ministry

There are some guidelines we need to note to help us move in this gifting. We must realize that the Spirit indwells us as the author of prophecy. On one notable occasion Jesus announced, "Whoever believes in me, as the Scripture has said, streams of living water will flow from within him." And the apostle John comments, "By this he meant the Spirit, whom those who believed in him were later to receive. Up to that time the Spirit had not been given, since Jesus had not yet been glorified" (John 7:38–39).

But now, at this time in the history of salvation, Jesus has been glorified and the Spirit has been given to his church and to individuals who have been born again and baptised in the Holy Spirit. We are to expect that there will be an outflow of the Spirit's life. I love that statement of Paul at the end of the epistle to the Romans, as he addresses his intentions for a place and church he had not yet visited: "I know that when I come to you, I will come in the full measure of the blessing of Christ" (Romans 15:29). Would that we could all say of ourselves, "I know that when I am around you, I will be present in the fullness of the Holy Spirit and there will be a flow of God's outpoured blessing upon many lives." Is that an arrogant statement to make? No. It displays an appropriate confidence in the Spirit and his call upon our lives, knowing that under his guidance we may all prophesy. That's what Paul made very clear to the Corinthians: "For you can all prophesy in turn so that everyone may be instructed and encouraged" (1 Corinthians 14:31).

These words should alert us to the reality that if our church is without this vital instrument of blessing, something is missing from our spiritual "toolbox". It's good and helpful to think of all the gifts of the Holy Spirit, including the nine listed in 1 Corinthians 12, along with the 18 or so others listed throughout the New Testament, as our Holy Spirit toolkit, and even these may not be an exhaustive list. When a handyman, electrician or plumber comes to your home he doesn't know exactly what problem he is going to encounter, so he brings a toolbox. It has all the usual tools like a hammer, saw, various types of spanners or screwdrivers, but it may contain more unusual tools. What he does, therefore, is rummage through the box for whatever tool is most needed on this particular occasion. We may do the same thing, spiritually speaking. It may be prophecy that is needed this evening, or healing or the gift of praying in tongues may be on God's agenda. So we all need to carry with us the Holy Spirit's toolkit, prepared and confident to use it.

Then, whenever healing or prophecy are necessary and appropriate for the situation, we are ready for God to use us. The gifts, the toolkit, belong to the Holy Spirit; they're his, not ours – but we do need to learn to use the tools; some regularly, some occasionally, all of them sometimes. The Spirit's gifts are both *possessional* as permanent abilities within our lives, and more *occasional* in their functioning. It is all down to how the Holy Spirit leads and directs and this is finally not under our personal control or sovereignty, but his.

Some say that each Christian receives only one gift of the Spirit, or at most two, and that the gifts then become a permanent possession to be used at will – the only gifts you can ever move in. By this way of thinking, if there doesn't happen to be a prophetically gifted person present in the meeting, we are not going to hear from God in that way. In fact, all the gifts belong to the Holy Spirit all of the time and are therefore all available, as and when appropriate, to those servants of Christ who live consistently under the direction of the Holy Spirit, obedient to his voice, familiar with his Word in Scripture and immersed in his presence.

Excuses, Excuses

Anyone who wants to get started in prophetic ministry sooner or later has to stop making excuses and just go for it. The excuses vary, but here are some of the most popular ones:

1. "It's not for today"

This is the theological position of those known as "cessationists" with regard to the miraculous or extraordinary gifts of the Holy Spirit. This stance, once dogmatically held, has now come to be widely seen as untenable in the light of Scripture taken as a whole. It also denies the plain evidence of church history, up to and including today. Throughout the New Testament there are many endorsements of the promise Christ made just before his ascension to heaven: "These signs will accompany those who believe: In my name they will drive out demons;

they will speak in new tongues; they will pick up snakes with their hands; and when they drink deadly poison, it will not hurt them at all; they will place their hands on sick people, and they will get well" (Mark 16:17–18).

It is clear from this that Christ's long-term intention was for all congregations and every believer to operate in such gifts, everywhere and always. These gifts are for all believers without exception, until the day the Lord Jesus returns from heaven at the end of history, as we now presently know it. Paul very clearly said much the same thing to the Corinthians when he wrote that though the gifts will one day be obsolete and eventually pass away, they will continue until "perfection comes" (1 Corinthians 13:8–12). This is not a reference to the completion of the canon of Scripture as some maintain, in order to justify their denial of the present-day availability of all of the gifts of the Spirit. It is rather a reference to the *parousia* or second coming of Jesus and the culmination or consummation of his reign at the end of history when full perfection will finally have arrived, as the context, and especially verse 12, clearly shows: "Now we see but a poor reflection as in a mirror; then we shall see face to face. Now I know in part; then I shall know fully, even as I am fully known."

Paul began this same epistle with a similar allusion to the permanency of the operation of all of the spiritual gifts until Christ's *parousia* at the end of the age: "Therefore you do not lack any spiritual gift as you eagerly wait for our Lord Jesus Christ to be revealed" (1 Corinthians 1:7). If the Corinthians needed all of the Spirit's gifts, then so do we. Our disadvantages and weaknesses are the same as theirs. Our challenges are just as great also. The Holy Spirit's gifts will no longer be needed and the people of God can cease eagerly desiring them when, and only when, Jesus comes again – not at some arbitrary expiry date imposed by sceptical scholars: spiritual killjoys, kingdom party-poopers and grim-faced "fire sale" receivers who have sold off the church's best assets at bargain-basement prices at some time in early church history when they concluded that not much else was likely to happen. To such sceptics, the most popular expiry dates for the spiritual gifts are AD 70 (the destruction of Jerusalem, when the gifts are said to have gone up in smoke along with the temple) or AD 90 (the death of John, the last eyewitness apostle).

2. "I'm too young for this"

That's what Jeremiah protested when God called him to be a prophet, but God refuted his objections and made clear to him that this was out of step with the mind of the Holy Spirit. Jeremiah recorded, "I said, 'I do not know how to speak; I am only a child.' But the Lord said to me, 'Do not say, "I am only a child." You must go to everyone I send you to and say whatever I command you. Do not be afraid of them, for I am with you and will rescue you,' declares the Lord" (Jeremiah 1:6–8). Jeremiah felt weak, immature, inexperienced and inadequate – just as many of us feel also. But God knows us better than we know ourselves. He makes no mistakes.

God often has to argue with his children as to the appropriateness of his call on our lives, overcoming objection after objection, until we finally cooperate with his wishes.

3. "People might not approve of me"

True! You can be absolutely certain of that, because you have our Lord's word for it. It's recorded in Matthew 5:11–12, as part of the Kingdom Manifesto – the Sermon on the Mount: "Blessed are you when people insult you, persecute you and falsely say all kinds of evil against you because of me. Rejoice and be glad, because great is your reward in heaven, for in the same way they persecuted the prophets who were before you."

Prophesying is not, and never has been, a popular ministry when it has been conducted faithfully, for such powerful words do not just constitute innocuous talk about pretty little flowers and the return of the butterflies in spring, or the sweet singing of the birds in summertime. Rather, true prophecy is the declaration of the mind and heart of Christ to his people, and sometimes it has such forcefulness, shattering effects and life-changing impact upon a sleepy, backslidden and apostate church, that it can drive people mad with rage and trigger fits of violent opposition. Prophecy is not guaranteed to make us popular, except perhaps in heaven where the only applause that really matters is finally going to be heard.

4. "I did it once, but it all went wrong!"

Maybe, but what would you say to a learner who told you that after his first driving lesson? Prophecy sometimes does go wrong. Recall that we only ever prophesy "in part" (1 Corinthians 13:9). Since everyone sometimes makes mistakes (that's how we learn), the thing to do with a mistake is discover where and how you went wrong, learn from it, seek forgiveness from God and anyone else who was hurt by your ineptitude, pick yourself up again and resolve to do better next time. Be very careful that you don't talk yourself out of a job. If we keep on making excuses when someone calls us to do a special task, then eventually that person may stop calling us and seek a more willing and cooperative agent or messenger to work with. In the same way, God will never force upon us a ministry we consistently refuse. We all make mistakes but with God failure is never final.

What's important here is that we don't wilfully renege on God's call and prove consistently unfaithful in this difficult ministry, especially by our stubborn refusals. Our criterion should be obedience, not a trail of unbroken successes. However, consistent unreliability has consequences. If you were a manufacturer and regularly used a transport company to distribute your company products all over the country and even abroad, and that firm regularly lost those products on railway sidings or minor country roads, so that they regularly turned up either at the wrong destination or two weeks late, what would you do? You would simply hire another firm. God wants reliable messengers who will pass on faithfully the things he has entrusted to them; otherwise he may decide to use somebody else.

Imperfect as I am, I would rather he used me. Surely, you feel the same?

Chapter Six

Learning to Prophesy

We have set out the principles for eagerly seeking and welcoming the ministry of prophecy in today's church, and established that all authentically Christian prophetic ministry must be rooted and grounded in the Scriptures. We have looked at how prophecy works in the community of the faithful and in the conviction and persuasion of those who do not yet know Christ, and we have dealt with the fears and objections that may hinder believers from getting started in this wonderful privilege of using the Holy Spirit's own toolkit to make our everyday lives work out as they should, to the glory of the living God. It's time now to move on to address the practicalities of how we get started in this ministry in the power of the Holy Spirit.

To prepare the way for a confident beginning in prophetic ministry, the first thing we have to examine is our attitudes. Here are the components of the appropriate attitude we need to adopt.

Stirring up the Gift of Prophesy

1. Resist the temptation to use the Holy Spirit's gift of prophecy as a means of establishing a personal reputation

It's not about me, or you; it's about Christ and his glory. It's about the welfare of his church. It's not about what people think of us, whether they like us or dislike us. It's about being faithful to the commission and call of God upon our lives. Somebody once put it like this: "There is no limit to what God can do through the man or woman who does not care who gets the glory." If you don't care who gets the credit, so long as God's will is done, you are well on the way to moving in the gifts of the Spirit.

Eliminate carnal personal ambition from your life, therefore (James 3:14–17), and recognize the fact that, as in any other area of life, promotion comes from the Lord. We don't have to blow our own trumpets or beat a drum and say, "Look at me!" or "Can you find an outlet for my outstanding talents?" "A man's gifts make room for him" (Proverbs 18:16 NKJV). The Lord will open the door for you and make a way where there was no way. He will also shut the door if that path is the wrong one for you (Revelation 3:7).

2. Recognize the value of the gift of prophecy

If, as Paul says, everyone who prophesies speaks to people for their strengthening, encouragement and comfort (1 Corinthians 14:3), then why would we ever want to neglect a gift that had such potential for blessing individuals and which is authentically of God and widely available to all of God's children today?

3. Ask God for the gift of prophecy and then stir it up

Are you stirring up a desire for this gift in your own life? If you have already known what it is to receive messages prophetically from God, are you asking that this gift will never again be ignored and allowed to lie dormant or neglected? Are you beginning to stir it into operation when you are in meetings, or when you are aware that people are facing difficult situations, or perhaps when you are engaged in working pastorally with individuals or in conversation with unbelievers? Prophetic words are not only for church contexts. God uses them, as we have seen, evangelistically among unbelievers as well. Ask God to continually stir up this gift in you and be always ready for the moment he deems appropriate. Paul says, "Follow the way of love and eagerly desire spiritual gifts, especially the gift of prophecy" (1 Corinthians 14:1). He adds later in the chapter, "Therefore, my brothers, be eager to prophesy, and do not forbid speaking in tongues. But everything should be done in a fitting and orderly way" (1 Corinthians 14:39–40).

Prophecy, once stirred, begins to bubble up within us. Sometimes this happens when we are eagerly wanting to hear from God about a situation that's puzzled us for some time: "How do you want us to use our buildings, Father?"; "What area of our discipleship do you feel we need to address next?"; "What word have you for the home and family life of our people?"; "Where could we improve our daily habits as biblical Christians?"; "Is there anything you want to say to us about the way we are using our time and our money?" And so on. Prayer is meant to be dialogue, not just monologue, so expect the Lord to reply. As we begin to wait on the Lord in an actively receptive attitude of mind and heart, he may lead us in surprising ways, imparting to us the revelatory information that will make the church and our walk as individual believers steady, wise, radiant and glorifying to God.

When Joshua was looking for the culprit who had stolen the forbidden Babylonian garment and wedge of gold, and who later occasioned the ignominious defeat at the battle of Ai, he used a prophetic tool for divine guidance under the Old Covenant – he cast lots. This was a legitimate way of hearing prophetically from God. Joshua began a process of elimination, working through the tribes of Israel, and then through their clans, households and families until he finally identified the culprit as Achan. We too can identify clearly the Holy Spirit's wise choice; but we don't need to throw dice any more. God, at the day of Pentecost, poured out his Spirit on all people, through the great victory of Christ on the cross. We can hear directly from the Holy Spirit now. All we have to do is open ourselves up and be available to Christ, then ask and seek, and stir up this gift within us.

4. Resolve to faithfully report what you hear and whatever God gives you to say

There is little point in God giving you things to say if, through fear of what people might think, uncertainty and self-doubt, you then keep them to yourself or water them down. We have to resolve to say what the Lord wants said, no matter how unpopular it is or how odd it may seem. We do so humbly, in that we submit it to others to assess properly, but we will not hold back simply out of anxiety about how it will make us look. Years ago, when I began preaching as a young man in Lancashire, I made a promise to the Lord, inspired by the examples of men like George Whitefield and Charles Haddon Spurgeon who seemed to model this attitude consistently. I said, "I don't know where you will take me or what you will have me do with my life in the future, Lord, but I thank you that these doors are opening for me to preach for you and I want to commit to a decision I've made. Lord, I promise you I will preach whatever you ask me to preach and whatever you summon me to say, whatever the audience and whatever the situation. And I promise you that for the rest of my life, Lord." And to the best of my knowledge I have kept to this. Whenever I feel hesitant in the pulpit, thinking, "I'm not sure whether I should say this or not", I have a motto: "Say it anyway!" – on the grounds that it's easier to obtain forgiveness than it is to get permission!

There is no point in asking the Lord to use you as a prophet if you are not willing to pass on accurately what he has to say. There is no way to become mature and experienced in prophetic ministry except by passing on what the Lord has to say. We must prove faithful, for if we are faithful in small matters, delegated responsibilities and material things, then God will trust us with even bigger things eventually (Luke 16:9–10). Paul counsels, "Do not put out the Spirit's fire" (1 Thessalonians 5:19). Don't be your own asbestos blanket. Don't extinguish the Spirit's blaze within you. This will take courage. It is not an easy resolution to keep.

5. Exercise strong faith that the Lord is with you

That's what he told Jeremiah: "I am with you" (Jeremiah 1:8). That's what he told Gideon too: "I will be with you" (Judges 6:16). That's what he told the returned exiles through the prophet Haggai: "'Be strong... I am with you,' declares the Lord Almighty" (Haggai 2:4). And the clear inference is that he is with you too, so learn to move out in faith upon God's prompting and become completely fearless. Try not to give in to doubt, thinking, *"It's just me. I'm sure it's just me."* God may encourage you strongly in the early days, as he encouraged me when I first began prophesying in the early 1980s. I often had clammy hands. I don't usually have clammy hands at all, so this was a real encouragement to me many times, an indicator that the Holy Spirit was working in me. Sometimes we feel an involuntary trembling or shaking in our bodies under God's power. Other times we feel a gut-wrenching stirring in our stomachs or intestines, butterflies in our stomachs or our hearts racing in our chests, and we know something unusual is going on. On occasions we are overwhelmed by the Holy Spirit's power and can barely stand. Other times we may feel hot all over. For a long time, one or both of my knees used to vibrate when the prophetic anointing came upon me, and this still happens occasionally. Yet we don't need to depend on those things for confirmation and, after a while, God may ask us to act in simple faith without the need for "putting out fleeces" to confirm it is really him, as Gideon did once. John Wimber spells "faith", "R.I.S.K"! You have to go out on a limb for God sometimes, but out on a limb is where the best fruit is so often found. So let's do it!

6. Ask a trusted leader/pastor/prophetic person to lay hands on you to receive this gift

Paul knew that when he came to Rome he would be bringing the fullness of the blessing of the gospel of Christ. What for? He explains that it would be to "impart to you some spiritual gift to make you strong – that is, that you and I may be mutually encouraged by each other's faith" (Romans 1:11). It is possible for the gifts of the Holy Spirit to be passed from one person to another through impartation; this is often how people get started with speaking in tongues in a new prayer language to God. Sometimes God will act sovereignly and sometimes he will use a human intermediary who lays hands upon someone while praying for him or her. Paul reminded Timothy of the gifts that were bestowed on him at his ministry ordination with the laying on of hands of both Paul and the team of church leaders (2 Timothy 1:6; 1 Timothy 4:14). Ask for this. Ask people to pray for you and lay hands for the impartation of the Holy Spirit upon you, particularly from those who are already moving in this gifting. Who knows, but that something of their spirit may come upon you as happened with Moses and the seventy elders in the passage that we looked at earlier on (Numbers 11:24–25). During seasons of heightened activity of the Holy Spirit, it is remarkable how prophetic activity begins to operate more strongly as we gather with other prophetically anointed people. We literally "catch the fire"!

Many of the stories I have told so far come from the years 1994 to 1997, because that was an unusually significant time for the prophetic. I was privileged to see God's anointing rest with great power at that time on gatherings of church leaders and others who were fully open to his Spirit and the movement of his presence in their midst. Sometimes it seemed that everywhere I went I was hearing something of tremendous weight and prophetic significance for my life, and the lapse of time only served to endorse the spot-on accuracy of those prophetic words. Thank God that there are special seasons like that. During dry seasons the movement of the Spirit may seem more infrequent and spasmodic, but these are the times when we are called to pray and grow and eagerly desire the anointing. It will always come to those who call out to God, walking in his way and trusting in his love.

7. Wait for God's timing

When we begin to move in the prophetic, we have to resist the "urge to splurge". We must exercise strong faith that the

Lord is with us and resolve to say what he wants said, no matter how unpopular it is or how odd it may seem – but with patience and discernment. Resist the impulse to impart your first impressions to someone, or just about anyone, even the first person in sight – so that you can pass on the package regardless of the addressee God has in mind! Timing and true destination are very important matters. Some prophecies are to be announced now; others are for intercession, and still others may even be for your ears alone. Some prophecies are to be put on file until God tells you when it is time to share them. Some must be written down, perhaps dated and shown to trusted leaders, helping to guard the gift against accusations of fraud when the events eventually transpire and you are accused of prophesying after it all happened!

My friend Genny Burgin, a prophetically gifted and godly woman from Sheffield, England, who receives incredible visions from God of national and international significance, saw well in advance many of the events that took place in August 1997 surrounding Princess Diana's death. She saw in advance a vivid depiction of masses of flowers laid in the streets of every major town in the United Kingdom. She knew that somehow God would work through an event that would occasion this display of national grief and mourning on an unprecedented scale. Ever since then, because of the unwanted publicity and even criticism her prophesying brought her, she has written down any subsequent dream and vision she has received, and puts them on file with the elders of her church until they come to pass. She saw something of the tragic events that occurred in New York on 11 September 2001, two years before they occurred, and prayed that it would be prevented, until God told her to stop praying. He said to her, "It's going to happen and it will shake the nations and I will use it to call to my people to pray for the countries in which they are placed so that revival mercy will flow, because judgement is the only other alternative." That is a weighty prophetic revelation, but I think you will agree that it is good that she records such disclosures on file in this way. It helps to preserve the integrity of this ministry when it is genuinely of God.

Some prophecies are for a specific individual, others for the group. You have to know the timing of when to deliver them and, of course, specifically for whom they are intended.

It is also wise to have the humility to check what the Lord shows you, seeking the wise judgement of others you trust. You may have a prayer partner, or be part of a prayer triplet, whose wisdom can help you weigh the message, in prayer and with honest common sense, to test the inspiration that has come to you. Prophetic words should agree with the tenor of Scripture and be passed on in an attitude of humble submission to the spiritual authority of church leaders, not least because prophetic ministry is very powerful and if it is not clearly submitted to the leadership and exercised within the ministry team of a church, it may appear to be pushing for a rival or independent authority over against them. Trust in God, act in faith, but keep a wise personal discipline and respect the judgement of other anointed servants of God.

8. Know that if you move in the prophetic, you'll pass through seasons of training and testing from the Lord

Prepare yourself for this. Ready yourself for more pain and more darkness than the average Christian will ever experience. Because God is interested in developing your character and your knowledge of him, the truth of Hebrews 12:6, "Those whom the Lord loves he beats the hell out of" (my favourite paraphrase of this text!), will be a clear description of your life. And this means that you will be tested and proven many times in private, in secret divine dealings with you that will make up your personal history with God, or you will know the experience of frustration and times of seemingly endless waiting periods and "wilderness experiences" as God keeps you hidden and your gift under wraps until the time for sudden disclosure arrives. Sometimes, you will experience the attacks of wicked people and demonic powers, or church leaders may simply squash and sit on both you and your gifting for a long time before you are allowed to go public again in prophecy. You may try to wriggle out from under this, but God wants you to be aware that somebody is out to get you and it isn't the Lord, so he strengthens your spirit, using this adversity to shape a godly character and strong fortitude within you. Satan wants to snuff out your ministry before it can prove truly effective. The Lord therefore wants you safely contained for a while, until you are ready.

Elijah was completely "shelved" at the Kerith Ravine for two years (1 Kings 17:2–6). Long times of hiddenness often precede occasions for sudden disclosure in our lives. Jonah was incarcerated in the "Fish Hotel" for three days and nights (Jonah 1:17). Jeremiah was isolated in a cesspit for weeks. Though you may not be set aside in such extreme ways as these, you will be sharpened by seasons of change and times of quietness when it seems like God has just forgotten about both you and your gifts and, try as you may, you can't hear a thing from him and you conclude that people have forgotten that you ever existed. You receive nothing. This can last for months and, in some cases, years. You begin to think and question: "Did I sin? Have I disobeyed the Lord? What's gone wrong with me?" The answer is: "Nothing". It is all part of the training. All is well. You are God's servant and you prayed for this ministry. No wonder God has taken you in hand for special training and preparation, including inevitable obstacles, hurdles and restraints. Even when the difficulties you encounter seem to be human antagonism or church politics, everything is part of God's good gift as he calls you, equips you and opens the way for you. There is no need to fret or chafe, no need for impatience or discouragement. Just humble yourself. "Suck it up!", as our American friends so bluntly advise godly sufferers. Dignify the trial, see through another winter and wait for God's springtime to come again.

Become Familiar with the Variety of Ways God Communicates with Us

I heard of a six-year-old girl who was drawing a picture of a bearded figure, using crayons and pencils in an art lesson at school. The teacher came over, looked over her shoulder and asked, "What's that?" The little girl responded confidently, "It's a picture of God." The teacher said, "I don't think so. Nobody knows what God looks like." The little girl replied, "Well, they do now!" If only things were that simple. God's ways are varied, sometimes cryptic and often mysterious, and certainly not predictable.

1. The Lord can give you a prophetic oracle

This is a very common way for prophecies to be delivered in the Old Testament. The prophets acted as though the Lord was speaking directly through them and they prefaced their announcements, more often than not, with words such as: "Thus says the Lord". In the New Testament, Agabus did the same: "The Holy Spirit says, 'In this way the Jews of Jerusalem will bind the owner of this belt and will hand him over to the Gentiles'" (Acts 21:11).

Because our prophesying is always imperfect, it's wise for us to refrain from prefacing a prophetic word in this kind of lofty way habitually, especially if its content may be quite mundane or even trivial. God does speak through us, but others must test it also and not be daunted in the task of doing so as though they were questioning the Almighty himself. In many cases, "Thus says the Lord" would be a premature assumption on our part – it's for those who have weighed it carefully to add that assessment. Such claims can often come across as overbearing and can prove intimidating, and even resistant to the holy scrutiny that the leadership must apply in order to discern what is and is not of God.

Even with these cautions in place, every now and then people are prompted by the Holy Spirit to speak in just this kind of way. I have done it myself. I have been so conscious of the authority, weight and significance of what I am saying that I felt very comfortable prefacing it with, "Thus says the Lord" or "The Lord says". Yet even then it must still be tested, just as Agabus' words were by his close associates and by Paul the apostle (Acts 21:12–14).

2. You can give a prophetic exhortation for either an individual or a group of people

God may lay on your heart a message calling on someone to act or speak or change in some way. You will know for sure who this message is meant for and what God wants them to do. Remember to be humble and gentle in the way you deliver it ("Thus says the Lord", as we've noted, doesn't always go down so well; "I believe this is what the Lord is saying" is often more palatable), and check it out with your church leader or prayer partner if you are concerned that its content may be alarming or upsetting. The messages to the seven churches in Revelation 2 and 3 are a helpful example or pattern for us. They affirm the good points of those faith communities; then they offer a strong challenge to change and reform, but even in the challenge there is hope and healing. Christ's words never left his hearers under condemnation or caused them to despair. The conviction of the Holy Spirit always offers a positive way forward for repentance and new life: "I counsel you to buy from me salve for your eyes"; "I counsel you to be earnest and repent"; "I counsel you to recover your first love"; "I counsel you to deal with that woman Jezebel", and so on.

Back in 1996 we heard from the Lord that he wanted to bring a significant increase in numbers to the church I was pastoring in Winchester. The building we had erected at great expense only five years beforehand was already filled nearly to capacity. The Lord kept saying to us, "You are going to have to provide more space; I want you to go looking for a building that will provide for a growth that will mean a doubling and a doubling again." I was given those very words by at least five prophets over a period of time. Knowing that we could never accommodate such growth in the church we had built, we went looking for a sizeable venue. This proved difficult in the small market town of Winchester. We explored everywhere. We checked out commercial buildings on industrial estates, but found nothing suitable. We looked at fresh "green" land (sites that had never had anything built upon them before and where building was restricted), only to find that such sites were inviolable in Winchester, a conservation area; the local authorities simply wouldn't allow us to build upon them.

We were scratching our heads in bewilderment until one morning, as we were praying about the issue in the elders' meeting, my associate pastor Guy Miller said, "I've just seen an incredibly vivid picture: The eldership team were all sitting in a car driving round the M25 motorway that circuits the city of London. We were simply going round and round in circles and the Lord was saying, 'Come off at the next exit and go right to the heart of the city'."

We were puzzled by this. We weren't looking for property in central London; we wanted guidance about a church location in Winchester. But Guy then explained, "I believe that the Lord's saying we are going all around the houses on this issue, looking at industrial estates at the edge of town, when he means us to go right to the very centre of the city." So we thought, "There aren't many buildings in the centre of the city. The only site that is even remotely suitable is the old cinema – the bingo hall near the High Street." As we followed this up and investigated the building, despite some serous reservations and no knowledge that it was even available, we concluded, "Yes. This could be the solution." We discovered that the bingo hall had been built as a cinema in 1940 to accommodate 1,500 people – exactly the figure we had in mind.

We began to feel excited. God was on the move! About four weeks later we were at a gathering of 300 pastors and elders where the meeting prayed for people searching for big buildings in their towns, to use as churches. We divided up to pray in groups, and Guy and I were separated. The moment Guy's turn came for his group to pray for him, an elder who had never met him before, did not know him personally and knew nothing about his situation, put his hand on his chest saying, "I feel that God wants your church to double and double again. The Lord has got a building earmarked for you, which you have hesitations about, because it's not the normal kind of church building. It's an unusual shape for one thing but, God says, this is my will for you. Everyone who passes through

Winchester will see this building [it's actually on the one-way system in Winchester] and it will become more prominent spiritually than Winchester Cathedral."

We didn't need to hear anything else. We went for it, purchased it, paid for in full from our very first church offering of £805,000, and now that building has been completely refurbished as a superb conference facility and is filling up nicely! Recall that all of this came from a prophetic exhortation in a prayer meeting.

3. You can pray prophetically

This, as we have seen already, is not the same thing as "getting something off your chest" under the guise of offering a pointed prophetic prayer! Standing up in the prayer meeting to take an indirect swipe at another person present, under the camouflage of prayer to God, is *not* from the Holy Spirit. Praying prophetically has a luminosity that enables us suddenly to see clearly into baffling situations, praying with conviction, precision and power. There will be times when you lay hands on someone in a prayer-ministry line-up at the end of a powerful message, when many have responded to a call, and find yourself praying more than you knew for a particular person or complete stranger; then you notice that tears are rolling down that person's cheeks as the Spirit accurately uncovers their deepest concerns. He or she eventually asks, "How did you know? That's amazing!" The fact is, you didn't know. The Holy Spirit did, however, and prayed through you with great accuracy and relevance into the life of that individual. There are some examples of prophetic praying in the Bible: for instance, Zechariah's psalm of praise to God about the coming of Jesus and the ministry of John the Baptist (Luke 1:67–79), the prayer of gratitude and repentance in Ezra 9:6–15, the song of God's faithfulness and plea for his aid in Nehemiah 9:6–37, and many others. This phenomenon still occurs today. It is part of what it means to "pray in the Spirit on all occasions" (Ephesians 6:18).

4. You can bring a prophetic song

Unless you are tone deaf of course, and can't sing at all, like me; but even then, I've known God use people who can't sing a note! Recall that God is the source of all musical and poetic abilities. They are the gifts of his common grace to all humankind. They will still be present in heaven, only more enhanced than ever. In the Bible, Revelation 4 and 5 give us several glimpses and confirmations of this. Prose is the language of the mind, but poetry is the language of the heart. It is designed to move and ignite the emotions so we *feel* God's truth and not just understand it.

This means that God's Spirit can inspire both words and melodies prophetically in a person so that he or she spontaneously sings a "new song" to or about the Lord. Music characterized the angelic praise of God's heavenly hosts at the dawn of creation (Job 38:7), and God himself sings prophetically over his people (Zephaniah 3:17). The book of Psalms is full of such God-inspired compositions, 150 in all, and amounts to a kind of alphabet of the whole gamut of spiritual experiences that believers of every age have passed through, from the highest of heights to the deepest of depths. The Bible celebrates the beauties of human marital love and sexual intimacy through the sustained poetry of the Song of Solomon. The canonical prophets frequently deployed poetry to speak out and record their oracles, and this is usually signified by the indented verse layout of modern Bible translations. The Lamentations of Jeremiah, for example, simply consist of one long poem alphabetically arranged in the original Hebrew. It could easily be set to music. The apostle Paul urges us to follow the promptings of the Spirit in using such psalms along with more contemporary hymns and Spirit-given songs in the life of the congregation (Ephesians 5:18–20). More classical but modern examples might include Bach's *Christmas Oratorio*, Mendelssohn's *Elijah* and George Friedrich Handel's great oratorio, *Messiah*, since the libretto of the latter consists entirely of selected scriptures concerning Jesus Christ, and the sublime music was composed in a few short weeks of "burning the midnight oil" on the part of the composer, all under the clear inspiration of God.

In our churches, a song may be imparted to someone in its entirety in a meeting. Many of the songs we sing regularly in our churches have come prophetically to the original songwriters. Some came spontaneously, complete with beautiful poetry and inspiring melody; some were carefully composed in private before they were launched in public, and others were given especially for that particular time of worship, never to be recorded and perhaps never to be sung again. Such a prophetic message or song of praise, intended for that one occasion only, is simply another way in which God encourages, comforts and exhorts his people prophetically. Indeed, music often triggers the manifestation of prophetic gifts generally (see 2 Kings 3:15; Hebrews 2:12). As the 1970s Christian singer Larry Norman once asked, "Why should the devil have all the good music?"

I have heard some truly remarkable prophetic songs delivered: you could mistakenly think it had taken six hours to compose that music and write those lyrics; but no, it came by the Spirit there and then, God's "now word" for that moment. Such songs can speak to one individual in pain, a specific group present or to the whole congregation, just as normal prophecy does. Mike Bickle suggests various ways in which God can prompt us to use prophetic song. These include our private devotions, spontaneous group singing in home groups and celebrations, sung prayers to God, Bible passages sung spontaneously and not read as prose, and musicians "jamming" and singers singing without rehearsal unto the Lord.[7]

5. You can deploy the clever use of wordplay and double meanings

A related phenomenon to music and poetry is the imaginative and poetic element that sometimes occurs in prophetic words based upon puns or clever wordplay. Jim Paul, a Canadian prophet from Toronto, passing through a large prayer and fasting gathering of over 400 leaders at which I was present, spoke prophetically about the movement then known as New Frontiers International. He said, "Your initials are NFI. From here on in you will no longer be known just as 'New Frontiers

International', but 'No Fear International' because you are going to move with increasing boldness, faithfulness and courage on dangerous ground: the Middle East, many Islamic countries. Some of you will be martyred for the faith in the years ahead." Since that time, the NFI movement has indeed commenced its work in Islamic nations; some of its people have been arrested and others have died. It's comforting and encouraging to know that the Lord saw all that. It's good to know that a death in the family does not mean that we are not in the will of God. It might mean that we are right in the centre of God's will.

Another occasion when a prophetic message centred on a play on words happened when I was on sabbatical leave in the United States. Chris and Michelle, a young couple in their twenties whom I had never met before, had graciously offered their hospitality for the duration of my stay. I arrived very late after a long flight that touched down at 11.00 pm. When I reached my destination, Chris had kindly stayed up to welcome me. We chatted for about twenty minutes, then I was ready for bed after my long journey and we planned to continue our conversation in the morning. That night I had a dream about this couple, even though I still hadn't met Michelle. The Lord spoke to me in my dream, saying: "Tell Chris and Michelle they *may* be having a baby." There was a peculiar intonation about the word "may". At breakfast, not wanting to blurt out my prophetic message without having first understood something of their situation, I asked conversationally, "Do you have any children?" Chris said, "No. We've actually been trying to conceive for three years but it would appear we cannot have children. In fact, Michelle is probably going to go back to work soon because she simply can't get pregnant." So I said (this occurred in the month of April), "The Lord said something odd to me that I just want to run by you. He asked me to tell you: 'You *may* be having a baby'; and I don't think he said it like this because he wasn't sure! I think it was a prophetic emphasis on 'May', the calendar month." As April came to a close, I was eager to hear if Michelle had conceived; but no news. When July came, and there were still no signs of pregnancy, I wondered, "What was all that about, then?" But guess what?

Some time in October/November Michelle discovered that she had become pregnant in September; so a quick calculation will tell you when that baby was born – in May of the following year! I am happy to report that Chris and Michelle have had a second beautiful child since then, as well.

This was a play on the words from the Holy Spirit, but it was far from frivolous. This was something vitally important and life-changing for this couple. The pun on the word "may", highlighting their uncertainty and the Lord's faithfulness, was not a joke but a message in code, promising them the desire of their hearts. The word play in both of these cases made the prophetic messages especially focused and personal for those who were to receive them. In the case of the NFI movement, the word play made clear that God knew them by name – cared about them and wove his encouragement perfectly into their identity, defined in their name, underlining the need for God-given courage and boldness, which was to prove a reassuring strength in the challenge of risky mission ahead. In the case of Chris and Michelle, nothing could have made clearer to them that God understood the agony of uncertainty that they had lived with for so long, and replaced it with the blessing of something definite, real and trustworthy.

6. You can read or recite Scripture prophetically

God often quickens and illuminates certain scriptural passages that have special relevance for a meeting or an individual. Scripture always edifies and instructs, but when it is offered with this prophetic sensitivity to how the Sprit is moving among us now, its inherent relevance becomes something of burning significance. I remember an occasion when Terry Virgo, Bible teacher and leader of Newfrontiers, was once very exercised about the possibility of closing down the annual Stoneleigh Bible Week, a huge Christian conference that gathered up to 25,000 people annually, making a tremendous impact upon their lives and home churches, and regularly seeing annual offerings of over £1 million for the work of training, missions and church planting. Terry gathered a group of church leaders to pray through this issue. He had already heard from God in a significant way about this matter, but the decision had serious implications and he wanted to be sure.

During the prayer meeting God moved and, during a time of intense prayer, quickened a scripture to one of the men present: "I tell you the truth, unless a grain of wheat falls to the ground and dies, it remains only a single seed. But if it dies, it produces many seeds" (John 12:24). A brief explanation was then added about the principle of the multiplication of seed-life that emerges from the apparently complete loss of a grain in closure and death underground. But essentially the Scripture itself was the important thing, for this made clear that this major conference had to be allowed to die before further growth could occur. Its time had come to an end. In the years ahead, the movement would see massive and multiplied fruit from that moment of relinquishment and courageous obedience. The decision was made and the Bible Week was closed down in an absolutely amazing final event that summer, and God continues to produce a staggering increase of the promised fruit that has grown from that act of obedience to his Word. A scripture quickened to our lives in this way can carry immense power to change our thinking, behaviour and outcomes.

7. You can pass on a personal prophecy

When I was in the process of being called into the ministry back in 1978, I had already been a full-time high school teacher for two years. My wife Ruth and I were very concerned about the stirrings in my heart to give all this up, take a risk and go to Bible college for further training. We were not eligible for a local authority educational grant but would need significant funding. Furthermore, we did not know for sure if there would be an opportunity to pastor a church at the end of the two years' training. As we were living with the complexity and uncertainty created by my sense of call, we received an invitation to a house group of about twenty people, where the gifts of the Holy Spirit were accepted and welcomed as normal. At that time, Ruth and I weren't too familiar with charismatic meetings, but we decided to give it a try. Twenty people is a lot to squeeze into somebody's living room and, in that crowded space, Ruth and I found places to sit where we could, one of us at each end of the room. During the time of praise and worship at the beginning of the meeting, a man prayed in tongues. The gift of tongues often triggers a flow of spiritual activity and a few seconds later a prophecy came: "My son, don't be afraid. This is the call of my heart upon your life, and I am about to open a door for you which no man can shut. You must not be afraid to go through it. I will provide for all of your needs according to my riches in Christ Jesus." Nobody present on that occasion knew us very well at all; certainly nobody knew of the call stirring in my heart and the future challenges (particularly financial) we were facing as a result. It had been a tense time and we needed so much to hear definite confirmation from the Lord, to give us the courage for this step of faith. The words meant such a lot to us and, in addition, when a prophecy is meant for an individual, it strikes like a spear of light into the heart, bringing conviction, gladness and the joy of the presence of God. The moment that prophecy began to unfold, tears rolled down my cheeks. I looked at Ruth over the crowded heads in that packed room and she burst into tears as well. It was all we needed. We both concluded, "Well, that's it, then!" I resigned my teaching post the next day and the rest is, as they say, history. That was thirty-one years ago. God has proved absolutely faithful to the word he spoke in that crowded room, through the obedience of a complete stranger. God encourages us with personal prophecy.

8. You can receive a prophetic vision or a dream

What is the difference between a vision and a dream? A vision is something you see screened before your mind when you are awake, and a dream is basically the same phenomenon occurring while you are asleep. They both consist of vivid and memorable visual mental imagery that God puts before your mind. To illustrate, I was once at a coffee shop in the heart of the city with Ruth, when we saw some non-Christian friends we had met through a family at our church. We had not seen these acquaintances for the best part of a year, so we sat and chatted with them, catching up on each other's news in the coffee shop. After a while, the wife of this couple excused herself, leaving rather hurriedly. Ruth also took the opportunity to continue her shopping at that point, leaving me with the husband.

A likable, highly intelligent, talkative man and a high flier in his work, he seemed to have nothing wrong at all in his life. But that night at 4.00 am, I had a dream about him. It was as though I saw his life unfolding before me in episode after episode, and it was so vivid that I got out of bed and went downstairs where I could put a light on without disturbing Ruth, to write down a whole series of fourteen startling things I had seen in the dream about his private life, before I forgot them – including the fact that he was having an extra-marital affair.

God's timing is not random or approximate. I was awake again by 7:00 am, knowing that although he would soon be setting off for work, it was important that I see him that same day. So I phoned him at his home. He greeted me: "Greg! Oh, wow! I was just about to ring you!"

"Really?" I said.

He continued, "Yeah, when we had that coffee I just felt I needed to talk with you. There's some stuff going on and I need to talk to somebody about it; and you're the best person I can think of. Can I come and see you today?"

God had gone before me, making this difficult situation far easier! We arranged for him to come around after work, which he did.

I welcomed him into our lounge, where we sat on the easy chairs across the room from each other. I said to him, "Listen, the reason I rang you is because I've had a dream about you and I want to share it with you." I got my notebook out and explained: "In my dream I saw vivid details about you." I started to describe them to him and, as I did so, he leaned forward and put his hands to his face and then lunged backwards and stretched his legs out, sighing deeply. Flinging his head backwards and forwards throughout my report, he squirmed and wriggled in the chair: all the body language of a man in great agitation.

This continued as I recounted all that I had seen, and when I had finished he said, "Wow! You have just described my life." Every single detail of what I had seen was accurate. I told him: "The Lord wants you to do something about this", and I began to speak directly to him about what this would mean, pointing him to Christ as the only one who could fix him and the mess he was in.

I wish I could say that he fully repented. I wish I could say that he came to faith in the Lord; but he didn't, though he had his chance to do so. He acknowledged the truth of what I had seen, but he chose not to heed the warning or take the opportunity it held out to him, to begin again. His marriage broke up and his life disintegrated into a mess. Yet the power and clarity of the way the prophetic sometimes comes to us in dreams and visions made an impact on him he will never forget. It is never too late to make a new start with God; and perhaps the memory of that prophetic dream will stay with him as a reminder that God is real, and cares about his life.

As the well-known story of Joseph (he of the "Amazing Technicolour Dreamcoat", Genesis 40 – 41) shows us, it's one thing to have prophetic dreams, but it's another thing entirely to be able to interpret them. There are three vital components to bear in mind in responsibly receiving prophetic dreams and visions: (i) *revelation,* (ii) *interpretation* and (iii) *application.* All three are necessary for the prophecy to be functionally complete. You need the content of the dream or vision (accurately recorded while you can still remember it); you need to know what it means; and you need to know who it's for and what he or she is supposed to do about it. God may show you something, asking you, "What do you see?" as he did with Jeremiah (Jeremiah 1:11–13). But you then need the prophetic insight to interpret it. What does it mean, who is it for, when should you give it? The answers to those questions also come from God (Jeremiah

1:14–16), and you must also be able to grasp some of the likely implications for the recipient's life.

Sometimes, as happened to Joseph in prison (Genesis, see reference above), the dream comes to someone who does not have the prophetic sight and cannot understand it, even though it is so vivid and weighty that they recognize it as of great importance. Then they may bring it to you to explain and, together, you create a prophetic team, in ways similar to speakers in tongues and interpreters working together (I Corinthians 14:6–13).

Such dreams in the Bible often came to people who did not know God. In this case, they were brought to Joseph to interpret because he was perceived to be a man of God. As the church matures in prophetic ministry, those whom God visits with dreams and visions should be developing the capacity in the Lord to interpret what he has shown them. Pastors are not unused to people rushing to share "pictures" with either them or the church before all three of these components have been properly understood. Someone will come forward during a morning service, saying, "'Pastor, I've seen a cow in a tutu and the cow is tightrope-walking across Niagara Falls; and it's carrying with it an umbrella, and I've seen a bell hanging from its neck. And the bell rings three times and then the cow falls off the line, but as it falls, halfway down, just before the great splash occurs, the umbrella opens to form a parachute and helps it to descend safely. I don't know what it means, but I will just leave that with you, pastor!'"

Great! What on earth do you do with that? Sometimes the answer is "Nothing", because it is so ridiculous (yes, church can sometimes be amazing, can't it?)! However, I usually say something like, "I don't know what it means, either! So, go and ask the Lord about it and come back when you do understand. In its present form it would not be helpful for you to share it." I don't want half-formed and half- baked prophecies brought to the church if they're clearly unhelpful. If the Lord has more to say, if it is really from him, he will provide an interpretation and an application for us as well.

Visions and dreams must be handled in this way or the quality of our ministry becomes devalued – what is good and life-changing gets all mixed up with what is bizarre and, in its half-baked state, simply useless.

9. You can perform a prophetic action

This is sometimes described as an "acted prophecy". The prophet Jeremiah once placed a heavy wooden yoke over his shoulders and told the nation of Judah that this was symbolic of what would happen to the whole population when the Babylonians eventually invaded. Meanwhile, the court prophets at the king's palace (imagine living in a nation where being a prophet was a prestigious job!) were offering reassuring, but entirely false, prophecies in the smoothest of words, predicting divine deliverance from military disaster. They were not tuned into the Lord but rather to what the king and people wanted to hear, reporting "Peace, peace" and promising there would be no invasion, for the Lord and his temple would be the protection of his people. Jeremiah's stark, grim, acted prophecy made unforgettable and clear the true outcome and tragedy of their rebellious stance and apostate situation before God (Jeremiah 27).

Similarly, the prophet Ezekiel cut his hair off and then began throwing it up in clumps into the air, attacking it with a flailing sword as it blew away in the wind. Now, this must have looked seriously weird to his observers. Ezekiel didn't care. This was a man who in a previously acted prophecy had lain naked on his side for over 300 days, eating animal dung for breakfast, drawing cartoons and pictures of Jerusalem on slates, then depicting ropes strung across the chalk drawings to evoke the long siege of the city that would soon follow (Ezekiel 5:1–4; 4:1–17). These were memorable communications. They brought home so graphically the imminent destruction of Judah and Jerusalem at the vicious hands of Nebuchadnezzar and the Babylonian army – God's final instrument of judgement on an apostate people. Ezekiel's audience could not have failed to see that the prophet's actions were of profound significance. This is a very powerful way of getting the attention of God's people when there is something they must not fail to heed or address. Sometimes God will direct you to do the same kind of thing.

Acted prophecies can go much deeper and be far more costly than a humorous dramatic sketch during Sunday morning worship or a guest service. Hosea was told to marry a prostitute as a picture of Yahweh's relationship with unfaithful Israel (Hosea 1–3). Christ cursed a barren fig tree (Mark 11:12–14, 20–21). Agabus tied his hands with Paul's belt to predict the apostle's future arrest and suffering (Acts 21:10–11). All of these actions spoke to people very powerfully. In the case of Hosea, the prophecy was undertaken at immense personal cost and over a lengthy period of time. This is another instance of the wisdom in humility. It would be sensible to share with the church leadership and trusted prayer partners before embarking on a course of action or behaviour that seems crazy or bizarre, but which may nevertheless be of God. We prophesy "only in part", and the flawed nature of our ministry means that it is always essential to check and double check that we are hearing correctly God's Word.

10. You can feel sympathetic sensations in your body or certain specific parts of it

This can sometimes be a prophetic indicator that God is going to do a healing work in the body of someone present in that gathering. I recall one particular Sunday evening gospel meeting when the Lord gave me a peculiar sensation in my teeth, augmenting the words he was putting into my mind. I stood up and said, "I think there is a girl here who has highly sensitive teeth. She can't drink hot or cold fluids and experiences pain in her gums and teeth every time she does so. I think the Lord wants to heal you." A young woman from the local teacher training college was there for the first time that night. She had been brought by a friend because she was curious about God, wondering whether he was real or not. She had suffered from this dental condition for a long time and in fact had been receiving treatment for some months, with no result.

When she identified herself, I placed my fingers on her lips, saying, "Be healed in the name of Jesus!", while praying in some real measure of faith. She went straightaway to the tea point at the back of the auditorium and checked the sensitivity of her teeth by drinking first a piping-hot drink and then some cold water – no discomfort whatsoever! She was definitely healed in those few moments and she stayed healed. She soon found the Lord and received him, and became a keen Christian. The word had come to me along with the prophetic, sympathetic sensation of the discomfort in her sensitive teeth only for a few moments. I did not suffer with this condition myself, before or since. So I concluded this was God speaking to me.

A similar incident occurred, again during a Sunday evening service when, as the Lord spoke to me, I felt a pain in my right knee like that of a sporting injury. Recognizing this as a prophetic indicator and not a problem of my own, I thought about it and then relayed my impressions, announcing, "There is a girl here who has injured her knee in some kind of sporting activity." A young woman was with us that night, Carmen, who had become a Christian some time before but had subsequently drifted away. I was not aware of her presence and I certainly didn't know she worked in a sports shop and offered fitness instruction in the course of this employment. She had injured her knee about six weeks earlier, could no longer do her work properly, and was really worried about losing her job. So I got her to lay her hands on her own knee and I put my hand on hers, saying, "Lord, we're looking to you to repair this damaged tissue – sinew, bone, knee cap, muscle, nerves and blood supply. Be healed in the name of Jesus!" Her knee was healed instantly. Carmen was so thrilled that God would single her out in that way that she ran around the auditorium, delighting in her pain-free movements and enjoying the reassurance of her job security for some time to come! She had drifted from Christ, but he still cared for her and had not stopped watching over her. Carmen came back to the Lord that night.

Whether it is for an individual or a community, whether it comes as a picture or a word, prophecy is given to us by God for the vital purpose of calling us back into his way of holiness and encouraging us to stay close to him.

None of these activities should ever be used as an opportunity for self-display or self-aggrandizement. This gift is designed to disclose God's best way for us and to bring glory to him. As God's prophet, a part of your responsibility will be to bear witness to the kind of God he is by your attitude and behaviour. God is loving and gentle, honest, trustworthy and kind. God is at work in the world reconciling people to himself, healing and restoring them by his compassion and unconditional love. As his prophet, two things are unquestionably required of you: to be a person of unimpeachable honesty and integrity, and to allow your everyday life to be formulated and conditioned by the principle of generous, sacrificial, forgiving love. Your daily life and your attitude to other people are the messages that speak loudest of all. In his first epistle, John, the apostle of love, wrote, "If anyone has material possessions and sees his brother in need but has no pity on him, how can the love of God be in him?" (1 John 3:17).

This sharing with others includes not only our material goods, but also our spiritual treasure. In the book of Proverbs we read, "Do not withhold good from those who deserve it, when it is in your power to act" (Proverbs 3:27). Scriptures like these challenge our sinful reticence to relay or give others the great blessings God has first given to us. We do not always see that the gifts of the Holy Spirit are a treasure trove but, once we have recognized this, we will realize that it is selfish not to share these gifts or to hold back when we could pass them on. Don't sit on a gift when it's in your power to minister it. Instead, use it. But remain teachable and submitted to God, the Scriptures and the godly leaders who are over you in the Lord and who will help you grow in the wise use of these gifts to bring untainted honour to the Lord. A wise leader can help you immensely in the confident deployment of spiritual gifts if you have the humility to trust their oversight of you and their goodwill towards you.

Chapter Seven

Delivering a Prophetic Word

Tongues, then, are a sign, not for believers but for unbelievers; prophecy, however, is for believers, not for unbelievers. So if the whole church comes together and everyone speaks in tongues, and some who do not understand or some unbelievers come in, will they not say that you are out of your mind?

But if an unbeliever or someone who does not understand comes in while everybody is prophesying, he will be convinced by all that he is a sinner and will be judged by all, and the secrets of his heart will be laid bare. So he will fall down and worship God, exclaiming, "God is really among you!"

What then shall we say, brothers? When you come together, everyone has a hymn, or a word of instruction, a revelation, a tongue or an interpretation. All of these must be done for the strengthening of the church. If anyone speaks in a tongue, two – or at the most three – should speak, one at a time, and someone must interpret. If there is no interpreter, the speaker should keep quiet in the church and speak to himself and God.

Two or three prophets should speak, and the others should weigh carefully what is said. And if a revelation comes to someone who is sitting down, the first speaker should stop. For you can all prophesy in turn so that everyone may be instructed and encouraged. The spirits of prophets are subject to the control of prophets. For God is not a God of disorder but of peace.

> As in all the congregations of the saints, women should remain silent in the churches. They are not allowed to speak, but must be in submission, as the Law says. If they want to inquire about something, they should ask their own husbands at home; for it is disgraceful for a woman to speak in the church.
>
> Did the word of God originate with you? Or are you the only people it has reached? If anybody thinks he is a prophet or spiritually gifted, let him acknowledge that what I am writing to you is the Lord's command. If he ignores this, he himself will be ignored.
>
> Therefore, my brothers, be eager to prophesy, and do not forbid speaking in tongues.
>
> 1 Corinthians 14:22–39

The reception and encouragement of prophetic ministry within the life of a local church does not always proceed without difficulty. We've already mentioned the immaturity that sometimes manifests as arrogance in those who refuse to be accountable to the church leadership in using and developing their gifts. Prophecy has serious potential for disturbing both individuals and whole congregations and, surprisingly, most of all when it is genuinely of God. Presbyterian pastor and author Frederick Buechner writes, "God comes in such a way that we can always turn him down." This is true: the humility God requires in us originates in himself. Yet, while those he speaks to in prophecy may resist or refuse his Word, his prophets should discipline themselves in accordance with the humility, submission and lowliness of Jesus. Sin is added to sin when people refuse God's Word to them, and this is particularly inappropriate when they do so because the prophet's attitude is so arrogant or overbearing that God's whisper is drowned out by the clamour of the prophet's approach.

However, even when prophecy is offered sensitively and within the discipline of the leadership structures and oversight of the church, sometimes God's Word to his people is rejected; the disruption it may create is unwelcome. In either case, whether the word is brought gracefully or clumsily, it is never in our interest to dismiss or refuse what is offered to us as God's Word.

We might imagine the situation of a church community in need of the refreshment of God's life-giving breath as a group of people in a stuffy room on a hot day with all of the windows shut. If they open the windows, it will let in the refreshing, cooling breeze: but then some people may be allergic to pollen brought in on the breeze, there may be a noisy din from passing traffic, and some stray insects and irritating flies might trouble the meeting.

Similarly, if we permit the activity of the Holy Spirit (setting aside for a moment the breathtaking presumption of saying "No" to God!) in the life of our church, then yes, some disconcerting inconveniences may enter our midst along with that life-giving breeze; but the alternative is miserable suffocation and refusal of God's blessings.

Proverbs 14:4 asserts, "Where there are no oxen, the manger is clean, but from the strength of an ox comes an abundant harvest." If we ban or exclude prophecy from church life, of course things may continue to remain tranquil and fairly safe for a while, even predictably boring. No obvious or embarrassing mistakes will be made. No extremism will be allowed to intrude. We won't risk our routine being messed up. Yet, given our fresh understanding of the positive value of authentic prophecy from all that we have considered so far, surely it is worth risking a few cow-flops in the stable in order for the church to prosper greatly? We need to look beyond any possible pains and see all of the likely gains. Nevertheless, it is right to acknowledge that prophecy requires careful handling on the part of both the recipients and those who deliver it. This is the theme of our present chapter.

Faithfully Delivering the Word

We have looked carefully at the forms in which prophecy may be delivered, but how can we be sure it is God speaking to us? Apart from checking with a church leader whom we trust, how might we determine when is the right moment to speak out what we have seen or heard from God? For those who are just getting started, what are the signs that will help us recognize when God wishes to pass on a message to his people through us? Those who have become more mature and confident in this gift have discovered a number of clues and indications that signal for them the movement of the Holy Spirit. Though each person is unique, and prophetic ministries vary according to circumstance, culture and temperament, some common themes emerge which may help us recognize the voice of the Spirit as we start to move in this gift.

1. You may experience a kind of "bubbling up" inside

This echoes the phraseology of the Old Testament itself, describing a kind of eruption inside, the point when divine activity is "coming to the boil" in the prophet's spirit. The Hebrew word *nataph* carries the idea of "to ooze", "distil gradually", "to fall in drops" and thence, "to speak by inspiration or prophecy" (Micah 2:6, 11)[8] A stirring occurs concerning an issue the prophet may not have been thinking about before, something not planned or prepared, and after some processing it comes to the surface and pours from his lips. This kind of experience occurs in counselling, preaching and teaching contexts, as well as in ordinary conversation. You may have been given a preaching topic, or be engaged in biblical study. Unexpectedly, as you read and think through the study material, a "bubbling up" occurs inside you, an insight, a compulsion. You want to say something about this insight to others. This is not the same as a feeling of joy or enthusiasm that we can link to an obvious cause or sight, external to ourselves; it is quite unpredictable and spontaneous.

The Hebrew word for prophesying in the Old Testament, meaning "to bubble up", indicates divine activity (and sometimes, as in Micah 2, the stirring of false prophecy from an alien source other than God's Spirit, i.e. a demonic spirit) within the human spirit that rises in its intensity and compelling power as well as its clarity and its purity, deepening in meaning and significance within us, then gripping us with a sense of urgency to pass it on. When this is of God, this divine intimation (recalling some of the ways we used earlier to describe God speaking to us, it is located more in the mouth than in the brain) creates a sense of compulsion to speak it out, even though you may not understand why at that moment and have no reasoned declaration prepared. As the Word from the Lord continues to fill your being, your thinking starts to focus intensely upon it as your mind tries to catch up with what you are receiving from God in your spirit.

2. A vision/picture or the vivid memory of a dream may continue to fill your mind and cannot be ignored

Imagination is a gift of God's common grace to all humankind. It enables people to literally picture things in their heads, to visualize them in their minds. This is how engineers, designers, artists and architects can all conceive machines, furniture, paintings and buildings before they appear on a drawing board, or later become a physical reality. How does this happen? Where do these pictures come from? How do we see and read them? No one knows for sure, but we know that this is part of the created humanity and capacity of our brains that God has given to us. Well, that same God who created this faculty of imagination can access it at any time, then use it to screen his own images there, images of great significance. This is not common grace, but an act of his special grace in speaking to us personally. If demons can do this, surely God can? He does this by supernatural visions and dreams that linger and demand interpretation. Our eyes constantly pick up visual data, and our brains routinely process it. Most of it is of no significance whatsoever. But when God gives us visions or dreams of significance that linger when we wake up, then they stand out with great detail and clarity in our minds. They simply will not go away. Even when we tell ourselves, "This is me. It's just me and not God", the vision or dream will still intrude and persistently remain. And so there is a compulsion to do something with it or to try to describe and understand it and, then, as a result, to interpret it and speak it out for the benefit of ourselves and others.

3. God may highlight a biblical text to you

Perhaps in your own quiet time as you have been reading through the Scriptures, a verse has particularly stood out to you, perhaps for personal reasons, or maybe for the benefit of someone else. It may prove to be burningly relevant to a situation your church is facing, or the pressures your pastor or a dear friend may be under. It occurs to you: "This is the word for them, I am sure." Sometimes it is a short and simple verse, at other times it may be a whole passage or chapter of Scripture; even the complete story of a Bible character, along with the details of his or her life, may seem apposite to your local situation. Or it may be a single event in Scripture carrying rich symbolism for this moment in your church's history. You may feel the Holy Spirit saying to you, "Don't just pass this on – meditate on it; I want you to bring this or that aspect of the scripture to the attention of the church; I want you to read it out at the prayer meeting; I want you to bring it to Sunday morning's meeting." As you listen, you will hear God's voice; as you obey it, it will strengthen you. You will grow in confidence as you discern the times when you are hearing from the Lord, seeing the affirmation of the word's authenticity as you watch it fly true to its target.

4. You may sense an impression or words coming to you

This may be no more than the beginning of a sentence; or it could be that information comes to you as if someone was whispering in your ear about a specific situation, and this intimation simply will not go away. A possible indicator that this is a genuine word from God may be the sense of weight attached to it that you feel in your spirit. You know that this is something you dare not dismiss lightly. Prophets of the Old Testament sometimes describe this as the "burden of the word of the Lord". Its weight has the effect of impelling you to deliver and offload it completely at its intended destination. You simply need to know where that is, for whom it is intended, and for what purpose God has given it to you.

5. You may have a "gut feeling" that something is so

This is not to be mistaken for a suspicious or paranoid attitude! There are too many people willing to suspect the worst about their fellow Christians, their church leaders, their denomination or movement. The "gut feeling" spoken of here is not a nagging anxiety, but usually comes as something that has suddenly occurred to you without you even looking for it. It is a hunch: a strong conviction or gut feeling, giving an unexpected sense of clarity about a situation that God wants you to speak into and address. And again, it cannot be ignored.

6. There may be a persistent but quiet "still, small voice"

This phrase was used by the biblical narrator, sometimes translated as a "gentle whisper" or the "sound of silence", to describe the gentle, hushed, intimate way God spoke to his anxious prophet Elijah on the run from Jezebel (1 Kings 19:12). Elijah had fled to a cave on Mount Sinai and, as he hid there, depressed, defeated and afraid, God ministered to him and began to encourage him again. Here is an example of a man mature in prophetic ministry. Always his ear was tuned to the voice of God and his heart was open to receive the approach of God's Spirit. This acts as a lesson to us, warning us not to limit our expectations to what we have experienced before – earthquakes, wind and fire. God came to Ezekiel's slain army of dry bones as the mighty wind of God's resuscitating breath. God went before the wandering Israelites in the desert as a pillar of fire. God's voice is often likened to thunder or earthquake. So when the earthquake, the wind and the fire visit the mountain, anyone expecting God might have understandably assumed: "Oh, yes! There he is!" But Elijah, a true prophet of God, was used to looking and listening for the unusual, and not necessarily a repetition of what the Lord had done in the past. And so there came a "still, small voice", a "gentle whisper", a "silent, thin sound" (1 Kings 19:11–12). Here was God in mustard seed mode, quietly sovereign in spite of all appearances to the contrary, unfazed by Jezebel's antics and intimidating threats. And Elijah knew it.

God's voice to us today can sometimes be little more than half a whisper: very quiet, almost imperceptible, like an undercurrent that catches our attention below the clamour of relationships, commitments, hobbies and duties. We are sometimes called to encounter God in gentleness and apparent weakness, as well as in the more spectacular arresting indications of his presence: God in the silence as well as in the spectacular. Never despise this.

7. Sometimes you will experience unusual physical sensations

Though your hands are not normally given to sweating, they may suddenly become unusually clammy. Your breathing may alter noticeably – you may pant or breathe deeply, your body may shake all over, or your limbs begin to tremble or vibrate – a frequent phenomenon during times of intense activity of the Holy Spirit and a common indicator of his movement in our midst. You may experience a warm flush or a sympathetic physical pain.

These are some of the ways God may use to indicate the stirrings of prophetic communication in your spirit. But when the signs come, what are you meant to do next?

Delivering a Prophetic Word: Some General Directives

1. Interact with what you are receiving by asking questions about it

We should try to avoid passing on a prophetic message prematurely, before it has had time to incubate and mature.

We want to get as much information about it as the Lord is prepared to give us. He may not tell you everything, but you should be sure you have heard all he has to tell you. Never be in such an impetuous hurry that you deliver a half-formed message. God does not mind us asking questions: "What are you saying in this, Lord?", "What does this mean?", "There are some details about this picture I am unclear about", "Who is this for? Is it for the whole church? Is it for an individual within the church?", "Is there something more I need to know? Am I missing something?" Usually, answers to all of these points will come quite quickly to you, even instantly, the more you mature in this gift. But if they are not there yet, feel free to ask the Lord for more insight, more information and clear directions about how and when and to whom the word must be delivered. For example, ask, "Is it for now or later? Do you simply want me to pray about this for the time being? Is it for me to tell straightaway or must I put it on hold for now?"

Once we have become familiar with the indicators that the gift of prophecy is stirring within us, and have also considered when and to whom a prophecy is to be delivered, we come to the matter of how we communicate this message from God. As we noted in the previous chapter, the three aspects that must always be present are *revelation, interpretation* and *application.*

Revelation is somewhat out of our hands since this is God's initiative alone; our responsibility is simply to make ourselves open to the Lord and receive from him. We can't dictate when God will speak to us or what he will say; we can only make ourselves available to him. Sometimes, for reasons we do not always understand, the flow of prophecy may dry up for long periods of time. It is all in the hands of a sovereign God who knows best when and how to use us. When revelation does come, it may be in the form of cryptic words or pictures that we do not fully understand at first so, next, we must seek the *interpretation* of what we have received. Then last, but not least, comes the *application* – what are people meant to do with this? How is God calling them to respond? In delivering a prophecy, it is helpful if we can report all of this as fully as possible.

On one occasion, at a church weekend in Torquay during one of the worship times of a gathering of forty or fifty people, I noticed a lady in her early fifties in the congregation. It was a hot summer's day, the weekend gathering was relaxed and informal, and everybody was dressed very casually – except this one lady. She was dressed in a manner appropriate to a formal funeral. She wore a black dress with lace trimmings, her hair neatly tied up in a bun, her appearance overall very prim, guarded and restrained. She caught my eye, because she seemed so out of place, and as I was watching her, I felt the Lord show me something. I saw, as it were, a picture superimposed over her: the same face, same body, but now she was dressed in jeans and a cheerful red top with a very colourful scarf tied at the neck. Her hair was down, loosened casually beyond her shoulders, and she was wearing pretty jewellery. I couldn't help thinking, "That picture does not fit this woman." But the image kept coming persistently and I felt God was speaking to me about her; so I asked him, "What does this mean?"

As I waited on the Lord, I felt I was receiving an interpretation and an application for her. When she later came forward for prayer ministry I thought, "This is the moment." I told her what I had been seeing, saying, "I sense that perhaps people have squashed your creativity or sat on your potential as you grew up, or you have simply set certain restraints upon yourself. The way you carry yourself does not truly represent who or what you are really like inside. I think there is a shyness about you; but there is a different kind of woman altogether within you who is just waiting to get out. On the inside, you are a colourful and imaginative person; a very creative and passionate soul. I feel the Lord wants to lift off the excessive restraints from your personality. He wants the creative life within you to be allowed to colour your interactions with people from now on. I think he even wants your imaginative, colourful inner being to influence the way you dress. I think God is telling you to start all over again with your wardrobe, choosing colours and styles that would reflect the real you inside, if only you had the courage to pick the clothes you would really love to wear."

She looked astonished. What I said had the profound

emotional impact God's Word so often has, as it finds its target. As I spoke to her, tears began to flow. She made no comment at the time, so I simply left all this with her to think about.

Four or five months later I was visiting the same church and this lady was the first person to greet me. She said, "That word was from God. You could surely tell that, because I was crying all the time that you spoke to me. You wouldn't believe the changes that have taken place in my life since then. Everything you said was true." She was beautifully dressed in vibrant colours that morning. She went on, "People will tell you, I have become a much more outgoing person. I'm less shy. I'm now able and willing to interact with people, and I've become involved in some new ministries within the church. I'm doing creative things in ways I have never done in my life before, *and* I have completely changed my wardrobe!"

The revelation in this case was the woman herself. The church is full of unique beings with all of their individual traits and even oddities, but the Lord kept drawing her to my attention, prompting me to notice that she needed the transforming touch of his love. The interpretation of the way God was drawing her to my attention, asking me to look at the way she was dressed, was that her warm and beautiful inner being was at variance with the repressed and timid self she showed to the world. The application of this was the permission, encouragement and even direction to focus on her wardrobe as one of the means of transformation. Like Lucy first entering into Narnia (in C.S. Lewis's famous novel), this lady found her way through into a wonderful place of freedom and friendship – and she arrived there through her wardrobe![9]

2. Wait for the peace of God

Paul told us that we should let the peace of God act like an umpire in our souls:

> And the peace of God, which transcends all understanding, will guard your hearts and your minds in Christ Jesus.

Finally, brothers, whatever is true, whatever is noble, whatever is right, whatever is pure, whatever is lovely, whatever is admirable – if anything is excellent or praiseworthy – think about such things. Whatever you have learned or received or heard from me, or seen in me – put it into practice. And the God of peace will be with you.

Philippians 4:7–9

Acting on this principle, be careful about speaking when you are hesitant or uneasy. We are not to feel afraid, nor coerced into producing a prophetic utterance. There is no pressure upon us to pass on prophecies, beyond the innately prophetic lifestyle of love, grace and the desire to serve God. Any artificial pressure because people are expecting us to prophesy, or because that's what they invited us here to do, or because we think that people would think badly of us if we didn't do it, is nearly always inappropriate and self-imposed. We need to be freed from any pressure other than the Lord's direction and timing. This is imperative. To accommodate the prophetic ministry of the Lord to human expectations is to emulate the behaviour of those court prophets in the Old Testament who, aiming to please their hearers said, "Peace, peace", when there was no peace, because that was what people wanted to hear. They reduced prophecy to performance; and that was a serious sin.

I spoke recently with a remarkably gifted, internationally recognized prophet who said it was an enormous pressure to be invited as a speaker at a major conference where everybody is expecting you to have amazing words for people, only to have the experience of spending all day in the hotel room, hearing nothing from God on that occasion. This experience may happen to all of us to some degree, from time to time. That prophet endeavours to be at peace at such times, since he cannot perform to order. He cannot, and should not, "turn it on" just to prove to people that he is a great prophet. He is dependent upon God, just as we all are; and we must therefore experience genuine inner peace and God's release in order to prophesy wisely and well.

It is wise to remember that, just as speaking in tongues is under your control and is not a kind of seizure, so also the utterance of prophecy is under your control. There is no irresistible compulsion to speak when the Holy Spirit is at work. The apostle Paul expressed it in this way: "The spirits of prophets are subject to the control of the prophets" (1 Corinthians 14:32). This means that you are able to decide, "No", "Not yet" or "Not like this – perhaps in this way?" You are able to decide, "I think I'll wait a little longer before sharing this one." It's fine to conclude, "No, the time is not right. I wonder if it is meant for today? I wonder if I should bring it at all at this meeting? Lord, I hope you will just give me a window of opportunity. I'll see how the worship goes. I'll see if there are specific Scripture readings or songs, perhaps other prophecies related to this theme. I'll wait for the appropriate time in the meeting." Wait for the peace of God. There is no driving compulsion upon us when the Holy Spirit is at work, no need for impetuosity – *"I couldn't help it! I had to say that."* That is simply not true. *You could help it.* You simply chose to say what you said at that time; no one forced you. Wise restraint, discretion and an eye to the Lord's timing are as essential to prophetic ministry as much as boldness, inspiration and courage.

This is in stark contrast to the activities of mediums or occultists when they testify to being "taken over" by a ghost or spirit. Control is a mark of unholy spirits or demons, not the Holy Spirit. We're not dealing with unholy spirits here, forces that drive and compel us to do things against our will. The Holy Spirit is simply not like that. The Holy Spirit may put a certain burden or urge within us, but he does not override our personal choices. That is one means of telling the difference between the Holy Spirit and unholy spirits, and one of the differences between authentic churches and the activities of the cults. Cults brainwash and coerce people, exercising unhealthy and dominant control over their lives. The Holy Spirit does not act this way and neither should his people.

3. Try to dial down emotionally

Of course, it's not inappropriate to feel emotion, excitement, joy and sometimes grief, or to feel totally engaged with the prophetic issue, or to feel burdened by it. But it's right to exercise restraint over merely fleshly excitement, and important that we don't allow ourselves to become all "psyched up" or "hyped up" to the point that we can't express ourselves without confusion of mind and garbled speech. Paul has directed us to do all things decently and in order, so that we may lovingly edify people (1 Corinthians 14:33, 39–40). Dial down. It can be off-putting and even offensive for us to be in an excitable state when we bring the Lord's Word to the people. We are not to get in the way of what the Lord has sent us to do, by prioritizing our own emotions and responses over the message itself.

Eliminate distractions in your mind. They are like "junk mail" coming through the door, or "spam" in your email inbox. Your mind can sometimes become distracted when ministering prophetically, wandering away to the décor of the building or to what the pastor is wearing, or to that woman's extraordinary hairstyle or that flamboyant hat in front of you. Try to simply focus on the task in hand and do not let distracting static or interference confuse your mind or divert you away from hearing from God.

Delivering a Prophetic Word: Some Specific Directives

Perhaps you have seen prophecies delivered in a less than helpful manner. Some of the most off-putting mannerisms can be corrected if we pay attention to factors that help rather than hinder the delivery of prophetic words. Here are some that I have found particularly useful.

1. Have a clear objective

Make sure that what you have to convey actually makes sense when you come to speak it. For example, it does little good simply to stand up and say, "Thus says the Lord: 'I see a flower. It's springing up in front of me, it's red and it's raining.' Amen." That is not a weighty word and I personally would have no clue as to what it might mean, any more than the speaker seems to have. It's simply a pretty image so far. There may be more to come, but until that happens there is no point or reason for speaking this out. Let's be sure we have a clear objective. Get rid of confusion, repetition, rambling. The Holy Spirit is not a Spirit of confusion. Say what the Holy Spirit gives you, then stop. Try not to talk nonsense. Prophecy is a mixed phenomenon and we have to get used to this fact, but good theology really does help.

2. Never prostitute your gift

The desire to impress others is often an indicator of immaturity. You may be unsure of yourself; perhaps you have only a vague impression of what God is saying, and so you try to firm it up with some good ideas of your own. Maybe you have not checked it out with the church leadership when you should have done so, and therefore try to add a little more weight to it by the language you use or by inserting an impression of urgency that was not really in what you heard God say. The desire to impress people must be resisted because, if you give in to it, you and your ministry will be spiritually weakened. If this is a big temptation to you, you must be especially particular about humbly submitting your words to be weighed, making clear that you are not quite sure about what you have heard; then those who are more mature can assist in the discernment process.

It is shameful to mouth pleasant words to gain popularity or approval, or to use your gift in any way for personal gain or profit. Some seek popularity or notoriety through prophecy, like the court prophets in the pay of the apostate king in ancient Israel (1 Kings 22:4ff). Genuine prophets seek truth, not popularity. They don't do it for reward, but for God's glory. Let God reward us if he wants to, but never pursue human favours.

3. Use clear language and stop when the Holy Spirit stops

You may not understand what the Lord means, and may be puzzled by why he should want to refer to *this* scripture or show a particular image to *that* person, but you can be sure his message is to be delivered in words that make sense and are not garbled or confused.

Similarly, when you prophesy, it does not add to the message to ramble on at length or repeat yourself, hoping to make a brief word feel more important. Say what the Holy Spirit has given you, and no more. It is a common temptation, as you are watching the faces in the congregation, to think to yourself, "They are not getting this. I'll elaborate a little more." This is a recipe for drifting away from the Spirit and into the flesh, and what's more, everybody knows it. When you believe that you have passed on what God wanted said on this occasion, add nothing more. Stop when God stops.

4. Write things down if you need to

This will help you to get the message clear. Habakkuk was told to do this: 'Write down the revelation and make it plain on tablets so that a herald may run with it" (Habakkuk 2:2) – and also, I guess, "so that whoever reads it may run". Jotting down the thoughts that occur to us is an excellent habit to develop in prophetic ministry, even during a meeting, because some of these will be God-given ideas. This helps to clarify the components of a word from the Lord so that they are properly ordered and, as we write it down, the prophetic flow may increase and other things may occur to us which are of real significance and should be added. So write these down, and submit the written prophecy to the church leaders for them to weigh it. This helps the process of serious consideration of genuine prophecy.

You can say, "During the week, pastor, the Lord gave me this message and I want you to read it carefully and let me know if I should bring it to one of the meetings, perhaps on Sunday."

People have done this with me personally many times, and I have read the message and carefully considered it, and then responded, "Yes. This is right, I'm sure it's of God and I'd like you to bring it at some point in the service on Sunday morning." At other times, I have sought to encourage the messenger with constructive observations that point out that this word, as it stands, is quite "heavy" and even condemnatory and, as such, is probably incomplete and lacking the right note of God's grace. I might then go on to suggest ways in which it could be better expressed to challenge yet encourage people. This brings security to the speaker, the church leaders and also to the whole congregation.

5. Be cheerfully submitted to the church's leadership

Cheerfully and responsively allow both the leadership and others to test your contributions. This is particularly valuable in the early days of learning to prophesy. For one thing, you will probably lack confidence and be scared of getting it wrong and making a fool of yourself. By submitting your words to others for testing before you deliver them (or at least when you deliver them), you will find that their comments are helpful to you and it is reassuring to know you have their support as you minister publicly. People who are not prepared to do this, the independently minded, the "mavericks" who "do their own thing" may eventually become proud and ostentatious about their abilities and are prime targets for satanic deception. The apostle Peter wrote in 1 Peter 5:5–7, "Young men, in the same way be submissive to those who are older. All of you, clothe yourselves with humility towards one another, because, 'God opposes the proud but gives grace to the humble.' Humble yourselves, therefore, under God's mighty hand, that he may lift you up in due time. Cast all your anxiety on him because he cares for you."

Elders and leaders of churches, as well as others who are more mature in the Lord, have been set in place for our protection and training, as well as for our maturation in these gifts. We should not willingly lose out on this benefit by remaining unsubmitted to godly people. Even if you think your leaders might be resistant to prophecy and would stop it as a matter of course, God is amazing at finding a way through for his Word. He will open the way for the word he has given you; and until he does you must trust him and wait. It would not be right for you to disrespect the church leaders, go behind their backs or bring something at the meeting when they had told you not to. If God has entrusted you with a message for the church, you must make this known to the leaders, but if they choose to suppress it, the responsibility passes to them.

Be submitted, then. Lack of humility in this matter can stunt your development, even deform your ministry, because alongside a genuine gift of the Holy Spirit the right attitude must develop as well. It is in the area of our attitude that an otherwise powerful ministry can be made useless. Listen to Paul in 1 Corinthians 13:2–4: "If I have the gift of prophecy and can fathom all mysteries and all knowledge... but have not love, I am nothing ... Love is patient, love is kind. It does not envy, it does not boast, it is not proud."

A good attitude is a key factor in developing the power and usefulness of this ministry.

6. Wait for the right timing for that person or in the meeting

We've commented on this before, but submission to the church leadership will help you on this point, because discerning the right timing will come into the process of weighing the prophecy. But sometimes, especially when the Lord is working through you out of the context of church worship, the decision about timing will be yours alone. The initiative as to when to speak is down to your discretion.

It is important to realize that there is a sense in which the timing is an intrinsic component of the prophecy. You can catch a person prematurely and take them completely unawares, when they are not ready. Perhaps you decided to visit someone at home to prophesy to them, but you arrive to find that the baby is crying, the dog is barking, and a pan is boiling over on the stove. That is not the best time to pass on the word of the Lord, is it? Your friend will be more receptive to anything you later have to say if you take the pan off the stove, clean up the mess it made, help to calm the baby down and offer to walk the dog first. The prophecy may receive a better reception later.

Because the "spirits of prophets are subject to the control of prophets" (1 Corinthians 14:32), we can afford to wait for the appropriate moment and leave the matter until the time is right. We can sense the kind of mood people are in. We know this may not be a good day for them. This word is best kept until later. A little sensitivity will tell us when the timing is right for them. And in much the same way in public meetings it is all too easy to cut across the flow of the whole meeting. If only we had waited a little while, the meeting might have shifted in its drift and direction under God's control, to the point where this word would now be entirely appropriate. But, for example, to give your word after the second chorus, thus bringing the worship to a grinding halt in a sudden, gear-crunching and dramatic change of pace and momentum that leaves all the musicians completely stranded and the pastor scratching his head in bewilderment as you leap to the platform and hold forth at the microphone, stunning everyone around you as the meeting is blown out of the water because you have "heard the word of the Lord" and are determined to get this off your chest… that really isn't helpful, is it? The fact is, you have probably got the timing wrong. It doesn't mean that you have heard the word incorrectly; it just means you also need the sensitivity to know when to come in, and the faith to trust God for his indicators as to when the timing is right. Prophecy is not only a question of "What?" but also of "How?" and "When?" If you're not sure of "When?" or "How?", ask someone in authority who might be.

In a meeting led by the Holy Spirit there is a beautiful divine orchestration of all that goes on, including the operation of the gifts of the Holy Spirit that occur in that meeting. The Holy Spirit can be trusted to be the heavenly conductor of the orchestra, not only summoning everybody to attention, but also bringing in the instrumentalists, each at just the right time. So we need to be sensitive to the Spirit's prompting, ensuring that our inner ear is always attuned to his urging or restraint and that our spirits are becoming well-adjusted to the wisdom of his love for Christ's people.

7. Try to conduct yourself as normally and naturally as possible

This seems an odd thing to say when we are operating in a supernatural gift, but our manner should be natural even when our words have come from God. True spirituality is not necessarily to be equated with "super-spirituality". Super-spirituality is a term that has been coined to describe behaviour that denies our true humanity and is disconnected from ordinary people and uncomfortable with normal social interaction, existing in its own rarefied, ivory-towered and separate world. It is the sort of spirituality that brings to mind the words, "Oh, lighten up, will you!" In prophetic ministry this super-spirituality is often displayed in flowery, abstruse or archaic language ("Thus sayeth the Lord…"), or trying to "gild the lily" as we succumb to the temptation to beef up what might otherwise appear to be a rather mundane, and not at all portentous, message from the Lord. But God is in the business of transforming lives and he knows what people really need to hear from him. In acting as his prophets, we are privileged to bring his word, and the word itself is enough; there is no need to develop a sideshow routine to catch the attention of the crowd.

Neither is there a need to shout raucously at people as we deliver a message to them, sometimes because we have the mistaken idea that this is what a prophet ought to do, other times because we really do feel passionate about the message and shouting it out feels good! There's no need to increase the volume as if people are deaf and need to be forcefully compelled to pay attention and take note. And there is certainly no need to use King James, 1611, Authorized Version English vocabulary and syntax to add a measure of authority to what we say: "Thus sayeth the Lord: 'Thou wentest out into the far country in prodigality, but I have regarded thy lost estate and am moved in my bowels to bestow mercy upon thee, though thou manifestly doth deservest it not'."

Why not just say, "I sense you have been away from the Lord for a long time, but he has never changed his heart towards you and he is telling me that he is longing for you to come back home"? This is natural language and actually conveys the feeling of what God is saying clearly, as distinct from sparking the suspicion that prophets are really weird.

Similarly, it is best to avoid putting on a pious or "holy voice" and sounding very "parsonic" and ecclesiastical like a TV sit-com vicar. Some people can't help speaking like that (all of the time), but the habit does no service to the prophetic ministry if that's not really you, because the Holy Spirit works most powerfully through unadorned attempts to act normally and without affectation, all within the context of what is simple, human and natural. The presence of God is enough to impress people without some of us resorting to special antics!

One woman saw this complete transformation to a more natural and unaffected spirituality in her husband, an elder of the Free Church of Scotland who had reluctantly attended one of the early Fountain Trust conferences and had been filled with the Holy Spirit for the first time while he was there. He had formerly been very stuffy and pompous whenever he attended church and even around the house at home. After his encounter with the Spirit of God, his wife saw the change and observed: "'Since he was baptised in the Holy Spirit, he's a lot less religious and a lot more normal." Precisely!

I believe that this is one of the evidences that the Holy Spirit is authentically at work. He makes us real, relational, human and normal. The Holy Spirit works best in that context. So, we need less melodrama and more common vernacular, less ham acting and more authenticity, less hype or trying to "help the Lord out" with the prophecy! You don't need to help the Lord out. If it is authentically of God the word will carry its own weight and inherent witness to its significance, as it reaches the individual lives for whom it is intended.

8. Use language that helps others to receive what you have to say

Avoid overbearing and heavily directional phraseology. Directional prophecy is a very real phenomenon, offering specific guidance from God related to a person's future. It sometimes happens that God will give us very specific directions about someone's future calling or change of direction, perhaps about a course of action God wants them to take. Such directions frequently confirm what people have already heard in their hearts so that in this way God encourages them that they have already heard his voice clearly (as happened to me in the charismatic prayer meeting I went to with Ruth at the time I was exploring my call to full-time ministry). Clear confirmation comes when the prophet says, "I have been sensing this about you and this is the direction I think God wants you to take."

This is different from heavy directional words that leave the hearer feeling pressurized, even controlled. For example, "Pastor, I believe that unless we start early morning prayer meetings for five mornings a week at 6.00 am, this church will have 'Ichabod' written all over it as God leaves the place for good, and it will become totally emptied of people within one month. Mark my words!" This is what I would call a "heavy" directional word, and it is simply not how God ordinarily motivates his people! Such a word may have begun with a genuine burden for more prayer in the church within the speaker's heart, but this kind of manipulation in the delivery is inappropriate, bringing the prophetic ministry into disrepute. It makes it rather difficult for people to do anything much with it, other than just stay silent and keep their mouths shut; because, if that really was the Lord, who are we to argue with it?

It would be better to preface such a word with something like this, "I think the Lord may be saying this to us…" or "Would you all please weigh this carefully, but I sense that…" or "I am receiving an impression, and I think it is from the Lord, that such and such is the case; am I right?"

This modest tone is especially important when passing on personal prophecies to individuals. Somebody may come to you and say, "The Lord has been speaking to me about you, Sarah. The Lord has told me that I am going to marry you, and now I am telling you, from the Lord, that you are going to marry me. And if you don't obey this word, then you are in rebellion against God. Pray about it!" That's a *very* "heavy" directional word! It is also manipulative and controlling. If God had indeed spoken to this person about Sarah, then we would expect that at the very least, he would have given Sarah a hint about the same issue as well. Calls to mission, ministry, generous giving, new directions in life, or major life changes, are accompanied by movements of joy and excitement in the hearts of the ones receiving the call. It would be inappropriate to give away your possessions, get married or offer yourself for ministerial training just because somebody else told you to.

Beware of telling people that they are going to marry. You may be right, but you may place unhelpful and unnecessary pressure on the couple themselves and on other parties concerned. Even if your prophecy inspires a corresponding witness of joy in the heart of one of the parties concerned, this may reflect a one-sided yearning that would result in the bitterest disappointment if the emotional attachment proves not to be reciprocated.

It is also wise to be very cautious about births. I have prophesied in at least half a dozen instances that a couple would conceive, and they did – often quite soon after the prediction was given and the stronghold of barrenness was broken over them. But I have also been mistaken once or twice and I have had to humbly apologize to the childless couples later. However, because in all of these cases I kept my approach low key and tentative, the damage was not what it might have been if I had assured them in ringing tones that they were about to conceive. I have taken great care to be sensitive in the way I have passed on such words, aware that such thoughts often come from our own longings and compassion towards childless couples, and not necessarily from the Holy Spirit.

In every case, the authority for the word we bring is not in our manner or style of delivery; it is in the content of what is being said. If that is genuinely from God, there will be a witness not only in the prophet's spirit that this is right, but also in the hearer's spirit, because the Holy Spirit will be saying, "This is me, and I want you to listen to this and receive it well."

We are not God's bounty hunters. We don't have to be like the Canadian Mounties who "always get their man". In a congregational setting, when we have only fairly vague information about a situation pertaining to an individual present, or we sense that there is someone unknown to us who is struggling spiritually in a specific way, we could, of course, walk down every row and ask, "Is it you? ... Is it you?" or "Are you the woman I'm describing?" But then, this is not really necessary, because we are not responsible for catching our victims like some zealous private investigator; we are simply to pass on God's message faithfully so that he can do the rest. The Holy Spirit will arrest and grip the man or woman intended through the words we pass on, because the authority lies in the word itself and the witness of the Holy Spirit to the person's heart; that's how supernatural gifts work. The hearer knows when God is speaking personally to him or her. Christ himself said, "My sheep listen to my voice."

9. Be especially careful and accountable with personal prophecies, avoiding a secretive, furtive approach

Secrecy and furtiveness can be indicators of false prophecy. We are all human and subject to temptation, and sometimes a genuine prophetic ministry is corrupted by baser motives. A secretive, furtive approach is often a sign that this has happened. Perhaps there is someone in the church whose company you personally enjoy; indeed, you are sexually attracted to him or her. Maybe you wouldn't be thrown together in this way under normal circumstances but, *if you had a prophetic word for that person… yes!* That would give you at least five minutes with that very attractive woman on Sunday morning after the meeting. Might impress her enormously too! It could be that you are suggesting something that is inappropriate for that person to do, simply for your own selfish ends. So you suggest to your chosen target, "Can we just slip outside for a moment? There's something I want to talk to you about, and I believe it's from the Lord." This underhand and secretive behaviour is appropriate for telling lies and behaving badly; it is not appropriate for the ministry of authentic prophecy which God entrusts to us. It's often a pretext for misleading people.

Where there is a genuine personal prophecy to individuals, as with all kinds of genuine Holy Spirit ministry, it is best to follow the New Testament principle and work together in pairs. This then involves at least one other witness for the sake of accountability and high integrity in the practice of this important ministry, as well as adding someone who can keep listening to God while you are delivering the prophecy, ministry of healing or other spiritual gift.

The sensitive pastoral nature of delivering personal prophecies must be taken very seriously. Never put pressure on individuals or appear to be manipulative and controlling in the way you speak to people. It is helpful to consult a church leader and share with him in advance the message you have been given; or, as you deliver the message, to take along with you someone of the same sex as the individual you are ministering to, especially if the content is about deeply personal matters. Then, if you are misrepresented afterwards or seriously challenged because the individual concerned believes you are wrong (and he or she may be motivated to say this even if you are right, if sin has been exposed or resentment aroused in the person), there will be someone else who heard what you had to say and the manner in which you said it. In this way mistakes can be corrected, and any potential damage can be limited or curtailed.

If a prophecy to an individual does cause great indignation or resentment, you should never apologize for God or your ministry unless the criticism is valid, in which case it is always very helpful to humble yourself, asking for forgiveness for giving offence and perhaps saying, "I am so sorry if you think I got this so wrong and it doesn't speak into your situation at all. I believed it was from God, but of course you will know best. Please forgive me if I have upset you. I assure you that only this church leader and I know about this word; and we will never share it with others. We respect your privacy and judgement on this." Gentleness and humility reduce defensiveness and resistance to the working of the Holy Spirit. Working in pairs makes it clear that both you and the person receiving the prophecy are accountable for what you say, and that you are not exploiting a reputation for spiritual ministry to get inappropriately close to vulnerable individuals.

It is important to be particularly tactful and gentle when dealing with people who have an established ministry and a leadership role, especially if what you have to say may cut across cherished ambitions or make them feel criticized. Unless you are sensitive in your handling of them, you may trigger a defensive and angry reaction, and even find yourself with an enemy who bears you a long-term grudge.

In summary, then, prophetic ministry places an extra responsibility upon a believer to be transparently honest, sensitive and compassionate, simple and humble. The work of prophecy leaves no place for ego trips and requires no extra drama to pep it up. Anyone who is called to prophesy quickly learns that it is wise to be cautious, quiet, low key and straightforward. It is also prudent, wherever possible, to work in pairs to avoid personal temptation, misunderstanding or misrepresentation; and you should bring all prophetic words that come to you under the covering of the church leadership, so that they may be thoroughly vetted and approved – for your own personal wellbeing and safety, the guarding of your reputation, and the protection of others from what may turn out to be some seriously damaging mistakes.

Time now to move on to a consideration of the weighing and sifting of prophetic words.

Chapter Eight

Testing a Prophetic Word

Having established the scriptural basis for continuing, contemporary prophetic ministry, considered the nature and ways that prophecy may begin to manifest in our lives and addressed some of the issues that may face us as we begin to move in this area of ministry, it is now time to look carefully at the all-important matter of weighing and testing words of prophecy, in faithfulness to the apostolic injunction to "test everything" (1 Thessalonians 5:21).

It will have been clear, in some of the real-life stories we have thought about, that there is always a temptation to embroider and elaborate the words that the Spirit has given us – whether from a desire to impress other people, or because the words we are saying do not seem to be understood or well received.

We acknowledged earlier that the prophetic ministry carries inherent risks – just as when we open the window to let in the fresh breeze, so we also open it to the less welcome flies and mosquitoes; we can't have one without the other.

We noted the principle in Proverbs 14:4: "Where there are no oxen, the manger is empty, but from the strength of an ox comes abundant harvest"', and we reflected that as well as strength and power, oxen are also likely to contribute a lot of unsavoury mess. Especially in the early days of prophetic ministry, as we begin to speak what the Lord has sent, and start experimenting with this wonderful gift, there are bound to be blunders. Not all the people God chooses as his prophets are models of tact and diplomacy, well-versed in oratorical skills and unusually sensitive and kind. People make mistakes;

sometimes feelings are hurt and apologies are necessary. But then, amazingly, along with these undesirable elements, the church starts moving forward as never before. Individual lives are changed. We feel a new momentum and hope entering our hearts and lives, as the Lord sends astonishing words to us through his willing servants.

Prophecy will always be a mixed phenomenon. Its purity cannot be guaranteed but, as we search the Scriptures and become more confident in handling the prophetic ministry, we find the teachings that will enable us to weigh and approve prophecy competently and wisely. There will never be perfection in the operation of this gift but there will be growth – which we may never see without it.

In this chapter we will be thinking about how to weigh prophetic words and prophetic ministries, distinguishing between different levels of experience and gifting, identifying the criteria that will enable us to discern authenticity and considering the necessity of a pastoral and sensitive approach to testing prophecy – because prophets are human beings capable of feeling wounded, uncertain, rejected and ashamed.

The World, the Flesh and the Devil

As the gospel stories unfold, we have so much to learn from the apostle Peter, who was always willing to venture, to speak up and to step out, as well as to risk failure in what was worth doing. Peter's errors, mistakes, and dogged determination to come back and start again, give us some of our most precious scriptural discipleship-training resources.

In Matthew 16:13–23, we read about the incident at Caesarea Philippi where Christ dialogues with his closest circle of disciples about his true identity. The text notes the fact that there were three "voices" operating in rapid succession through the disciples that day, and especially through the apostle Peter.

Jesus has asked them the question, "Who do people say the Son of Man is?", and they reply, "Some say John the Baptist; others say Elijah; and still others, Jeremiah or one of the prophets." They are simply reporting mere human opinion, the *status quo* consensus of the populace at large, the voice of the world in its inability to discern the person of Christ. Perhaps even at this late stage of association with Jesus, this viewpoint tallied with what the majority of the disciples still believed about Jesus themselves.

Jesus then asks them, "But what about you? Who do you say I am?" Simon Peter answers ahead of the rest, "You are the Christ, the Son of the living God." This is an amazing opportunity to see prophecy weighed by Jesus himself; for he replies, "Blessed are you, Simon son of Jonah, for this was not revealed to you by man, but by my Father in heaven." This clearly identifies Peter's confession of faith as inspired by an internal divine revelation from the Holy Spirit.

However, as Jesus broadens their understanding of what it means for him to be the Christ, predicting his violent, imminent death by crucifixion at the hands of wicked men, Peter is horrified. He begins to respond out of simple human emotion, too upset to listen for the word of truth in the grim prospect Jesus unfolds before them. When Peter speaks again, he has let go of the Holy Spirit's leading and reverted to the "flesh" – his own unaided mind. Even though this is understandable, the danger of such a lapse is brought home to us by what happens next.

Peter says, "Never, Lord! This shall never happen to you!" Jesus weighs these words also, making the shocking diagnosis that, in so saying, Peter has momentarily been transformed into an unwitting agent of the demonic. Jesus turns to face him, saying, "Get behind me, Satan! You are a stumbling-block to me; you do not have in mind the things of God, but the things of men."

It is important to note that this is not unkindness or insensitivity on Christ's part. He loved Peter. What it should bring into focus for us is the real and serious nature of the words we choose to say and of the prophetic power that lies within us. People who have been filled with the Holy Spirit, and are operating in the Spirit's gifts, will still make mistakes; the church leadership owes it to them to be watchful, to affirm what is true and rebuke what is off-centre. This is not being critical or picky; it is what our formation in discipleship requires. Weighing and testing prophecy is, and should feel like, a ministry of love.

It is simply amazing that, in the space of a few moments, Peter could move from the flesh, into the Spirit and then come under the power of the demonic, albeit temporarily. That ought to be a sober warning to all of us that different voices can operate under the guise of prophecy and, indeed, this can happen in any of our sincere attempts to speak to others for God – in preaching, in counselling and even in normal conversation. The flesh and the devil may intrude in some subversive ways that we are often unaware of. This is one reason why the apostle James has such striking things to say about the use of our tongues (James 3:1–18). Our tongues have a terrible power for good – or ill. We must use them wisely, and the best wisdom will come from the careful listening of mature leaders; we cannot always trust ourselves. Once a church congregation takes the brave step of opening up the worship to the movement of the Holy Spirit, an element of the unpredictable is inevitably added to their meetings (fresh air, yes, but the flies too).

If the Holy Spirit can inspire you on Sunday, he can inspire you in advance on Thursday. Much of what is unhelpful can be sifted out, ensuring that the worship is edifying, proceeding decently and in order, if we take the trouble to prepare, to seek the Lord, and to hear from him in advance what he would like us to contribute. Even when this is done, the spontaneity and freedom that we treasure in charismatic worship will always leave us with a certain rogue element of undisciplined spirituality.

If you are a church leader, entrusted with the task of weighing the words of others, you will always have to be alert to the reality that you might not like the brother or sister bringing the word. He or she may irritate you intensely. This may arise from the immaturity and unhelpful manner of the prophet; or it may just be a personality issue.

Your meeting may be invaded by maverick and unaccountable visitors, blithely unaware of any requirement to submit prophetic words to be weighed in advance or of the necessity to weigh them at all, firing prophetic silver bullets in the meeting rather like the Lone Ranger in the 1950s TV western series. As soon as the meeting is over, it's "Hi-oh, Silver, and away!", and suddenly they are gone, leaving us all to ask in bewilderment, "Who was that masked man?"!

A pastor friend of mine in Oxfordshire was leading a Sunday morning meeting that was already heavy with a sense of the manifest presence of God, when he felt led to announce, "God's here. I want us to be totally silent in his presence right now. I don't want anybody to pray or read the Bible. I just want us to be quiet, totally silent, and to wait upon God as he has dealings with us." You may be aware that charismatics generally don't like silence. So the congregation had gone into a hushed silence for probably less than thirty seconds when a woman suddenly stood up and cried out loudly, "I see a plane! I see a plane! It is high… It is flying across the sky…!" Exasperated, the pastor interrupted her with the strong words, "Yes, and I wish you were on it!" Pastors regularly feel like this: but not many of us express frustrations and indignant feelings so forthrightly!

On another occasion, during a public prayer ministry time one Sunday morning, a man in all sincerity prayed for someone at the front of the church with the words, "Thus sayeth the Lord: 'I forgetest thy name, but… '"!

At another church, one enthusiastic member of the congregation was greatly enjoying the worship that morning and suddenly announced a message from God, blurting out "prophetically", "Thus sayeth the Lord: 'I am so pleased, my children, with the worship this morning! It has been a joy to my heart to see you praise me as you did and to experience real joy with your dancing before me. Had I got here earlier, I would have joined in myself!'". Oops! As we noted earlier, prophecy is a mixed phenomenon and sound theology could improve our prophesying significantly and minimize the risk of silly comments like this one!

However, if we are to welcome the work of the Holy Spirit in our midst we simply have to get used to that possibility and deal with it sensitively and pastorally, as best we can.

While it can be oppressive and heavy-handed to attempt to *police* prophets and prophecies of this kind, we always need to *pastor* them, and so it is important for Christian leaders in particular, as well as for others also, to note that we are *never to become intimidated by prophetic people*. They are ordinary people like us with perhaps an extraordinary gift, that's all. And God has anointed them by his Spirit to act as our servants, not our masters, just as in any other ministry!

Prophecy, because it is frequently a mixed phenomenon of both the human and the divine, can become adulterated and sometimes spoilt at each stage of its transmission from God in the journey from initial reception to actual reporting. Though the weighing and sifting of prophecy is important – the dialogue between Jesus and Peter at Caesarea Philippi shows just how serious the adulteration of prophetic words can be – it should be accomplished with the gentleness and respect that should characterize all of our dealings with one another. We are not here to act as God's "thought police", exercising a kind of dictatorial control over people. We must always be watchful, but never heavy-handed or oppressive. Our task is to kindle the fire, not to quench the Spirit.

With this in mind, it is important for Christian leaders to find within themselves the maturity and confidence not to be scared by truly gifted prophetic people. It is more difficult to discern the authentic content of prophetic words if we are overawed by those who bring them and even a little bit afraid of them. Even if their gifts are extraordinary, they themselves are imperfect people just like us, people who are relying on us to love them enough to pastor them faithfully and responsibly while gladly hearing and wisely weighing their inspired messages.

At each stage of prophetic inspiration (revelation, interpretation, application), careful sifting should be applied both by the prophet and by the church leaders to whom he or she is submitted. Is the *revelation*, whether in words or through a picture, spoiled by flights of fancy? Is it clear or obscure? Has it obviously been suggested by something said earlier or does it really seem to be prompted by the Spirit alone? Is it edifying, decent and uplifting? Is it respectful, kind and healing whenever the mention of other specific people comes into it? Can the one who received the message honestly say that this is what he or she saw or heard – or have extra ingredients been added to help make more sense of it? If so, which bits were the add-ons?

Is the *delivery* of the word natural, honest and straightforward? As Wayne Grudem expresses this, "Prophecy is putting into human words, something God has previously brought to mind." Is the prophet struggling to find the right words to describe what he or she has seen? If this task is not easy, is the person staying faithful to describe what was seen, or making up statements that have little to do with the main message?

When it comes to the *interpretation*, which is at the heart of the message, constituting the core substance of the revelation, does it ring true and fit well with the words or picture described? Is it in accordance with scriptural principles? Does it bring conviction, release and joy – or shame and despair to God's people? Is there a witness that it is true in the spirit of the person for whom it is intended?

The final part of a prophetic word is its *application*. Is it liberating and healing, or condemning and oppressive? Is it appropriate and relevant – or has the imagination of the prophet tweaked the application out of kilter with reality, so that the word no longer sits right with the souls of those for whom it is intended? There is the real possibility of faulty perception or transmission of the word at any point in the process, and perhaps it would be helpful to see this matter visually. The diagram overleaf, adapted from Mike Bickle's book *Growing in the Prophetic,* is very helpful in this connection. You can see that the graph depicts accurately the kind of mixture that we often find in the prophetic. On the left-hand side we note that what is voiced is totally man's words, or at least a strong mixture of them. Over to the right-hand side there is the possibility of something that is 100% pure as a transmission of God's words to man. But most genuine prophecy today is usually located somewhere on the spectrum midway between these two extremes. This ministry can move from very weak prophetic

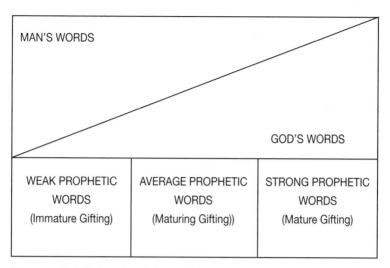

Diagram 1: Mixing the divine and human in prophecy

words where there is immature gifting characterized by more of man than God. But as sensitivity and accuracy mature in the prophet, then more of the authentically divine will enter into prophetic utterances and less of self because the gift is growing. This can increase to the point where consistently accurate prophetic words that are more God than man become the norm, and not the exception. So there is the real possibility for all of us to experience steady growth and maturity in prophetic ministry. You need to bear in mind also, that people themselves can vary in prophetic ability, depending on their experience, gifting and maturity.

The second diagram (overleaf) also makes this clear. If we look at this carefully from left to right we can suggest four categories of prophetic ministry. Most genuine prophecy today is located somewhere on the spectrum between the two extremities of an entirely human opinion or observation and an absolutely pure word from the Lord. Prophecy begins with an immature gifting of very simple and at times weak prophetic words with more of humanity than divinity about them. This can manifest either as erratic inspiration, like that of Peter at Caesarea Philippi, swinging chaotically

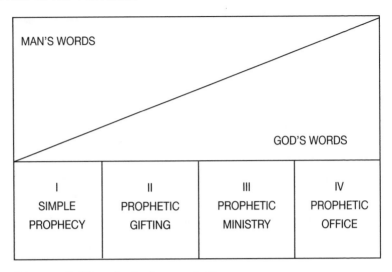

Diagram 2: Maturing in the prophetic

between the Spirit and the flesh, or as adulterated prophecies with a spark of inspiration that has become clogged by an abundance of human commentary and elaboration. But as sensitivity and accuracy mature in the prophet, then more of the authentically divine will enter into prophetic utterances and less of self, because the gift is growing. This can increase to the point where consistently accurate prophetic words that are more divine than human become the norm, and not the exception. The gift of prophecy does not usually drop intact and full-grown from heaven; it must be given time and experience to grow and mature. As it does so, it passes through identifiable stages. Recognizing these can help in the weighing and discerning of the prophetic word. As church leaders develop an eye for the maturity of the gift in a person, they can respond more appropriately and pastorally to messages submitted to them because, after all, this discernment itself is a gift of the Holy Spirit which has to develop and mature in us all, just as the prophetic gift does itself.

It may help to identify some of the stages we pass through as we become more confident and mature in hearing and passing on the Spirit's message.

• *Simple prophetic gifting* – There comes a time when individuals are regularly receiving impressions and intimations from God. Dreams, visions and other revelatory communications are experienced with some frequency. They could be puzzling to the recipient at first and there could be many riddles in connection with them. They may appear to be rather cloudy in their meaning for a while but, again, this doesn't mean that they have no genuine touch of God upon them; they may carry real significance for us, even if the recipient doesn't always know what to do with them as yet. There is a maturing process going on. After a while such a person can emerge with a recognized prophetic ministry.

• *Prophetic ministry* – This describes a person whose gifting has been consistently strengthened and has increased in quality and quantity over time. The church leaders know that this individual can be trusted to get the revelation clear, to spend adequate time in understanding the accurate interpretation and to have discerned the features of a powerful application of the message to the lives of the people. The church really listens when this person speaks, and he or she is consistently honoured and appreciated for the blessings they bring. Although all of us are capable of making mistakes and nobody gets everything right all of the time, someone with as trustworthy a ministry as this rarely needs to check contributions with the elders beforehand; there is every reason to believe that what is brought will be authentic and well worth hearing.

• *Prophetic office* – Eventually comes the point when someone rightly becomes known by the title "prophet", though the use of such a title is actually rare in my experience. Nevertheless a Christian conference brochure listing the names of the guest speakers might well describe such a person as a prophet, for this is now the dominant ministry operating in this individual's life and universally recognized as commanding widespread credibility and able to bring evident blessing. Yet, even among those who highly honour prophetic ministry, there still remains a certain reticence about using the title "prophet", even where there is a case of clear, consistent, established, effective prophetic ministry operating. We are reluctant to bestow such a title partly due to the fear of fostering pride in the individual, or the danger that this may lead to an unhealthy adulation and unquestioning submission to the prophet, or simply because the designation could be misunderstood. It is a wise reticence; the title could all too easily bring a burden of people's expectation and a whiff of carnal presumption in the prophet, which might prove a serious impediment to the kind of proper listening and attending to God that such ministry requires. But all of these reservations do not mean that the office of a prophet doesn't exist today, for it clearly does. Passages like 1 Corinthians 12:27–29 and Ephesians 4:11–16 assure us that this is the case.

With true prophets, clear, authoritative and weighty utterances are often combined with skill in handling the Word of God in Scripture as well as the prophetic word itself, combined with an ability to draw out the appropriate response from the people and possibly lead them into a time of dynamic ministry in the power of the Holy Spirit related to that specific word. Prophetic authority brings with it clear leadership gifts. Some prophets have a preaching and teaching ministry as well, and the prophetic gift blends and entwines with these other gifts as they expound God's Word in the Bible. They may regularly move in signs and wonders to accompany the truths they have spoken. They have a deep credibility with God's people because they have a long-term, proven track record of accurate and clear prophecies over a considerable period of time. Such prophets travel widely, ideally together with larger apostolic teams (for apostles and prophets often work very effectively when they partner together in tandem to serve the wider church), and therefore bring much blessing in the form of lives transformed and whole churches renewed.

As we address the task of weighing and sifting a prophetic word, it is helpful to us to have identified the stage of prophetic maturity reached by the person who has submitted a message to be heard and weighed. Even so, we should not allow ourselves to be dismissive or sceptical because the individual is new to this kind of ministry or somewhat unsure of themselves and of how to handle the gift. Neither should we relax our vigilance when somebody with a respected and established ministry brings a word from the Lord. In every case, as we hear the revelation, as well as its interpretation and application, we should be alert and watchful as to how our own spirits bear witness to what is said. There should be a checklist – a series of questions – always running through our minds.

A Checklist for Weighing Prophetic Contributions

Generally speaking, honesty, common sense, a willingness to risk looking naïve, and a total commitment to listening to God are at the heart of weighing prophecy. But we need to be aware that the Scriptures themselves offer a considerable amount of guidance to us on this matter. And this counsel is relevant to every one of us. Jesus said that his sheep "know his voice" (John 10:1–4). We can all have a witness within us from Christ, and an anointing from the Holy Spirit, enabling us to discern and know the truth. The apostle assures us that " … you have an anointing from the Holy One… and all of you know the truth… and you do not need anyone to teach you" (1 John 2:20, 27). This means that it is incumbent upon all believers, and not just their leaders, to weigh and test prophetic words that are delivered to us. There are three areas in which we must test the prophetic: the character of the speaker, the content of the prophecy and the effect upon the hearers.

1. The character of the speaker

The foremost indicator of prophetic authenticity is the life and character of the speaker. How someone lives is a very important and reliable sign of their faith and the genuine sincerity and pure attitude of their heart. Jesus warned his church in the Sermon on the Mount:

Watch out for false prophets. They come to you in sheep's clothing, but inwardly they are ferocious wolves. By their fruit you will recognize them. Do people pick grapes from thornbushes, or figs from thistles? Likewise every good tree bears good fruit, but a bad tree bears bad fruit. A good tree cannot bear good fruit, and a bad tree cannot bear good fruit. Every tree that does not bear good fruit is cut down and thrown into the fire. Thus, by their fruit you will recognize them.

Matthew 7:15–20

Christ's preoccupation here was with false prophets rather than false prophecies. Even true prophets can occasionally give false prophecies, but this is not such a great danger because we are urged to test what they have brought and we know that the overall trend and direction of their lives in this ministry is towards maturity and reliable authenticity. We don't worry too much about the odd mistakes that they make. But false prophets are another matter altogether. There is something so deeply dangerous and flawed about their lives and their teaching, so seductive and questionable about their demeanour, that Jesus described them as "wolves in sheep's clothing".

Jesus affirms that it is impossible to gather figs from thistles; in other words, that we will not be able to receive lasting edification from a corrupt life. There is a tendency in public life to adopt the view that the moral character of a politician or statesman is irrelevant so long as slick professional standards are met in the context of public service. This attitude simply cannot carry across into Christian life and ministry: "Do people pick… figs from thistles?" No matter how erudite, accurate and insightful his or her revelations might be, a prophet's ministry would be rendered useless and all its messages inadmissible if the individual concerned proved to be morally corrupt. Of course, all of us are flawed and infallibility is not the standard; every one of us has sinned and fallen short of the glory of God. We are the community of the redeemed and it is a waste of time looking for perfection as yet. No doubt this is why prophecy will nearly always be imperfect in this life. It is not ordinary human imperfection or the occasional slip-up that disqualifies the false prophet but rather a sustained pattern of wrong choices and deeply flawed motives that mark a double life of dishonesty; this is what concerns us. Nobody who is trying to develop a false reputation as a prophet will be advertising this, so it is important we ask all the right questions about their character.

a) Are they full of the Holy Spirit and godly in lifestyle (Matthew 7:15–20)?

Do they live a pure life free of scandal in the realms of money, sex and the abuse of power, and have they a true heart for God? If character deficiencies are visible and characteristic of this person, then beware. We should see the fruit of the Spirit" (Galatians 5:22–23), consistently present and growing in their lives. Their marriages should be strong, loving and secure, their children spiritually healthy and believing, their relationships warm and their private life open for all to see. There is a class of people the ancient Hebrews called the *anawim*, a word meaning "little ones", referring to the lowly and forgotten people, for example, children, the poor and the socially disregarded. In assessing the character of someone who aspires to ministry it is often wise to ask, "What do the *little ones* think of him?", for they often have the opportunity to see reality with much greater clarity than the ruling classes.

b) Are they under the authority of God, his Word, and local church leaders?

If the answer is "No" to each one of these elements, then you are probably dealing with a false prophet. You are dealing with someone who is essentially a "loose cannon" and is simply doing his own thing, so that not even God is permitted to correct this situation because "the prophet" wouldn't allow it. These dangerous people abuse the Scriptures and say things like, "I don't care what the Bible says – it's what my 'revelation' says that matters." They resist commitment to, and deep rootedness within, the church, for some are always on the road and others seek to dodge any proper accountability to pastoral leaders. A pride that feels too superior and too spiritual to be submitted to the elders of the church is often a mark of a false prophet. By contrast, true prophets cheerfully submit to appropriate higher authority.

Prophetic people really need to learn to minister out of good relationships with other people of God. They must work in harmony with the local church eldership as well as with trans-local travelling ministries, particularly with apostles. If this is not the case they will be both vulnerable to attack and harm towards themselves, and also dangerous to others.

c) Are they exhibiting proper self-control?

In 1 Corinthians 14:30–32 Paul counsels, "And if a revelation comes to someone who is sitting down, the first speaker should stop. For you can all prophesy in turn so that everyone may be instructed and encouraged. The spirits of prophets are subject to the control of prophets." True prophets never run off at the mouth, saying, "I couldn't help it – the Spirit made me do it." This is not true, for "the spirits of prophets are subject to… prophets." This self-control will be evident in other aspects of their character, as well as in the way they handle themselves in church – in humility, gentleness and a teachable spirit. They should not be quick-tempered, touchy people, hasty and resentful of criticism, but patient, good-humoured and able to bide their time.

d) Are they seen to fully honour the supremacy and authority of Scripture?

Again, Paul asked the Corinthians, "Did the word of God originate with you? Or are you the only people it has reached? If anybody thinks he is a prophet or spiritually gifted, let him acknowledge that what I am writing to you is the Lord's command. If he ignores this, he himself will be ignored" (1 Corinthians 14:36–38). This principle helps to ensure that prophetic people become increasingly more mature in their doctrinal understanding and thinking as they grow in their familiarity with the Bible in its entirety. They ought to be hungry to hear the finest biblical preaching of others, read as widely as they can in the best theological works available to them, and become humbly open to correction from the Scriptures. The life of anyone with a prophetic ministry should be founded in detail on the ethics and wisdom of Scripture. Wherever you look into their affairs – the way they look after their money and business interests, the way they steward their time, their approach to relationships, to hobbies and pastimes as well as to the goods of this world – all should spring from the Scriptures in which their lives are steeped. Everything about a prophet should remind you of Jesus, and tug your heart again to following in the way of his Word.

e) Are they anointed? Is it the Spirit rather than the flesh that is prominent in their ministry?

This may be a little more abstract in terms of its application, but you can usually discern if the Holy Spirit is present in a person because you have the same Holy Spirit at work within you personally, and there is a resonance between you and the prophet as a result. You know in your "knower" that a word given by such a person is from God. You may be backslidden and even arguing with this reality. You may dismiss it impetuously as a word that was given to you "in the flesh". But if you are walking in the Spirit, and the prophet is walking in the Spirit, then you'll know if it was from God. You will also know it was in the flesh if it was not of God. To safeguard against falling into the trap of discerning according to personal prejudices when determining if someone else is anointed of God, we also have the double-check of the evidence of the fruit of the Spirit (see the previous points on character and submission to Scripture). Though it's certainly true that we cannot "gather figs from thistles", and so judgement is easier here, we sometimes feel a strong revulsion towards the prophetic message of a gentle, blameless, wise and God-fearing person. It's worth asking if this is not simply a case of prejudicial and awry discernment rather than a prophecy that has gone adrift. This is one of the reasons why it is always wise to keep the responsibility for the public testing of prophets in the hands of the elders or other prophets, for it is serious sin to quench the Holy Spirit by denouncing someone as a false prophet when he or she is in fact bringing an occasionally unwelcome and unpopular word from the Lord that we most need to hear.

f) Are they free of serious error in both belief and practice?

Are they clear on the full deity of Christ, the way of salvation, the doctrine of the cross, the miracle power of God and the plenary inspiration of the Bible? Are they clear on all of the key doctrines of the faith, such as the Trinity, the central importance of the church, the future visible return of Jesus Christ and the full-blown reality of Christ's expanding kingdom? Prophetic people need to be sound in both doctrine and life, so that you know there will be no trickery or double-dealing on their part. They fear God, so they will not run off with the choir mistress or have their hand in the offering bags. There is nothing questionable about their lifestyle, habits, entertainments, spending or leisure activities. They are not involved in dubious financial dealings. They are not molesting little children or secretly indulging in same-sex relationships, let alone dabbling in the occult. They are clean, and they even look clean.

g) Are they humble enough to receive correction, challenge or feedback?

We should never get the feeling that we are walking on eggshells around such people, or that we are being manipulated or controlled as we attempt to challenge any dubious things that they say. I am not really interested in people prophesying in church regularly who aren't open to teaching, correction and feedback concerning their ministry, because this reveals that their spirit is wrong and out of order in some way and this will affect the quality and impact of what they bring, every time they speak. Prophetic ministry carries with it an innate temptation to play power games and to indulge in displays of ego, which makes it especially important that those who are called to operate in it have the strength of character to nurture a quiet and peaceable spirit, and be willing to listen to others and accept the possibility that they may occasionally be wrong.

Once we are satisfied that the character of the person who brings the message is fitted to bear this responsibility without giving way, and that they can be trusted to be translucently honest and clear, we move on to the next aspect of weighing prophetic words.

2. The content of the prophecy

We must next ask a further series of important questions concerning the substance of what we heard and was spoken (those two things are not always the same!). Again, we will be working with the three factors of revelation, interpretation and application, considering what was described to us, how it was expounded or explained, and what is urged upon us as a response.

a)　Is it scriptural both in content and general drift?

In Isaiah 8:19–20 the prophet warns his contemporaries, "When men tell you to consult mediums and spiritists, who whisper and mutter, should not a people inquire of their God? Why consult the dead on behalf of the living? To the law and to the testimony! If they do not speak according to this word, they have no light of dawn." Everything in a prophetic message should cohere with scriptural teaching; its doctrine should be clearly derived from Scripture and the related comments reveal an accurate understanding of Scripture. In other words, we should ask, "Is this biblically sound?"

In asking this question, we should not presume that our knowledge of scriptural truth is all sown up! Asking, "Is this sound?", is not the same as inquiring, "Does this agree with my personal theology, scriptural interpretation and deeply ingrained prejudices?" Sometimes God uses a prophetic voice to call us back to a more accurate understanding of Scripture when we have been adrift for years and not realized this. We must remain open to challenge, but the person bringing the message that so surprised us with his unusual reading of Scripture should himself be able to demonstrate that his interpretation fits well with the message of the Word of God in Scripture when considered as a whole, and is not simply a spin on that text taken out of its context. The Bible read as a whole, with an open and honest spirit, will move us on both to explore the wider horizons of Scripture and also to remain protected from error.

b) Does it glorify Christ?

If "the testimony of Jesus is the spirit of prophecy" (Revelation 19:10), then true prophecy will draw us closer to the Lord, shining a light upon Jesus and enabling us to see more of his greatness and glory and so to love him more. It ought to help us live better lives for him and so increase his fame and renown in the world. If prophecy leads us off at a tangent to follow after a celebrity figure or promulgate a new peculiar doctrine, to chase after a silly fad or idea and sidetrack us into a crippling preoccupation with something that diminishes our love for Christ and our allegiance to him – then surely it is false prophecy. Jesus said of the Holy Spirit that "when he… comes, he will not speak on his own… He will bring glory to me" (John 16:13–14). In my former home town of Winchester, the Cathedral tower is floodlit at night with a wonderful golden light. The eye of the observer is drawn to the magnificent tower rearing up dramatically against the night sky, visible from every part of the town centre, while the dark bulk of the rest of the building is lost in obscurity. In some ways that is very similar to the way the Holy Spirit works. He shines the spotlight on Jesus, allowing his own presence to remain somewhat hidden. The more powerfully the Holy Spirit is at work among us, the more intensely aware we become that Jesus is here, that Jesus is ministering and that he should have the credit for doing so. The spotlight, the glory, the wonder are directed towards Jesus; and this is as it should be, for these outcomes are his by right.

c) Did this come by revelation?

Paul refers to the way prophecy arrives by God's sovereign actions in our minds: "... if a revelation comes to someone who is sitting down, the first speaker should stop" (1 Corinthians 14:30). A revelation is something we could not have known through natural inquiry, investigation, study, personal experience or the activity of the natural mind alone, but it is something that God himself has supernaturally revealed to us, a vivid disclosure of something previously unknown or hidden from us. This is not a revelation of eternal weight and central importance or value, akin to that of Old Testament prophets and New Testament apostles, but a contextual, existential revelation in the here and now, relevant for our circumstances today and therefore totally subordinate to Scripture, as we have discussed earlier.

Occasionally, it may happen that another individual knows about something in your life which they would like to see changed. Subconsciously motivated to voice this or, frankly, attempting to manipulate the situation, they bring a "prophecy" advancing their point of view. When such a contribution is shared publicly in this way, it is usually instantly obvious that it is most likely a spurious prophecy. Yet it is precisely this factor of previously known information that makes it very much harder to prophesy with integrity when you have been the pastor of a congregation for a long time. You already know so much about the people that it becomes harder for either them or you to differentiate for sure between God's revelation and your own pastoral observation and judgement. What you say may be right, wise and good, but not necessarily prophetic. For this reason, the prophetic gift works much more powerfully and clearly when you are visiting groups or churches where you are not personally acquainted with the lives of the people. You are then free to prophesy more purely and the people can receive the word as from God, with no unspoken suspicion that you may be manipulating them. In such a setting, where people are not personally known to you, any words relating to the details of their private and personal lives are more readily received as being of the Lord. Nevertheless, in your eagerness to demonstrate the authenticity of this ministry, be careful that you do not casually trespass the barriers of kindness, respect and compassion for people. Do not reveal in a public setting anything that would be damaging to someone, or even distressing and shaming to them. Some things are best addressed gently, tentatively and preferably in private counsel.

d) Do the church leaders endorse it?

"'Two or three prophets should speak, and the others should weigh carefully what is said" (1 Corinthians 14:29). The question, "Who are 'the others'?" is sometimes raised about this verse. Does "the others" mean everyone else in the meeting? Perhaps. But we have several clues that something else is intended. Firstly, the word "others" obviously links with the earlier phrase "two or three prophets"; so some of the prophets speak and the other prophets weigh what is said. Secondly, the following verse says that when one prophet is speaking and another receives a revelation, the first should finish and allow the other one to speak. So this word "others" sits in a context of discussing the activity and ministry of a group of prophets in the congregation, in both of these verses. Thirdly, the word "others", in Greek, is the word *allos* ("another of the same kind"), not *heteros* ("another of a different kind") – a clear reference to others with similar anointing and gifting to the speaker, those who move in prophetic gifting themselves. Since these are the ones who are often (but not always) best placed to be able to judge and weigh prophetic contributions and properly assess what has been said, we conclude that the meaning of the text is that prophetic utterances are to be weighed by the others present who themselves have a prophetic ministry, though other pastoral leaders will doubtless have important input to offer. They will ask regarding the message, "Does it complement the scriptural teaching currently under focus in this church?" Often the prophetic will endorse the regular preaching ministry, applying it in new, creative ways. They may also ask if the prophecy ties in with what other sensitive people in the congregation are currently hearing from God. This helps to establish the burning relevance of the prophecy and whether or not it is in harmony with similar dealings of God we are experiencing and with his present leading of the congregation.

e) Does it contribute anything of substance?

Someone may address the congregation with what they feel is a revelation that is in line with Scripture, glorifying to Christ, supportive of the teaching emphasis of the leaders and surely impossible for anybody to disagree with. But if it leaves everyone present thinking, "Yes, but *so what?*", then it is unlikely to be a message from God. A prophetic word brings fresh insight, inspiration, instruction or information of significance; it is never merely general commentary, though we should never despise the simple gift of prophecy (I Thessalonians 5:20).

Having considered the character of the speaker and assessed the quality of the message content, the next indication to consider is how the word ministers to the people.

3. The effect upon the hearers

a) Did it "strengthen, encourage and comfort"? (1 Corinthians 14:3)

Some so-called prophecy has the effect of figuratively demolishing people. It agitates, crushes us and tears us down, like a crane swinging a wrecking ball at a building. It leaves us feeling condemned and hopeless with little or no idea at all of how God wants us to change. How can that be truly prophetic? The Holy Spirit is always positive in the ends he has in mind for our lives, even when he exposes error and sin. He holds out hope, even in the midst of challenge or rebukes, pointing the way forward and the way out.

b) Was it "in the flow" of the way the Lord had led the meeting so far?

Or did it have the "gear-crunching" effect of sounding a jarring note with an intrusive, unwelcome outburst of strange words at an otherwise harmonious and happy family occasion, leaving everybody asking, "Where did that come from?"

c) Do you feel loved by God as you listen to it?

Even when God tells us things we don't want to hear, uncovering secret sins, for example, or challenging character deficiencies and signalling radical change in our lives, sometimes revealing ways in which we have displeased him, nevertheless, we are still aware that he is speaking lovingly to us. You simply know that he is telling you the truth in love. In fact, we may all feel even more greatly loved by God because he took the time and trouble to bring one of his messengers to tell us about this characteristic of the church, or that dangerous feature in our lives, making clear that he wants genuine change to occur and being very specific as to exactly how that can happen. That's the love of God. So, it is important to ask, "Do I feel loved?" The great chapter on "Christian love and the gifts of the Spirit" in 1 Corinthians 13 is our guide here.

d) Does it provoke cynicism and criticism in otherwise positive people?

"Oh no, not her again!"; "I can't stand that look on his face; that look of superiority and pride, and that patronizing tone of voice." These may be the kind of common reactions that some prophetic contributions regularly provoke. Sometimes cynicism is the first response from normally positive people when there is something wrong with the speaker and everybody knows it. People struggle to receive what is being said. This may be a clue that it is not a true or pure ministry. Its content, tone and spirit are off key.

e) If it was a predictive prophecy, did it come to pass?

This can only be properly assessed in the longer term and usually applies only to predictive prophecies. Sometimes, if the prediction has not been fulfilled as yet and is taking far longer than we thought to be so, it may nevertheless still be true, and the Lord is asking us to exercise faith and patience as we wait for the promised fulfilment (read Hebrews 11). On the other hand, it may simply be that the speaker got it wrong. If a specific date was given and if by this time next year the event hasn't happened as he or she predicted, then the prophet needs to admit honestly, "I got it wrong", asking for everybody's forgiveness – which should be readily granted.

f) Do people feel condemned, controlled or manipulated – or convicted and challenged to change?

This is the flipside of the first test above, for it may indicate the work of an unholy spirit in the speaker. We saw that the Holy Spirit will always speak specifically and offer us hope concerning destructive moral issues in our lives. But an unholy spirit will leave us feeling oppressed and guilty, with little or no clue as to what the problem specifically is or what can best be done about it. What has been unmasked by the prophecy may be accurate and true, but an unholy spirit will offer no hope along with that exposure, so that we just feel abandoned by God. Prophecies that are all "mustery" and "oughtery", and often spoken in a legalistic or accusatory tone, may be the result of anger or deep malice on the part of the speaker, and even prove to be demonic in origin. Satan is called the "accuser of our brothers" (Revelation 12:10) and he is often the true source of much that is manipulative, critical, condemnatory and controlling in our lives.

g) Do you feel closer to God as a result of this?

Where the Spirit of prophecy is genuinely operating, the congregation (as individuals and as a corporate whole) senses the Lord's presence drawing near and will move closer to the Lord in its walk with him, over time: "The blessing of the Lord brings wealth, and he adds no trouble to it" (Proverbs 10:22).

h) Does the prophecy "put a dampener" on the meeting?

Everything may have been flowing well, with a sense of cohesion and a clear theme unfolding beautifully in all that has been said or sung so far. There was a wonderful time of worship, the prayers, readings and other contributions have been flowing, and then somebody stands up to speak and everything goes flat. A fog descends and a real "dampener" falls on the people. Heads hang low, nobody wants to sing any more, some sit down despondently and the leader cannot pick up the lost momentum. The reason may be that both the content of the prophecy and the person who said it were simply not right. The effects on the people bear witness to that. This should be publicly and clearly addressed by a leader and not ignored as if nothing happened. Learn to be real about such things. It brings release and security to the people.

> i) Is there a witness in all of our spirits that we have heard the "burden of the word of the Lord"?

The same Holy Spirit is at work in both the speaker and hearers alike. The issue that weighed heavily upon the prophet will also carry the same weight and significance among discerning people in the congregation. They will know that God was in this. We all have an anointing of God's Spirit to enable us to discern truth accurately (1 John 2:20). Learn to rely on it.

It remains to be said that in this matter of testing prophecy, a spirit of discernment is not the same as a spirit of suspicion or a critical spirit. We are not to treat prophecies with contempt (1 Thessalonians 5:19–20). Test prophecy with *sincerity*. Test prophecy with *love*. Test prophecy with *grace*.

Test prophecy with *sincerity*, because it would be inappropriate to sift prophetic words unless we truly want to know if this is genuinely a work of God or not. If someone has already dismissed the very possibility of the validity of prophecy today, they are not honestly testing the prophetic word as they stand in the meeting, arms folded, stiff-lipped and thinking, "Very well then, come on; impress me, you so-called prophet with your pretentious nonsense!" Such critics are already blinded by their unbiblical prejudices and are not in a fit state to weigh a prophetic word: they are usually still waiting to be filled with the Holy Spirit, personally, and are in need of healing and illumination before they are able to hear and evaluate the Holy Spirit's work properly.

Test the word with *love*, because it's obvious that you really delight in the operation of the gift of prophecy and that you love the people who have the courage to prophesy, as well as the way God graciously uses his people. You truly want to hear what he has to say.

Finally, test it with *grace*, eager to encourage people as they learn and grow in this ministry, and careful not to quench the work of the Holy Spirit or discourage his children. Be honest, but see these disciples of the Lord as great gifts to the church, yet often carrying the warning label: "Fragile: Handle With Care". How you weigh their words may make the difference between people growing in confidence and maturity in the prophetic, or shutting down completely in discouragement, resolving never to do it again.

Chapter Nine

Finding Prophetic Vision and Direction for Your Life (Part 1)

In previous chapters we have emphasized the practicalities and theology of the gift of prophecy. In the remaining sections of this book we shall consider its broader applications and developments as we mature in the exercise of this gift and grow in understanding of God's goodness in revealing his will for our lives. In the letter to the Ephesians, having outlined God's glorious eternal plan, Paul then turns to prayer and writes,

> For this reason, ever since I heard about your faith in the Lord Jesus and your love for all the saints, I have not stopped giving thanks for you, remembering you in my prayers. I keep asking that the God of our Lord Jesus Christ, the glorious Father, may give you the Spirit of wisdom and revelation, so that you may know him better. I pray also that the eyes of your heart may be enlightened in order that you may know the hope to which he has called you, the riches of his glorious inheritance in the saints, and his incomparably great power for us who believe. That power is like the working of his mighty strength, which he exerted in Christ when he raised him from the dead and seated him at his right hand in the heavenly realms, far above all rule and authority, power and dominion, and every title that can be given, not only in the present age but also in the one to come. And God placed all things

> under his feet and appointed him to be head over
> everything for the church, which is his body, the fulness
> of him who fills everything in every way.
>
> Ephesians 1:15–23

Here, it is easy to discern and feel something of the impact of Paul's confident response to God's cosmic plan in Christ as he gives voice to his conviction that this will be fully realized partly through the body of Christ functioning as Christ directs. This is why Paul prays that the eyes of our heart may be enlightened that we might know Christ better, and also know the hope to which he has called us.

In Paul's thinking, the hope to which God has called us is not just the ultimate hope of the eternal state and our safe arrival in the new heavens and new earth. Paul's understanding of eschatology involves an overlap of two ages during this intermediate era of time called the "Last Days". The former "evil age" is now overlapped by the "age to come", which has already arrived. This "age to come" is not, as contemporary first-century Jews and even many present-day Christians think, going to arrive at the very end of history as we know it but has already commenced right in the middle of history, in our present space–time continuum, with the announcement of God's rule and the arrival of the kingdom of God inaugurated with the coming of Jesus (see Luke 4:21 where Jesus declares of Isaiah 61, "Today this scripture is fulfilled in your hearing"). Already in place today, the new age of his kingdom is presently advancing daily and will be fully consummated when he comes again in glory at his *parousia*.

We may infer from this that knowing the "hope of our calling" means comprehending not merely the long-term future that God has planned for us after the *parousia*, but what he has devised for us right now, in the time between Christ's first and second coming. That hope is meant to affect the rest of our lives, starting this very moment and continuing into all eternity.

A little boy was travelling on a bus with his father. Being very young and having little grasp of the route for their journey, he inquired of his father, "Daddy, where will we be when we get to where we are going?" That is a very good question for all of us to ask God from time to time: "Father, where will we be when we get to where we are going?" Our heavenly Father wants us to know his will for our lives; he loves to reveal glimpses and insights of the way ahead and its eventual destination. He knows that, if we have a clear grasp of where we are headed, this will help keep us on track in the here and now. If we know we are going home, by his grace our feet will remember the significance of each step of the way that we take. Yet many Christians regard this matter of guidance and growing insight into our earthly destiny as an elusive, mysterious thing. It is not God's unwillingness to share the vision with us, but our own shy reluctance to enquire and seek, that has made a confident sense of purpose and direction a scarce commodity, attained only by some of God's choicest saints. The rest simply don't have a clue.

A God-Given Vision

The great American jazz pianist and musician Duke Ellington was once asked to provide a definition of "rhythm" because, of course, he possessed this quality to an exceptional degree. He thought for a moment and said, "If you got it, you don't need no definition. If you don't have it, ain't no definition gonna help you!" This is rather like the way many of us regard supernatural guidance from God, and the impartation of personal vision for our lives. If God has already given it to you, then you don't need people to talk to you about it and, if he hasn't, then talking about it isn't going to help you very much. I disagree. You *can* learn about rhythm and be helped to get in touch with your inner talents, then encouraged to explore and discover musical confidence and ability with the aid of the right teacher. In the same way, God wants us to know from his word what he also can do for us through his Holy Spirit, so that we may rise in faith to receive the vision and prophetic direction he has prepared for us. Not everyone will develop the performance skills of Duke Ellington, but everyone can at least learn to clap along. Not every believer will one day be revered for their awesome prophetic ministry, but every believer was born to be filled with the Holy Spirit and walk daily in his chosen service for them.

Some people think that this is just a vague and elusive concept, or simply an instinctive hunch in the hearts of some very privileged people, a kind of indefinable reality that you either have or don't have and there's nothing much that the rest of us can do about it. Leaving the railway station on my way to a gathering in south-east London, I noticed a woman in her thirties walking slowly towards me with her head down, looking at the ground. She was carefully pacing and scanning the pavement in front of her. Then she suddenly stopped, picked something up from the ground, examined it and slipped it into her pocket. She then resumed her journey and walked on, clearly still scouring the pavement. Had she lost something, I wondered? Or was she one of those habitual scavengers?

I heard of such a "scavenger" years ago in the days when £5 notes were really worth something. Leaving his apartment block on his way to work one morning, this man chanced to glance down at the pavement and catch sight of a lost £5 note that was lying there! So delighted was he with this find that, from that day on, he never left his house without continually scanning the pavement each step of the way, his gaze firmly fixed on the ground everywhere he went. After some thirty years of diligently pursuing this strange habit, he had acquired 2,950 buttons, 587 pins, twelve pence, a painful bent back and a miserly disposition! He had missed the beauty of the trees, years of seasonal changes in the weather, the sounds and sights of children playing in the streets, and the many faces that greeted him as he passed with his eyes to the ground. He missed out on so much in pursuit of what was ultimately not worth having. Tragically, that is also the case with many believers. They are so fixated on small and trivial things – on bargains and acquisitions and glittery bits of "bling" or accumulating total rubbish along the way – that life, hope and insight pass them by unnoticed. They never give themselves the chance to discover what God has planned for them. They desperately need a true vision. They ought to look up more often.

We may define it like this: "Vision is seeing the invisible with a view to making it visible." Vision comes from God. Vision is a form of sanctified dreaming, the result of the Holy Spirit's operation on the minds and imaginations of God's children, allowing them to see and hear the wonders of what God is keen to reveal to them. Ultimately, this is how we find out how to precisely answer the questions: "What does God want *for* me?" and "What does God want *of* me?"

"According To The Pattern"

Consider the design and building of the tent of meeting or tabernacle in the wilderness, as an illustration of God's willingness to reveal information to his people. You will know that Moses was destined for greatness from the moment of his birth and was miraculously preserved from the genocide that Pharaoh had planned for all of the Hebrew infant slave boys in Goshen (Exodus 1–2). Moses was miraculously rescued from being drowned and becoming crocodile bait in the river Nile which Pharaoh intended to become a river of death to others, and was providentially elevated to full adoption as a son in the Egyptian royal family, eventually emerging as the prince of Egypt. Over eighty years later, after the miracle story of the Exodus, God met with Moses on Mount Sinai and began to reveal his plans to him for the nation he was to help and deliver from slavery in Egypt. There are three significant statements in Scripture that indicate what happened when Moses climbed Mount Sinai for a private meeting with God to receive the Law and to design God's meeting place with his chosen people.

The Lord told him, "Make this tabernacle and all its furnishings exactly like the pattern I will show you" (Exodus 25:9). It was to be a unique structure, sanctified exclusively for God's use, replete with amazing symbolism that indicated the means of access to God for sinners and the channels by which his grace could come to them. Later in the same chapter we read, "See that you make them according to the pattern shown you on the mountain" (Exodus 25:40). These instructions are later recalled in the New Testament as part of Stephen's speech recorded in Acts 7:44: "Our forefathers had the tabernacle of the Testimony with them in the desert. It had been made as God directed Moses, according to the pattern he had seen." Nothing was left to chance or mere human design.

Note the operative words here: "...the pattern I will show you" (Exodus 25:9); "... the pattern shown you" (Exodus 25:40); "...the pattern he had seen" (Acts 7:44). It is clear that when God wants something important accomplished in his name (and for Moses this was nothing less than the building of a dwelling place for God on earth), then he does not leave the discovery of its details to mere human guesswork. This is an important principle for us to take on board. I sometimes discuss with people the issue of what kind of churches God wants and what our ecclesiology should look like if church life is to manifest something of God's glory. I am frequently told by some that there is no definite ecclesiology revealed in the pages of the New Testament. If that were true, it would leave the development of the church almost entirely to us, to human guesswork, because there would be no revelation and we would be left without a plan. And this is exactly how some historic denominations have behaved and acted in the past. But I couldn't disagree more with this understanding.

There is a very clear ecclesiology revealed to us in the New Testament and it is a kind of "revelation" of its own to church leaders, when they eventually discover it! It is of crucial importance that they do so. Watchman Nee, the outstanding and courageous leader of part of the persecuted underground church in China during the mid-twentieth century, once wrote, "The necessity of a revelation of the Church of Jesus Christ to the believer is as great as the necessity of a revelation of Christ himself to the unbeliever." He is right. God wants us all to receive a revelation of what the church can be in her glory, as much as he enabled us to catch a revelation of the glory of Christ in the first place when we were converted.

God's words to Moses make clear that he is willing to reveal the details of his intention: "Make this tabernacle and all its furnishings exactly like the pattern I will show you." In the case of the tabernacle, these details included even the gold and silver furnishings and the decorative work that went into the embroidered cloth. God cares about the details as well as the grand sweep of an authentic vision from God. Note, too, that this complex information was imparted to an individual in a private encounter with God on the mountain top. This was clearly a place of withdrawal from the normal hubbub and bustle of daily life; it was "time out" with God.

While it may be valuable to read the latest paperback success story of a mega-church on another continent, or to attend a conference on church growth, exploring vital truths God might want for his church today, there is really no shortcut to actually spending time alone with God and quietly hearing what he has to say to you about your life, your family, your daily work, your ministry and your local congregation. It is imperative that we take time to commune with God in seclusion, because he reveals things to people who take the time and trouble to listen and are willing to implement what he says. This quiet time of retreat, alone with God, will help to order our priorities aright. Most of us ask ourselves from time to time, "Am I on course? Am I doing the right thing?" However much good advice we receive from respected friends, we still need to hear from the Lord ourselves, not least because our choices and decisions are our own responsibility before God.

God has a pattern to reveal to each one of us, which will disclose the details of our personal destiny. This may well affect the lives of others, having local implications for our family, our church, our neighbourhood or the wider region in which we live. It may have national or international implications also, because sometimes God-given vision is not subject to human limitations and expectations. When Martin Luther met with God back in early sixteenth century Saxony, (in a terrifying lightning storm that nearly killed him) he subsequently decided, in his fear-ridden state, to become a monk in order to save his soul. He hungrily devoured the Scriptures and eventually made his great rediscovery of the gospel principle of justification by faith, recovered the central importance of the final authority of the Bible over faith and conscience, and re-established the central importance of biblical preaching of the Word of God in church life. These developments eventually affected the lives of millions and subsequently changed the entire spiritual landscape of Europe. At the time, Martin Luther would have had no idea that the things God was revealing personally to him were eventually going to shake nations. And who knows but this may be part of the happy outcome of some of the things that God is willing to show us today.

Whether in the life of an individual or a church congregation, vision is what motivates us to grow, make radical changes and move on – and our vision should develop out of supernatural revelation. There will also be practical implications to be worked out as we implement what the Lord requires of us. These will make a visible difference to our lives and perhaps to our church's life, to our family, our business and our earthly career in three, five or ten years' time, as we follow through on the vision that God has given to us. To realize the vision it is important that we stay faithful to the revelation: nothing is left to chance or to human guesswork or design – everything is accomplished according to the pattern we have seen. Without revelation, there is no pattern and no coherent vision to guide us, for example, in the development of our lives and churches, so things may simply limp along without direction indefinitely – a recipe for complete aimlessness.

Once we have listened to God, however, and then received the revelation and established the vision, we need to understand that preaching alone cannot bring about such changes. Action is also required. The common misconception of pastors who faithfully deliver consecutive series of expository ministry on biblical themes week after week is that, in the end, this is the only factor needed to change the church. Thank God, in some measure such teaching does cause change, but talk alone will not see it through. There must be strong, committed, practical application of the things God has been showing us in the

Bible. We do not merely preach theories. We preach for visible change. And it is the responsibility of leaders to ensure that such changes happen. Endless recycling of truth, even through well-researched expository biblical preaching that reiterates the same scriptural concepts again and again, will not build a church in the way that God wants it built without the accompaniment of genuine spiritual impact and the believing response of our hearers. There must be a strong determination to obey what we have seen and heard in the Scriptures, and to implement the pattern revealed to us as we have taken time to seek the prophetic word of God for our lives today.

Called for a Purpose

So the ability to receive vision from God is not only a result of our faith, but is part of the reason you and I were called to faith in the first place. In Ephesians 1:17, Paul prays that "God... may give you the Spirit of wisdom and revelation, so that you may know him better. I pray also that the eyes of your heart may be enlightened in order that you may know the hope to which he has called you, the riches of his glorious inheritance in the saints."

Here, Paul is indicating that we must make practical responses to God's calling. Most of us know, by background and teaching, if not from strong personal conviction, that God has chosen us. We were chosen in Christ before the creation of the world, so that we might be holy and blameless in his sight (Ephesians 1:4). This word, to "choose" or "elect", is one we still use in common parlance today when we elect political candidates to become councillors or members of parliament. We elect those people not simply so that they have the letters "MP" after their names, but to engage in a specific task and to fulfil a key role in society, implementing the will of the electorate. We have chosen them because there is a job to be done, and we have confidence that these are the candidates equal to the task. That's why they won our votes in the first place.

Similarly, when God sets his love upon us, choosing or electing us to salvation and a restored relationship with him, this privilege also includes a summons or call to a specific task, namely, to assist him in the tremendous work of bringing the rule and reign of Jesus Christ to visible expression in the world through the agency of redeemed lives. He has called us for a purpose.

When my sons were little boys growing up, often, as I was doing small repair jobs in the home, I would call one of them to me: "James... *James*, please come here. I need your help!" I would call him for a reason. I didn't want to hear him merely reply, "Yes?", the sound faintly wafting from some distant region of the house – though obviously that was the first step. I wanted him actually to come to me. When he appeared I would have instructions ready for him: "Will you please go and fetch me a screwdriver?" or "Would you go out to the shed in the back garden and fetch me an oil can, please?" I often called him to me in order to send him away again, to accomplish some particular purpose. And that is precisely what the Lord has done in calling us. He calls us to himself in order to send us away; to commission us with a purpose no less specific than the directions I would give to my sons when I called them by name.

Vision is a kind of unveiling, as God lifts the cover on a future previously hidden from us. He allows us to see through and beyond present circumstances to his hidden purposes for our life, our locale, our people and the sphere of influence that the Lord has given us. When we read the catalogue of commendations recorded in "God's Hall of Fame" in Hebrews 11, concerning the great heroes of the faith – people like Abel, Enoch, Noah, Abraham, Moses – it becomes obvious that all of them heard from God, received a vision, and then "by faith" did what God told them to do. Theologian and biblical counsellor Jay Adams, commenting on this "Hall of Fame" observes that "The notable Saints in Hebrews 11, all gained their power to act meaningfully in the present because of their orientation towards the future." God wants us to experience a similar call and motivation in our lives.

Vision therefore relates to your most basic convictions,

values and beliefs, eventually becoming an inseparable part of you. It is something you carry around with you all of the time. It quietly exercises its secret, silent influence all through life's journey, once you have genuinely received it from God. It's something you cannot suppress or deny. It is something that will act like an internal dynamo within you, constantly energising you. No opposition, no deterrent, no discouragement can ultimately succeed in diverting you because God has spoken to you. Human pressure or opinions take a decidedly second place; would that more of God's children had received such a God-given vision. It is important to ask why many do not.

What Hinders Our Receiving Personal Vision?

Any one of us may experience one or more of the common blockages to hearing from God concerning our energising and transforming life vision. Let me suggest three of the most significant.

1. Spiritual malnutrition

Here, something is missing from the believer's "diet". Often, when young children are fussy eaters, anxious parents try to persuade them to eat things they don't like. We give them good reasons why they ought to eat everything on their plate. We tell them, "Fish makes you brainy"; "Carrots help you see in the dark", "Cabbage puts iron in your blood!" In the 1940s and 50s, spinach growers in America commissioned the creation of the enormously popular sailorman, the muscular, one-eyed, pipe-smoking cartoon hero – Popeye. Whenever he got into a jam, Popeye would open a can of spinach and swallow it, with immediate effects on his expanding muscles and subsequent mighty deeds of strength. Each cartoon carried the overt propaganda that "spinach makes you very, very strong". Millions of cans of spinach were sold as a result and presumably eaten by millions of schoolchildren who didn't like their greens! Sales rocketed because of those cartoons.

Whenever Popeye ate a can of spinach his muscles bulged, and I can still remember as a child begging my mother to buy some. I was a spindly kid, easily bullied, and I wanted to put everything to rights with a can of spinach.

Even as adults we are told that sprouts will help prevent certain types of cancer, broccoli will help prevent testicular diseases or that daily bran will help keep our bowels "regular", and we readily believe it. There is often a good medical reason to eat the very things some of us don't like very much, because it's certainly the case that a good diet affects our overall wellbeing and helps us function to full physical capacity. It's also true that likes and dislikes are created more from habit that anything else and that often we are disinclined to try new foods in our diet for trivial reasons. However, as we include some unusual food (of which we may feel deeply suspicious), over time we discover to our surprise that we like it after all – "Can I have some more, please?"

In exactly the same way, we have to feed on the right things spiritually. God's Word really does help you to "see in the dark"! Good theology, inspiring preaching, informative biographies and sound biblical counsel can all help attune you; they help you to gain "night vision" when others can see nothing or very little at all. We all need a healthy, multivitamin intake of divine insights and divine perspectives on God's plans for his world. We need to expose ourselves to large quantities of Christian doctrine, and to hear prophetic teaching also, so that we can understand what God is doing in the world at this time and align ourselves with his priorities for our lives. We need to share in worship and fellowship with others whose hearts are open and yielded to God. It's equally true that a steady intake of the toxic rubbish of half-baked philosophies and ideological fads that the world, the flesh and the devil tempt us to feed on, will make our souls really sick, even to the point of death.

2. Spiritual distraction

This occurs when our gaze is not fixed where it ought to be – on Jesus – but is wandering elsewhere. There is too much "rearview mirror" Christianity around. Instead of keeping our eyes on the road that God has mapped out for us, some of us act like bad drivers perpetually watching what's going on behind them in the rearview mirror, while ignoring the road ahead. An occasional glance in the rearview mirror on a regular basis is important – everyone needs to watch their back – but it is dangerous if your attention is fixed there permanently, worrying about who's coming up behind you, trying to see if that lady really did turn left, admiring the sunset as you drive east, and so on. It's equally bad practice to be forever looking back spiritually, obsessed with past mistakes, worried about what others think of you, wondering what might have been and what's happening in other people's lives now that might be different from yours.

Over-concentration on the past can paralyse us for the future. A preoccupation with our personal histories, always looking backwards and inwards to a painful and traumatic childhood or a disastrous, wrecked marriage, or to major losses and errors of judgement, can all serve to prevent us from receiving fresh vision from God. We need to look upward, outward and onward, not backward and inward.

Some people have a personal motto: "If at first you don't succeed… destroy all the evidence that you ever even tried!" But with God, failure is never final. Even several serious falls may not be the end of us (Psalm 37:24; Proverbs 24:16): "Though a righteous man falls seven times, he rises again…".

The vocal opinions of others can be a distraction – especially if you live with a Greek chorus of negative commentary on everything you do: "Well, you know, pastor, I don't think that's possible here. I've been around a long time and I can tell you, they won't receive that here. No, it can't be done!" "That's interesting, but I think we should really be doing this instead… "; "We've never done it like that before; we just don't work like that in our denomination!" Vociferous minorities (or majorities!) can keep us from pursuing a genuine God-given vision, but when God has truly revealed something to us, as he did to Moses, there can be no popular vote on the matter, as if God didn't make himself very clear. We can have dialogue and discussion, but we don't vote on the will of God; we just get on with it!

Moses didn't go down the mountain and say, "I think God spoke to me about our future, a promised land of plenty, and something about the way and the means of getting there. Let me tell you about it and then we'll ask for feedback and arrange a vote as to whether we'll go for it or not." God's will is rarely revealed to us, or even recognized at all clearly, by a democratic, majority vote. History tells us that majorities are rarely in the right. We need to hear from God first and then have the courage and faith to do what he told us to do, persuading as many others as we can to be in faith for the same thing.

Fads and fashions are a distraction. The latest Christian success story urges us to duplicate other people's methods in our situation; rumours of what has "worked" in Korea, for example, pressurise us to believe it will "work" here too. It may not. Sometimes it's the buzz talk of our denomination that we heed, or what a neighbourhood church is effectively doing, or the latest church growth manual. We receive mailings from a multitude of unconnected organisations, all urging us to support a decade of prayer for *this* cause, a Sunday of celebration for *that* wonderful outcome, a week of mission for another reason, and a night of intercession for something different again. It's good to keep in touch with other Christians, but so often this excessive input can create confusion, distracting us from the vision God meant for us, the clear revelation of what God told us specifically to do.

People will also challenge us with their own agenda. They have their own personal definition of who we are and what we are meant to do, and it is therefore very important that we know that we have heard from God for ourselves about what the Lord wants for us, and what is required of us, if we are to be true to the person God made us to be. Let's remember that ten Hebrew tribal leaders at Kadesh Barnea, sent on a spying mission into the promised land but possessing poor vision and even less faith, succeeded only in talking three million Hebrew slaves out of their destiny; and their bodies all eventually perished in the wilderness (see Numbers 13)! Don't let people talk you out of your "promised land" or your earthly destiny when God has already begun to show it to you. Welcome advice, receive helpful input and remain accountable to others, of course; but ultimately we have to hear personally from God, and refuse to be distracted from what he has asked of us.

3. Spiritual declension

Sometimes we stop moving on because we face setbacks, discouragements and opposition in the Christian life; or we just get tired, "weary in doing good" (Galatians 6:9). It's easy to retreat into the security of our comfort zone, the cosy and the familiar, where we resist growth and change because we dread the turmoil it may create. Most churches are founded on some form of historic tradition and, of course, godly traditions can be helpful, enriching, strengthening, inspiring and wise. But as we look back on the activities, programmes and methods that God anointed in the past when our church was just beginning, we have to make sure that he is still anointing them in the present, otherwise tradition has dwindled away into nothing more than traditionalism. It has been well said that "tradition is the living faith of those now dead; but traditionalism is the dead faith of those now living".

People will resist calls to change, preferring to hold on to the safe ground formerly occupied in the past. Mark Twain, the American writer and humorist, once observed, "The only thing that likes change is a wet baby!" For everybody else, change is uncomfortable to go through, but fresh vision always necessitates substantial and unsettling change. The physical sciences, and particularly biology, have agreed upon a term that accurately describes entities and organisms which are no longer undergoing change – they are "dead"! The late former UK prime minister, Sir Winston Churchill, once announced, "To improve is to change. To be perfect, is to have changed often." And so God has planned frequent change for individuals and for whole churches. So, when did you last do something for the very first time? The call is to keep up to date with the Holy Spirit and what he requires of his people.

When we hear protests such as, "I don't like this, pastor!" or "I liked things the way they were", then it's important to keep in mind that it is utterly irrelevant what you and I personally like or dislike. The only questions we need to decide on are: "What does God like in our worship? What does God like in our church life? How does Christ want his church to be run? What kind of vibrant spiritual life does God want to pervade the place and to transform the relationships of the people?" It's not what you and I like, or have grown comfortable with and used to, that really matters. We shouldn't want to impose our likes and personal preferences upon other people at all, nor should we resist something because we personally dislike it. Our aim is to find out what God wants for his people and then be determined to do it. Our churches need to adopt a simple motto: "Change is here to stay."

The Necessity of Receiving Vision

Vision is a necessity: without it, our lives will cease to count for very much. It's simple: "Where there is no vision, the people perish" (Proverbs 29:18 KJV). We will be ineffectual. Our personal life as individual believers, and our corporate life as communities of the Lord's people, will both fall far short of what God has planned for us. This is why denominationalism is such a danger. I define denominationalism as "loyalty to something other than Jesus himself". It may be loyalty to a particular mode of baptism. It may be loyalty to a particular form of church government. It may be loyalty to a particular experience of the Spirit that your movement emphasizes. But if it isn't enabling you to hear from the Lord Jesus Christ himself, the king and head of the church, as to his current mind and wishes for your church and people, then such loyalty can become a spiritual killer.

Denominations are only crutches to help the broken body of Christ get along until it heals up again. During the long history of the Christian church various essential truths were lost and then finally recovered and restored to the church once again. The process is most likely to continue. As each vital emphasis was rediscovered in Holy Scripture (personal holiness, believers' baptism, justification by faith, team leadership, the baptism and gifts of the Spirit, etc.), determined and courageous believers corporately grouped together to hold fast to that vital truth from the New Testament until others could eventually reap the benefits of it. Many were even satirized and cruelly nicknamed or labelled according to that particular truth, as "Congregationalists", "Baptists", "Presbyterians", "Anglicans", "Methodists", "Pentecostals", "Catholics" and "Charismatics". The inevitable result was the birth of denominations. But as time passes and others acknowledge that this truth is truly biblical after all, then the Body of Christ can recover its strength and the denominational crutch can be discarded. That group's particular label is now somewhat redundant because many others practise the same thing. Once that broken leg is healed, we don't need to rely on a denominational splint any more. We can embrace that truth and unite in agreement together over it. Jesus commanded others to aid his friend Lazarus, newly emerging alive again from the tomb, but still smothered in a now obsolete burial shroud: "Take off the grave clothes and let him go" (John 11:44); likewise, isn't it time that the grave clothes of restrictive denominationalism were taken off our renewed and revived churches everywhere, so that we can move about freely again?

Paul wrote to his friend Timothy from a death-row prison cell, where he was awaiting capital punishment by beheading, "I have fought the good fight, I have finished the race, I have kept the faith" (2 Timothy 4:7). There is a race that has been marked out for each one of us and we have to run to the finishing line in order to win the prize! Finishing well is very important in any athletic competition. But nobody will finish anything unless they first begin. Before you can cross that finishing line, you have to know what and where it is. It is important that each one of us hears from God about our personal race and ultimate goals in life. What has God earmarked you to achieve in life? Someone expressed it like this, "A vision without a task is a dream; a task without a vision is drudgery; but a vision with a task is the hope of the world."[10] God is prepared to plot the course of our race for us. Nothing worthwhile happens without such a dream.

Everything important in life and in God's kingdom begins with God sanctifying our imagination to see something that we never saw before. If something great is ever to happen in and through our lives, then we have to have a great dream. What are you dreaming? Where do your thoughts drift between the tasks that fill up the day? What do you really want? What would you like God to do with your life? These are important questions. Because our lives affect others it is vital that leaders have a dream from God. The emperor Napoleon once said this: "The only way to lead people is to show them a future. A leader is a dealer in hope." The future is God's business and, because of his grace, it is our business also.

The key text quoted above in this connection is Proverbs 29:18: "Where there is no revelation, the people cast off restraint; but blessed is he who keeps the law" (NIV). The Hebrew for "revelation" here is *chazon*, which refers to a divine communication, given especially to prophets by way of guidance and direction, and is variously translated as "revelation" (NIV), "vision" (KJV) and "prophecy" (RSV). Each translation implies the availability of some kind of specific and significant "divine disclosure" to our hearts, such as revelation, vision, prophecy. Therefore, the vision comes from the Lord, and this verse underlines five important implications of this.

1. It points to the dire consequences for individuals who have no vision at all

It tells us that where there is no revelation "the people cast off restraint". What does this mean? It describes two results, personal and corporate. It means that an individual without vision will decay into a general experience of weariness with life. This will lead to dissipation of energy. It may lead to decadence and immorality. It will ultimately lead to a life of impotence and ineffectiveness.

The reason people so often waste their lives is that they haven't seen what God has planned for them – *or they have chosen not to see it.* They have never been truly excited. They are bored and empty, vainly trying to fill the vacuum created by their boredom. Some are trying to anaesthetise themselves against the pain of living or, in some futile and wilful bid for autonomy, frantically running away from God.

2. This carries implications for whole Christian communities who are devoid of vision

The greatest tragedy occurs when those called to Christian leadership also lack vision. Robert Greenleaf comments, "Foresight is the 'lead' that the leader has. Once he loses this lead and events start to force his hand, he is leader in name only. He is not leading; he is reacting to immediate events, and he probably will not long be leader."[11] Many, many churches in our nation at this time are lead by visionless leaders who have lost the way and who are wasting their own and their people's time! When people lose their vision they can lose their first love for Christ, along with their spiritual fervour. There are all too many pastors leading churches and turning up every Sunday for one reason only: they are *paid* to do it. It provides their home, their income, their travel expenses and pension; and they don't know how to do anything else. They have lost the joy; they have lost the fire of their calling and no longer have any vision of what God wants to do. Sometimes their faith is in crisis; sometimes they are simply burnt out.

Somebody put it like this: "He who thinketh he leadeth and hath no one following him, is only taking a walk."[12] By this definition, tragically a lot of leaders are simply out for a long walk, because they are not headed anywhere personally, nor are their people.

3. There is an implication that confusion results wherever people lose their vision

The people "cast off restraint", blurring the edges of sin and righteousness, then crossing boundaries that God has put in place and straying into areas where the Spirit never led them to go. Then comes competitiveness, as people jockey for position and power, seeking public recognition because they don't know what it is to be promoted by God and secure in his will for their lives. In church life it has been known for a prominent and wealthy individual to stand up and say, "Look, I don't like to boast, but I pay most of the bills around here because I am one of your biggest givers!", with the thinly veiled hint that this giving will soon cease unless the community adhere to his or her agenda. Always wave goodbye to people like that. There's plenty more money where that came from. Our Father owns the cattle on a thousand hills. There are others who say, "Wait a minute, pastor, my family have been here for generations!" ("*So?* And your point is... ?"). The truth is, it is not and never has been *their* church – it's *God's* church! Another might threaten, "I have already seen four pastors off, and if you're not careful you'll be the fifth!" In such circumstances you need to know who really appointed you. If it wasn't God himself, then you are in trouble!

Where the people have lost their vision, those who are not motivated by power are often motivated by fun. They come to church to have a good time – because the preaching is entertaining and the band plays all the latest music. People should be having fun in church but that shouldn't be their prime motivation for going to worship.

Churches and organizations thus fragment into factions wherever there is no vision. Rampant individualism results in people simply "doing their own thing", rather than God's thing. Christians wander from church to church, conference to conference, experience to experience – seeking but never settling.

4. Where there is no revelation, resources are wasted

We all have time, money and energy. We all have our allotted number of days (Psalms 90:12; 139:16) but none of us really knows how many days we have left. Nevertheless, we are spending them, one day at a time. Without vision, our resources are simply squandered and our money often goes down the drain.

Few things frustrate me more than seeing people wasting their lives. It may be in front of a computer screen playing video games hour upon hour, day after day. It might be the monotonous lifestyle of nights out at the pub, every night of the week. It could be an obsession with the betting shop. Some live a life of homelessness and little responsibility on the streets, through their own choice in some cases. At the other extreme, but equally wasteful, someone may squander valuable resources on a life of leisure as a "playboy", dedicating all the wealth and talents God gave them to a totally sensual, prodigal, selfish and empty life. It's tragic in the extreme! But the writer of Proverbs is saying that without vision that's exactly what people will do.

Just how completely it is possible to waste your life was vividly illustrated by an incident that happened in the UK parliament some time back. Decades ago, a man was actually employed at the Houses of Parliament in London, simply to stand at the foot of the stairs in the House of Commons. That job lasted for over 20 years. He eventually retired and passed the job on to his own son, who in turn passed it on to his grandson. What were these men doing at the bottom of those stairs? Apparently, the post originated when someone ordered the repainting of the grand stairway, and the grandfather was employed to stand at the bottom of the stairs to steer people over to the left while the right-hand side of the stairs was being painted and then, in turn, steer them over to the right while the left-hand side was being painted. But when the paint job was finished and they tidied up and stored the pots, brushes and work clothes, they forgot to tell the stair-minder he could go home, even though he was now superfluous to requirements. He was able to hang on to his job for over twenty years, no questions asked, standing at the foot of those stairs. People forgot why he was there – it was as simple as that. The paint dried up, but the job didn't. What a waste of a working man's life! But how many churches and denominations go on for decade after decade, staffing something that was only significant, useful and important long ago.

Apparently, the Tartar tribes of Central Asia have a curse for their enemies. When someone offends them, they don't say to them: "'Go to hell!'", but something comparable to that: "May you stay in one place forever." This is truly a damning curse, for it means that you will never improve, never change, never move on, never accomplish anything, and never experience success as God defines it to be. Thank God that such success is God's will for all of us. It begins to unfold when people receive vision that they are motivated to accomplish, and cease to resist the required changes.

5. The positive benefits of having vision

These are also spelt out in the verse, "Where there is no revelation, the people cast off restraint; but blessed is he who keeps the Law." Our lives are meant to be on course, fruitful and effective when we walk in God's way: "… blessed is he who keeps the Law."

The power of vision operates like the laws of nature – the law of gravity, for example, or the first and second laws of thermodynamics. A law, in this sense, is something we can rely on – the whole of human experience assures us that the predicted outcome should always happen. The power of vision, like the laws of physics, is a revelation of God's divine direction and will inevitably move and steer events into God's future. It is the way God has ordained things to be and therefore it will help to steer our lives purposefully and keep them headed towards the destination that God has in mind for us. Vision will make short work of obstacles and will surely bring what we dream about finally into being. Vision will drive and compel us. R. Judson Carlberg writes, "Vision is compounding a deep dissatisfaction of what is and a clear grasp of what could be."[13] When you are dissatisfied with what is, and you have a clear grasp of what could be, your life is going to be steered on course, as if by law. Vision is a God-given ability to see what *could* happen, what *can* happen and indeed what *will* happen if we follow the will of God faithfully.

Vision is Vital

Vision is vital for a number of positive reasons.

1. Vision gives direction to our lives

We are all looking for a lead in our lives, whatever role we are called to play. We need to know where we are going with our lives so that energy is generated to help us push ourselves through all of the problems and obstacles on the way. Obstacles are not a problem to men and women who have a vision. Neither are setbacks and discouragements. Delays are merely *delays*. A vision may be a dream with a deadline, but we usually don't know the timing of the deadline. God doesn't give us his timetable and, anyway, it is shot through with intentional delays. Visionaries keep going because they know that the goal hasn't changed. In this matter of vision there are leaders and there are followers, and the responsibility of followers is to find a leader with a vision that witnesses to their hearts. How do you know if you are a leader or a follower? You are a leader if people are following you. The responsibility of the leader is to find the vision and then the followers will come to him or her. Either way, vision is crucial to keep people moving in the direction God has indicated for them.

Edwin Land, president for many years of the Polaroid organization, had this to say about recruiting new staff for top positions in the company: "The first thing you do is teach the person that the vision is very, very important and well-nigh impossible to accomplish; and that draws out the drive in all of the winners around you."

2. Vision enhances unity

Vision creates focus and direction, and also attracts others who already have those qualities. People pull together when there is a God-given vision. After years of waiting, former shepherd-boy David became king over all Israel (the story is told in 1 Chronicles 11–12):

> David and all the Israelites marched to Jerusalem (that
> is, Jebus). The Jebusites who lived there said to David,
> "You will not get in here." Nevertheless, David captured
> the fortress of Zion, the City of David.
>
> David had said, "Whoever leads the attack on
> the Jebusites will become commander-in-chief." Joab
> son of Zeruiah went up first, and so he received the
> command.
>
> David then took up residence in the fortress, and
> so it was called the City of David.
>
> 1 Chronicles 11:4–7

So there was no question who was the visionary leader in this
context – it was David. The story continues: "He built up the
city around it, from the supporting terraces to the surrounding
wall, while Joab restored the rest of the city. And David became
more and more powerful" (1 Chronicles 11:8–9). Vision does
that. And the reason it does so? God's anointing attends both
the vision and the visionaries who are seeking to implement it
– as the text explains: "…because the Lord Almighty was with
him". A long narrative follows in chapter 12, describing the
rapid recruitment of David's mighty men, the chiefs of David's
military forces who, together with all the people of Israel, gave
his kingship strong support as it extended over the land just as
God had promised.

Typical of the descriptions recorded of such men is this
one: "Jashobeam, a Hacmonite, was chief of the officers; he
raised his spear against three hundred men, whom he killed
in one encounter" (1 Chronicles 11:11). That's a truly mighty
man, isn't it? I'm glad he was on David's side and not that of
David's opponents. But what about the next man? "Eleazar
son of Dodai the Ahohite, [was] one of the three mighty
men. He was with David at Pas Dammim when the Philistines
gathered there for battle. At a place where there was a field
full of barley, the troops fled from the Philistines. But they
took their stand in the middle of the field. They defended it
and struck the Philistines down, and the Lord brought about

a great victory" (1 Chronicles 11:12–14). And the list goes on and on, in this style. It is sobering to realize that these men would never have stepped into their full stature and achieved what they did – we would never even have heard of them – but for one thing: they joined David, sublimating their own personal agendas, achievements and renown to something far greater, the goal and vision God had given to King David. Their sole aim was to build the kingdom, to make David great. Vision enhances unity.

3. Vision also motivates change

People will not move anywhere important unless they think it's worth moving, but they'll climb out of a rut for a vision worth following. Vision motivates change. The leader's task is to identify with people's hunger for God and for his glory: when you help people to get what they want, they will help you get what you want – because we both want the same things. Ralph Waldo Emerson tells of how he once stayed on a farm in the countryside and was given the responsibility for moving a stubborn young calf from one cattle shed to another. Although this was only a young animal, he simply couldn't get it to budge. He tried everything. He pushed it sideways; he got behind it and pushed on its rump. But the animal just dug in and refused to move in spite of his cajoling and shouting and physical manoeuvring. The calf would not move.

Soon after, the milkmaid came across the yard, carrying a bucket, and noticed what was going on. She then did a very simple thing. She took her middle finger and dipped it into the bucket where she had been collecting cow's milk. She then put her wet finger to the nose of the little calf and it smelt the milk, then she began slowly retreating towards the other cattle shed. You can guess what happened. The calf meekly followed her. As she offered to give the calf what it wanted, the calf gave her what she wanted. And that's what vision does – it motivates people to change; it gets them out of a rut; it gently shifts them from one place to another.

4. Vision lifts the level of faithful giving among God's people

Building the kingdom of God is not a money-making exercise, but it still costs a great deal. Being a church leader is not a selfish get-rich-quick scheme. The church is not, as some people cynically suppose, forever after people's money, its leaders getting fat on the savings of pensioners. But if the church is to build and extend the kingdom of Christ, if it is to lift up the downtrodden and heal the sick and feed the hungry and unite congregations in worship, it has to have funds. Vision releases finances. It is exciting; it fills people with joy when they know they are giving to God. Prudent and practical provision for old age and times of adversity is wise and essential, but all the funds people can pour into their personal pensions, ISAs and other saving schemes, whatever the security, whatever the interest rates, have no returns to compare with the exhilaration of building the kingdom together – the sheer joy of giving to God.

Leonard Lauder, the founder and president of the cosmetics and perfume company, Estée Lauder, once remarked, "When a person with vision meets a person with money, the person with the money gets a vision and the person with the vision gets the money!" That's absolutely right – and what a wonderful arrangement! A God-given vision will attract resources of people, talent and generous financial giving, to see that vision realized, to make a dream come true. People need motivation to sacrifice, so it's prudent, when someone touches us for our hard-earned cash, to ask, "Is this worth it?" And if we do not think it is worthwhile, then we won't give. A church or organization that's going nowhere will usually be cripplingly short of cash. And the converse is also true. A God-given vision will release finances on an unprecedented scale, because people are motivated by a dream they can believe in. As Jesus said, "Where your treasure is, there your heart will be also" (Matthew 6:21). People will invest their hearts where they have first invested their treasure, and surprisingly, Jesus did not express this the other way round.

5. Vision orders priorities aright

Most of us wonder from time to time, "Am I on track? Am I still in the will of God? Is this the right place for me? Am I meant to be here right now? What am I supposed to do next? What am I here for? What shall I do with my life?" If you aim at nothing, you will hit it every single time. What does the Holy Spirit tell us when we listen to him? What kind of vision does he reveal as we wait upon him? Remember the principle we looked at earlier of receiving a specific revelation and then remaining faithful to what we have seen, acting only "according to the pattern". We must refuse every job opportunity or ministry invitation that doesn't feature in the vision God has given us for our lives. Too many of us are engaged in "un-commanded work".

This is so for individuals and it's true for churches too. No one church, of course, can do all that needs to be done in realizing God's plan for the neighbourhood. In a town or borough where there are many congregations, there will inevitably be things some churches are doing which yours simply cannot do. You haven't got the people or the resources or the right building in the right place to do it – but, much more importantly, you haven't received the vision to do it; it doesn't ring your bell in any way. Each congregation must find out what God has called them to do. Specialize in what God has gifted and told *you* to do, and then become really good at it. Then you can relax in the realisation that no one church is called to everything; that's why we have the body of Christ.

God's plan for your life and your church will be very concrete and specific. We are not talking about a vague aspiration like, "Well, I hope to be used in evangelism" or "I really want to have a ministry from the Lord." If you are a healthy Christian, of course you want a ministry from the Lord. But when we have received our vision, it will disclose a very specific direction for us to follow.

In the city I formerly pastored in, some churches have extraordinary social action projects going on, involving tens of thousands of pounds of expenditure every year – hundreds of thousands in some cases – supported partly by generous giving and partly by public funds. Not every church has the people or capacity to run projects of that kind, yet I rejoice in the vision and commitment of those who are called to that work. I am glad that the church as a whole is engaged cooperatively on that work in the city, because no one church can do everything. Neither can all churches have the outstanding worship teams, the outstanding preachers and the outstanding evangelists that some congregations seem to recruit, but maybe they are not required to do that. There is a place for the smaller congregation that feels like a family, where the worship is intimate and quiet, and the people know each other's stories and names.

We should be asking, "What has God given us the ability to do? What has he earmarked us to contribute to the overall picture of what is happening in this town?" We must order our priorities according to the vision that is real for us, so that we know what we are (and are not) called to do, and don't spend our time chasing around like headless chickens trying to achieve what others are doing so wonderfully, but we never will.

6. Vision engenders confidence

Vision releases heroism in people, along with extraordinary measures of courage and boldness. It releases their inner spiritual resources as they commit themselves wholeheartedly to it and become prepared to pay any price to see the vision realized in the world. People feel good when they are pursuing a God-given vision, and they perform even better. They endure longer and are less likely to experience burn-out. Everything they do feels worth the effort. If someone tries to stop them or criticize them, they'll brush it off, saying defiantly, "I don't care what you say, we're on course; God is in this place, God is working here. We can't change our minds and we won't change our direction. I am sorry but that's the way it is."

Jacques Plante used to be a member of the Canadian national ice hockey team. Every play he made was watched by up to 20,000 people in the arena and on television by millions. Every fault was logged. Quite suddenly, at the height of his career, he tendered his resignation and left the team, much to the shock and surprise of his fans and the media who loved him. Asked why he had resigned at the peak of his career, Jacques replied, "How would you like to have a job in which every time you made a mistake a horn blew, a red light went off and 20,000 people booed loudly?" It makes you think, doesn't it? How *would* you like it? Not many of us have to put up with such intense, sustained levels of criticism and expectation, but we do suffer from weariness, discouragement and self-doubt. When we stand together as a people, and know absolutely what God has told us to do, we find the confidence to keep putting one foot in front of the other and keep walking into the wind. Even when things are going badly wrong and we are wounded and battle-weary, we have no option other than to pursue what the Lord has said: because that's our vision – that's all we can see – we have no other options! But it's just a matter of time and we will see things take shape: "For the revelation awaits an appointed time; it speaks of the end and will not prove false. Though it linger, wait for it; it will certainly come and will not delay" (Habakkuk 2:3).

Catch the Vision!

We didn't come here just to fill up the days until we die. Our lives were not meant to be squandered, nor even spent on fairly good things. They are meant to be invested in God's wonderful plan for our corporate life together, the kingdom of heaven on earth. And paradoxically, the size of a vision doesn't always determine how hard it is to accomplish. You would think there would be a correlation between the magnitude of the vision and the degree of difficulty involved in its accomplishment, but often an inverse ratio applies. God often calls us to go for bigger goals rather than small ones and, as we are faithful, we find to our surprise that bigger goals are easier to accomplish than smaller goals. Why? Because people will simply not be stirred to sacrifice at all for trivial goals; people won't even cross the road for a small vision – it's just not worth it. It's not worth getting out of bed in the morning for a small vision. Why bother? We presently live in a "Why bother?" generation, and that tells me loud and clear that we live in a generation with little or no vision. You insult people if you offer them a superficial task that is not worth turning aside or turning up for.

Big demands attract more commitment from people: they will give their all to see those goals attained. They will give thousands of pounds, sometimes hundreds of thousands of pounds, if they think the vision is really worth it. So when God gives you a vision, speak it out in faith; talk in line with what God has said, and watch what happens.

Some years ago a TV Christmas special was produced in the European Community as part of the seasonal programme. This particular broadcast was to be aired in many nations and consisted of interviews with ambassadors from various European countries who were asked their views on hot topics of the hour. One of the lighter questions that each of them was posed was: "What would you most like for Christmas?" The British ambassador thought tentatively for a moment about this question, quietly speculating that it might be intended to catch him out. He thought, "This is going to be broadcast to millions and I don't want to sound proud or ambitious, and I certainly don't want to court any gifts or unwelcome favours from anyone." So he finally said, "You know, what I'd really love, actually, is a small box of crystallised fruit." When the programme was eventually aired, this particular section had a number of foreign ambassadors speak about their Christmas wish list, and the German ambassador said; "I want to see hunger and poverty ended all over the world by the sharing of our massive resources to raise the poor from the dirt." The French ambassador replied, "I would like to see the end of world conflict, a finish to the appalling arms race – and the beginning of world peace." Then the British ambassador added his ambition: "You know, what I'd really love, actually, is *a small box of crystallised fruit*"! It truly doesn't pay to have a small vision!

Big visions can serve to dwarf our petty ambitions and make them seem small and poverty-stricken, and indeed even selfish. Millions are familiar with the cartoon strip *Peanuts* by Charles Schultz. In one of them Linus and Lucy are toying with a wishbone from a chicken that they have obviously eaten for Sunday lunch. Lucy is holding one end of the wishbone, then offers it to Linus and says, "Let's make a wish and say it out loud. If you don't, it won't come true." So Lucy says, "I'm first! I wish for four new sweaters, a new bike, a pair of shiny rollerskates, a new dress, and $100 in cash. Now it's your turn, Linus." He ponders carefully and then responds, "I wish for long life for all of my friends; and I wish for world peace. Oh, and I wish for great advancements in medical research …" Lucy angrily interrupts him: "That's the trouble with you, Linus! You're always going around spoiling everybody else's fun!" The truth is, that's what visionaries are supposed to do. They are meant to spoil everybody else's idea of "fun" in order to get them out of the minor leagues of their own small dreams and into the major league of God's vast purposes – and that's where the real fun truly begins!

A former French prime minister once said, "If you are doing big things, you attract big men. If you are doing little things, you attract little men. And little men usually cause a lot of trouble!" My desire for the church of Jesus Christ everywhere is to see it filled with "big" men and women, because "little" men and women really do cause a lot of trouble. Only a vision from God will make that desire a reality.

Chapter Ten

Finding Prophetic Vision and Direction for Your Life (Part 2)

Anyone who holds responsibility as a church leader, or who carries a vision for positive change in situations marked by decay or defeat, can find real inspiration in the story of Nehemiah's courageous faith and perseverance in following a God-given vision to completion. This is how it began:

> In the month of Kislev in the twentieth year, while I was in the citadel of Susa, Hanani, one of my brothers, came from Judah with some other men, and I questioned them about the Jewish remnant that survived the exile, and also about Jerusalem.
>
> They said to me, "Those who survived the exile and are back in the province are in great trouble and disgrace. The wall of Jerusalem is broken down, and its gates have been burned with fire."
>
> When I heard these things, I sat down and wept. For some days I mourned and fasted and prayed before the God of heaven.
>
> Nehemiah 1:1–4

We can almost feel the mood of shock, gut-wrenching concern and overwhelming grief that seized Nehemiah as he absorbed this brief but stunning report. He was gripped by the strong summons of God to become the key agent for change in this devastated situation. Eventually, he went into the presence of the king, no longer able to disguise the grief and dismay he felt upon hearing this news. And we're told in verses 4–6 of chapter 2 that,

> The king said to me, "What is it you want?"
>
> Then I prayed to the God of heaven, and I answered the king, "If it pleases the king and if your servant has found favour in his sight, let him send me to the city in Judah where my fathers are buried so that I can rebuild it."
>
> Then the king, with the queen sitting beside him, asked me, "How long will your journey take, and when will you get back?" It pleased the king to send me; so I set a time.

All of our lives can turn around completely in a moment like this. It is then that we discover not only the goodwill and support of our fellow human beings, but the blessing of God upon a genuine call to launch and complete a seemingly impossible task that will recover the glory of his name in the earth. In Nehemiah 2:11–12, the restorer and reformer relates the secret commencement of this mighty project to rebuild Jerusalem's burned and broken city walls: "I went to Jerusalem, and after staying there three days I set out during the night with a few men. I had not told anyone what my God had put in my heart to do for Jerusalem. There were no mounts with me except the one I was riding on."

Then, as we rush to the end of the chapter, Nehemiah's firm resolve is voiced defiantly in his reply to his critics: "I answered them by saying, 'The God of heaven will give us success. We his servants will start rebuilding, but as for you, you have no share in Jerusalem or any claim or historic right to it'" (verse 20).

This pronouncement is a declaration of absolute trust in God's faithfulness, and makes clear that there is to be no sitting on the fence; there is no "observer" category or "neutral zone" available. Each of us is either for or against the work of

God in this world. Nehemiah accepts the challenge to his own life and circumstances, and throws it uncompromisingly at the stony faces of the onlookers and mutterers. Such is the power of prophetic vision and direction in a person's life.

So far, we have been seeking to demonstrate the importance and necessity of prophetic vision for each one of us resolved to live the Christian life, and for all who exercise any form of leadership or ministry for Christ. We have also explored the necessity of vision and noted some of the hindrances to receiving vision from God. Now it is time to explore some of the details of how such vision arrives in our hearts.

How Vision Comes to Us

God's call was a complete surprise to Nehemiah. He had made no preparations for his forthcoming leadership role. He was shocked and overwhelmed by the news of destruction in Jerusalem and the low morale of the returning exiles. As we read the story, we begin to see the life-changing power of authentic vision. No one who has been through such an experience can ever be the same again. It is utterly transformative. Something of that level of seeing must take hold of each one of us too, until our lives are transformed by truly having seen the role Christ has ordained for us to play in the church and wider world of today. As the vision catches hold in our hearts and lives, its transforming power will be the crucial element in launching our ministry. This is what will make us effective and influential in brokering much-needed change.

As John C. Maxwell so graphically expresses it, "All great leaders possess two things. They know where they are going and they are able to persuade others to follow." So, if God has entrusted us with any position of influence at all, in order to fulfil our responsibilities we must have both a God-given vision and the ability to share it. We need to hear from God and then communicate with authority what we have seen and heard. As we speak out in this way, the contagious influence of the Holy Spirit will stir people's hearts. Their spirits will witness to the truth of what we say, and we shall see our vision gain momentum. How then do we experience this kind of clarity, receive our vision and discover accurately where we are headed in our life and ministry? This is the substance of this present chapter.

We all live under the same *sky* but we don't share the same *horizon*. There are those who can see further than others; people who can hear what others cannot hear, and see what they cannot see, and are therefore able to identify clearly and confidently what others, squinting into the distance, can only hesitantly describe. These visionaries can then explain with authority what they see. The result is that both they and the people who have heard from God through them will dare to venture where those without vision have not yet dared to go. This is how vision becomes reality. When a God-given dream enters into your heart it's infectious – it spreads! Get close to someone with a vision, and you are likely to catch it yourself.

Field Marshall Montgomery, the famous Second World War British army commander, made this observation about the vital role that visionary leaders play: "Leadership is the capacity and will to rally men and women to a common purpose, and the character which inspires confidence." US president Harry S. Truman similarly commented that "A leader is a person who has the ability to get others to do what they don't want to do, and like it." The wonderful thing about a God-given vision is that it excites and exhilarates both you and others around you; and though it may terrify you when you contemplate the opposition and difficulties you will have to overcome, nothing will finally daunt you, because your eyes have seen beyond ordinary horizons to the new world you can reach if you receive the challenge and risk the great journey.

Vision is the clear, God-given picture of what you see your church, your business and your life becoming, being and doing for the Lord in the future. It's the ability to articulate clearly the answer to the question, "What am I and my church supposed to be accomplishing for God in our ministry together?" Vision is a clear mental image of the preferred future that God has planned for us. It changes the future forever; once God has spoken to us, our old cosy world is blown right out of the water.

Robert Woodruff had vision. He served as president of the US Coca-Cola company from 1923 to 1955, in its early years. His vision was not about building Christ's kingdom – it was commercial vision; but nevertheless it expresses exactly the power of focus and determination to realize change. He said this: "It is my dream that no one on this planet should die without having tasted Coca-Cola." As you know, the Coca-Cola company more or less realized that dream in Woodruff's lifetime, and his influence has continued to increase, realizing almost complete fulfilment in the decades since his death. You can cross the Sahara desert and find empty Coke bottles sticking up out of the sand. Visit any part of the world, places where the gospel has not yet gone, and people there will have drunk Coca-Cola. They call it "The Real Thing"!

If Coca-Cola did that for Robert Woodruff, how can it be that so many of God's people, as numerous as we are and empowered by God's Holy Spirit as we are, have not yet fully caught a vision like this for the expansion of the gospel – that no one should die without having at least tasted the truth that is found in Jesus Christ?

Vision gets things done because it sees the far horizon; it orientates us towards the future. The link between where we *are* and where we *will be* is our vision.

In practical terms, then, to become people of vision, we must be prepared to make a number of commitments. If you want to be a prophet, a visionary, you will need to put in place the following goals.

1. Develop a hunger for God

We must live in the light of something and someone greater than ourselves. No one ever became a visionary by thinking: *I want to be known as a visionary. What shall I dream about?* Until you care about something else more than you care about yourself, you can have no vision. A dream can start small and grow, of course; but it is only at the point where it becomes your consuming passion that we can talk in terms of the kind of transformative vision only the living God can impart. Of course, you cannot *make* something ignite you and then take hold of you, but if at present you have no vision, you can at least put yourself in the way of great ideas. The best of them come from God. Search. Be curious. Hang around groups where life and excitement and enthusiasm are buzzing because of the activity of the Holy Spirit. Go to conferences and festivals from which you have previously seen people return with new hope and shining eyes. Take time to visit churches that are growing. Listen to inspirational speakers. Look in the most needy places as well as among the stars, and see if the Lord stirs something in you or speaks to you. Many who have much to teach us live quiet, unadvertised, unremarkable lives of stunning service. Seek some of them out. Listen to children, to old people, to people who are chronically and terminally ill in nursing homes, to carers and others who work for subsistence wages because they care about what they do. Go through life with your eyes open if you want to catch a vision. Look beyond the obvious. Find God in unexpected places. Jesus frequently moved among spiritual deadbeats, despised foreigners, compromised traitors such as tax-collectors, and broken-down whores. He burned with a vision to rescue them.

2. Find the truly great ones

Get close to people of vision. If you hear of someone with a wonderful ministry, take the trouble to listen to them, spend time with them. Look into the background and lifestyle of that person to see the fruit of the Spirit as well as his gifts. Ask them to let you meet with them for a while or start some kind of apprenticeship with them, until you see what they are seeing and give yourself a chance to catch the vision that grips them.

3. Draw on the support of like-minded spirits

If you already have a vision then you will need the help of spiritual veterans, experienced coaches who are willing to encourage you, as well as followers who admire you. Seek out others in whom you recognize the fire of Holy Spirit passion and commitment: determined, God-intimate fighters to whom you can turn at times when your hope falters. They'll lift you up and help you persevere. Look for those of some stature whose faith has matured into something big, generous, selfless and infectious, then spend time with them on a regular basis.

4. Become disciplined and rigorously trained in your chosen area

Vision seems like a fiery, spontaneous, vital thing. It is, but vision is also nourished by discipline. Visionaries, surprisingly, live disciplined lives; they are not impulsive, flighty and uncommitted types. They get up early. They read and study voraciously everything pertinent that they can get their hands on to nourish their vision. They pray as a priority, not just when they get round to it. They eat correctly, usually wholesome, nourishing food that keeps their bodies fit and their minds alert; and they exercise regularly to clear their minds and prevent weariness and depression. They avoid toxic, dissolute lifestyles that dissipate energy and fog the mind. They keep away from poisonous gossip and frivolous occupations. Their Bibles are worn out with daily use.

5. Keep your life simple

Without this, you will neither acquire, nor sustain, a vision. A dream, a real dream, must be nourished by all the resources you have: time, energy, money, prayer – everything. In order to pursue it, you'll need to streamline your life, chuck the ballast overboard, and perhaps shed some needless baggage. If your life is full of debts, life-dominating hobbies and endless partying; if you are perpetually occupied with acquiring and maintaining possessions, you may find that there are too many distractions and tight strangleholds on your life. Visionaries – all visionaries – live simply and hold on to things lightly. Like Jesus, they spend as much time as they can in solitude, alone with God, soaking up truth and insight. When they give away their time to others, it is to a purpose, as it was with Jesus: to heal, to teach, to share the truth they have learned. They do not get sucked into the world's priorities or sweat and collapse on the treadmill of serving Mammon. They guard their freedom jealously, knowing that debt, the "Money Monster" and excessive partying erode freedom. Their greatest treasures lie elsewhere. Yes, they relax; but, yes – they are, as you are beginning to suspect, fanatics.

Now let me say a few things about the source of authentic vision.

Where Vision Comes From

1. Negatively, it is important to be clear that vision is never spun from our own ego

We have all met Christians characterized by an inflated ego, who brag and boast about what they have done, what they are planning to do, and what they are about to do for the Lord. This can be irritating when we do not sense the Holy Spirit's voice in what they are saying. It seems to be all about them and their personal ambitions, all about making a name for themselves. When vision comes from God it is not based upon hype. It's not about voicing exaggerated "big shot" ideas in order to sound important or make ourselves look good. It is not to get people to talk about us, or to give us sway over them. If, in your mind's eye, making yourself look good is your primary goal, then you are likely to become a candidate for trouble, because godly vision isn't about that at all. It's not about making us rising stars and minor celebrities in the Christian scene or the night sky of the charismatic universe, so that we get to twinkle more brightly than anybody else! That kind of fleshly ambition has led to the fall of many.

You may recall the scandal that became connected with Jim Bakker, the American televangelist who, during the late

1980s, built the PTL ("Praise the Lord") empire in South Carolina which included a Christian holiday centre to rival Disney World. He and his business manager Richard Dortch were both imprisoned for mishandling donors' money. When he was later interviewed about this, Richard Dortch had come to a completely different perspective about all that had happened and commented, "Well, the real reason we got here was pride. Vision appeals to our ego. I saw something big and great that could make me bigger and greater. And to maintain it we got involved in 'funny money', fundraising and lying and cheating to maintain that vision."

When our own ego ambitions are prominent in what we like to think of as a God-given vision, we are setting ourselves up for a fall, because the line between doing something great for Christ and doing something great for ourselves is a very fine line. Some people are ambitious to stand up on platforms and become like some hero they admire, so their vision is to have a ministry like his – a very public one. This will probably lead to frustration because they can't fulfil the dreams of their own inflated ego. It is like a donkey chasing a carrot on a stick. The dream is always out there just ahead of them, elusive and unobtainable. God will see to that!

But there is no limit to the good we can do if we don't care who gets the credit, when we are truly more concerned about God and his glory than about having our name up in lights. If other people receive some of the praise, it doesn't matter to us as long as the job gets done and the goal is realized. So don't let your vision be a mere reflection of your own face. Let me ask you a personal question at this point: "Who is centre stage in your vision?" If what comes to mind is dominated by _you_, then you are in danger, because it ought to be dominated by Christ.

I had a big vision for the first church I pastored for more than two decades. I preached, taught and encouraged the people to pray and give in support of that vision as it advanced in increasingly expanding phases, and they did. We had building projects in place to facilitate church growth. But when the call came to move to Westminster Chapel, London, towards the end of 2001, my vision for the church and the city I formerly lived in had not been fully realized. We had made a good beginning and the work was gathering momentum, but we still had a long way to go. How did I feel about that? *Great!* – because I knew that what God had in mind for me next was in the will of God for my life at that time, surprising as it was, and it would be dangerous to linger any longer where I had been. It is the danger that has been called "feathered nest syndrome"; and so God takes us out of our comfort zone.

Someone else has picked up the vision for my previous pastorate, and will see it through to some kind of completion, perhaps different from what I had envisaged, but in line with how the Lord leads them. But hopefully, neither of us will get the credit for whatever is accomplished – Christ will. It was Christ who gave the vision in the first place. He sustained it, he fuelled it and imparted faith for it, he released all the finances and he gave us the people. It's all to his glory, and that should always rejoice our hearts. For truly any work of God is not ours, it is his – we are not doing God a favour, or generously allowing him to take credit for something we really did ourselves. The glory really does belong to *him*. If it wasn't *his work* then it wasn't worth doing in the first place. Vision does not come from our own ego.

2. Positively, we should know that true vision comes from the Holy Spirit

Watchman Nee, the Chinese underground church leader during the toughest years of communist rule, said, "The start of a true work of God with us is not when we consecrate ourselves to him, but when we *see*. Consecration should result from spiritual vision; it can never take its place."

We will never commit ourselves seriously, or offer our bodies as living sacrifices, or give away all that we have, unless we know what it is for. All of those things demand a prior seeing, that can inspire enthusiasm and passion. It is the Holy Spirit who enables us to see a God-given vision worth giving our all to, to eventually see it realized. He is the Spirit of wisdom and revelation, and he conveys these things to us as we pray, as we wait upon him and become receptive to his movements within us. We then conceive the new thing by his revelation. It is as though he makes us pregnant.

During strong visitations of the Holy Spirit's presence at certain special periods, I have seen even *men* become pregnant – with revelation from God! As they lay on their backs on the floor, they would sometimes clutch their bellies and groan loudly like a woman in labour. They would go through all the motions of giving birth, groaning in almost physical agony over what they saw in the Spirit. The strong prophetic yearning within them, the deep urge to bring to birth what they had seen, was as powerful as a mother's labour pains throughout their whole being. In subsequent years I have witnessed the results of this in many cases that I'm personally aware of. Significant projects and vital new ministries emerged from those early "labour pains" in the Spirit during the mid-1990s. And therefore, when we truly conceive the revelation of God within our inner being, its time will surely come: sooner or later we will be compelled to give birth to what he has spoken to us. It may be a long and painful process of gestation, but it will eventually lead to labour pains and ultimate delivery. The promise of God does not fail; the Word of God is trustworthy and true.

The Voice of the Spirit

What does the Holy Spirit tell us at such times? When we experience such powerful visitations or seek and wait upon him in prayer, remaining open to his Word and movements in our midst, the Holy Spirit tells us three things:

1. WHAT we are to do

The instructions from the Holy Spirit will be specific. Maybe he will prompt you to rescue street children, open a soup kitchen, begin composing and recording songs, get involved in the political arena or develop a ministry to elderly and housebound people. Some are stirring right now with a burden for the modern slave trade of trafficking children and vulnerable young men and women for prostitution in the West, in cities such as London. The Spirit may even tell you to spend some more time in your own home with your own family, and less time on social action projects. Whatever he tells you will both surprise and convict you – it will feel right, feel sure and real, but it will usually come to you unexpectedly. As you pray, though you may have a vague sense within you, such as, "Lord, I wish I could do more with my music for you" or "I have such a heart for evangelism" or "I don't seem to do anything that amounts to a ministry of my own", this is not the revelation of the Holy Spirit; it is the longing of your own heart. But as you commit this vague feeling to God in prayer, it may provide the doorway through which authentic revelation can enter. Note that, when the Spirit speaks, his Word is compelling, specific, surprising and convicting. You will *know*. Even so, it is important to have the humility to test the word with those who are your guides, prayer partners and leaders. Mere wishful thinking can feel a lot like revelation on occasion. It is better to check it out.

2. HOW we are to do it

When God gives us a revelation he's calling us to join him in his creative and redeeming work, to embark upon a hands-on involvement and a lengthy journey that will take us through many important, successive steps that will be required of us, as we see through to completion the task God has laid on our hearts. The goal we have seen will never come about automatically while we sit, watch and wait like mere spectators. The Holy Spirit has intermediate stages for us to pass through in the realization of our goals, the means by which the dream can come into being. This may involve a study course or training programme in a specialized area. It may be that huge character adjustments will be needed, to make us trustworthy for this responsibility. It may mean that we have to become more knowledgeable about the Bible than we have ever been before, because we are called to teach it to others as workmen who have no need to be ashamed but who can correctly handle the Word of God (2 Timothy 2:15). It may mean that we have to attend some special conferences, purchase study materials, learn another language or apply to a college and undertake an undergraduate or post-graduate degree course. We may have to shed other commitments or make changes in our habits and lifestyle. Whatever is required of us, the Holy Spirit will make clear what the intermediate stages are, and the necessary preparation for the end he has in mind. Sometimes he shows us step by step as we go forward in faith; in this case we may see only the first step – but that first step will be apparent to us and will be a concrete and specific course of action.

3. WHEN it is likely to happen

This, of course, may take far longer than we at first assumed. Sometimes we become impatient or discouraged, and then the Spirit may give us an insight into the true timescale of the vision – which could be a matter of years or even decades, when we were hoping to have everything ready in time for Christmas! He helps us to see that realizing the vision will involve effort, preparation, huge investment and considerable time. On the other hand, he may reveal a vision as a "dream with a deadline" in the near future. We can learn from the way God revealed his intentions to his servants in the Old and New Testaments. When we look at the time intervals involved, we realize that this can be anything from a matter of days to several decades or even longer. It could take a whole generation or, perhaps, a hundred years or more.

Noah was building his ark for a hundred years before the flood came, and Abraham, Joseph, Moses, David, Nehemiah and Paul all went through long periods of waiting. Some, like Joseph, were thrown into prison and endured circumstances without any outward sign of the reality that God had promised for their lives, in his case for seventeen years or more. So think in terms of decades in some cases today.

Abraham was promised descendants as numerous as the grains of sand in the desert or the stars in the sky, but he began with an infertility problem; when that was miraculously solved he later progressed though the call and promise of God to be commanded to offer up his and Sarah's only child, their miracle son Isaac. It made little sense. It was in the nature of the promise that only the unfolding of generations could see his visions fully realized, but Abraham still continued to believe it, often in spite of appearances to the contrary. The reason why all of these men are now household names to us was because the Holy Spirit spoke to them about the "what", "how" and "when" of a God-given vision, even if it took a long time before they saw the vision come to pass.

Noah built a wooden ship the size of the *Canberra* passenger liner in the middle of a desert plain. Noah's obedience became a lived, acted prophecy for his generation. It must have taken a long while to build his boat and, in all of that time, thousands of lives were at risk through corruption and sin. Noah was a sign of the mercy and judgement of the living God in their midst: at any time the people could have repented and averted disaster, just as the people of Nineveh did in the story of the prophet Jonah. So it is with us in our generation. Thousands of lives are also at stake, as children grow up in broken homes, unhappy teenagers with empty lives turn to substance abuse and addiction, harassed householders are sucked into the grip of unrepayable debt, marriages are driven onto the rocks, and businesses founder. God speaks to us about all these things because he loves people; he cares about their lives and he wants to show them the way of salvation and repair for their broken lives.

What About You?

As you wait upon God concerning the timing of your revelation unfolding, you could find yourself in a similar situation to Joseph. You may have dreamed wonderful things in your youth but gone public with them prematurely and been ridiculed or mocked, perhaps even experienced jealousy and hostility in your family or in the church for the sake of those dreams.

People may even have developed real enmity towards you because of the things you have seen. But a God-given dream will not lie. It may be slow to unfold, but it will come to pass in the end. In the divine timing for your revelation it may be that, like Moses, you have felt pulled towards a place or a people all of your life, because, in spite of your circumstances and career path so far, you know whose child you really are and what God, not other powerful figures in your life, has in mind for you – just as Moses did.

Moses knew he was a Hebrew, though he was a prince of Egypt, and he had seen his people in dreadful oppression and slavery. He made a few false starts in his attempt to rescue his fellow Hebrews, for example, his reckless, inappropriate and violent action in murdering one of their Egyptian overseers, but though his methods may have been faulty, his vision wasn't. He was going to be a deliverer of millions of enslaved people. And, of course, although his mistake led to seemingly endless delays and almost overwhelming human resistance, God brought the vision to pass in the end. That's the thing about vision: stick with it, believe it, and God will bring it to pass.

It may be that, as with David, your vision has no other dimension than the sole purpose of bringing glory to God. God put it on David's heart to build him a house, a temple, a place for the presence and glory of God to be manifested on earth. David began to gather the materials for such a project and even enlisted the help of pagan kings like Hiram of Tyre who helped him fund everything God was calling him to do. Then came the bombshell, when David was told that he would not be the one to build the temple; his son Solomon would finish the task. This did not negate the vision or mean that it wasn't real, or that David had no part to play in seeing it realized – he just wasn't going to be the person to finish it. It may be like that with us. Conversely, it may be that, as with Nehemiah, God stirs the deepest emotions within us in preparation for a task that we alone can accomplish because God has put it on our hearts to see it through. The timing, the "when", is as essential a part of our vision as the "what" and the "how": it is in the slow, patient unfolding of the vision, and the journey we make as we travel towards the fulfilment of our dream, that God's Spirit works transformatively upon us. The vision was never totally about *us* but, as we are faithful to it, God shapes us and our souls along with it.

The Personal Element

A God-given vision is highly personal. George Barna, an American church growth expert, wrote, "Vision for Ministry is a clear mental image of a preferred future imparted by God to His chosen servants and is based upon an accurate understanding of God, self and circumstances."

Vision is thus highly personal and individual, though it may eventually affect many other people's lives within a corporate body of people, such as a business, or by transforming a whole church or inspiring a movement; but God usually begins by speaking personally to an individual. A dream begins in a one-to-one encounter with God. And this is always exciting and highly motivating.

In the Old Testament, one of the words that carries the idea of a vision is *chephets*, meaning "pleasure", "delight", "thing desired", "purpose", "valuable thing", "the will of God" (Job 22:3; Psalms 5:4, 111:2; Isaiah 44:28, 46:10, 48:14, 53:10)[14]. In the New Testament the Greek word *prothesis*, meaning "the setting forth of a thing, placing it in view", "a purpose" or "plan" (Acts 27:13; Romans 8:28; Ephesians 1:11; 2 Timothy 1:9),[15] is a word that carries the same idea of God-ordained vision and literally means, "the thing set before you". If you combine the two meanings together this gives us a wonderful definition of what vision is: Vision is something that God sets before you, which brings you pleasure and delight. And the implication of this is that you and I will never be happy or feel remotely fulfilled until we have discovered God's plan for our lives and are actually carrying it out.

I have now been a pastor for twenty-nine years and regularly preached for ten years before that. It has always been my greatest delight, since I was a teenager, to open up the Word of God to people. A wonderful surprise for me in connection with this life calling is that I now get paid to do it! I get paid to do what I always wanted to do! It's a bit like Moses' mother when Pharaoh summoned her to look after the tiny baby in the basket that had recently been rescued from the deadly river Nile where Moses' mother had launched him by faith. Pharaoh didn't know who she was but, at his command, she got to do exactly what she'd always wanted to do: look after her precious son whose life had been under threat – only now, she got fully paid to do it. That's what God is like in his goodness. He arranges for us to do what we have always wanted to do, and often to be remunerated for it as well.

It's highly unlikely, therefore, that if you hate snakes and spiders, can't stand jungles and intense humidity, and heat drives you crazy, that God will call you to be a missionary in Mozambique. Some people are fascinated by snakes and tarantulas, and can't wait to see them crawling through their tent; these are the ones God is likely to call to the tropics and subtropics to adventure for him there. And if some are still nervous, the Lord will help them to get over it and begin to enjoy it! God usually calls us to do the very things we already feel inclined and gifted to do – we actually grow to *like* it, even if we didn't to start with. Vision helps us finally to do what we always wanted to do.

Zig Ziglar, an American businessman and Christian leader, once observed, "You can get everything in life that you want if you help enough people to get what they want." That is a profound statement because it touches upon the element of mutuality that makes human societies work successfully. It is how we were designed to function in community and it isn't the same as being selfish. As the old proverb says, "Help thou thy brother's boat across and, lo, thine own has touched the shore!" As you share your God-given vision with others, they in turn help you to reach your goal, and you help them to reach theirs, in an experience of mutual blessing and fulfilment. What a wonderful arrangement – and God is the one who is behind it!

Vision works in this way, energizing people with eagerness, gladness and enthusiasm, because it becomes the dominant factor, the core reality, in a person's life. It's the thing that makes you tick, that "rings your bell", every time – not in the way an addiction draws and compels you, for an addiction will always leave you empty, unsatisfied and craving for more, since addiction is a form of idolatry. A God-given vision, however, is a means to worship and serve the living God. When you find your vision, it will lead you to do what you always wanted to do, and become whom you always aspired to be, because this is what God planned for you in the beginning.

What Rings Your Bell?

If you want to find out what your vision is, ask yourself, "What's dominating my mind and imagination much of the time?" Even if you aren't fulfilling it right now, what's the thing that is actually overshadowing your life and has been doing so for a long time? It's whatever is there deep down inside you when, like an onion, all the outer layers of your life are peeled away and you find out what's right at the core of your being. If your circumstances changed and you lost your present job or role, or your possessions and status and reputation, what's the thing you would still be clinging to because it's not an add-on or accessory but a central part of you? That's your vision. It's what is sticking to your insides, like your breakfast porridge to the inside of your ribcage. It's what spurts out of your spirit like juice squeezed from a lemon, when people put you under pressure and ask, "OK, I want you to open up with me, I want you to tell me what's really on your heart, what you really want from God. I am not going to let you leave this room until you've been honest with me." And out it comes. It's what you really feel and care most deeply about. It's where your thoughts automatically go to when they are not legitimately engaged somewhere else. It's what you daydream and think about often. In moments of quietness this is what you think about. It's just there.

Furthermore, it's what governs your choices. It has probably governed the type of church you have chosen to join because, in some way that you can't even define, the preaching, worship, conversations and main priorities there all help to foster your vision. Vision can also determine the music you listen to, the films that most move you, and the places you most like to visit. It's what governs the best friends that you make, the people you would regard as your soulmates, the characters you're most drawn to. You come alive when you are with these individuals and, even if there is a long time gap between seeing them, you just pick up where you left off, because there is a special dynamic when you are together. Such people are rare. The reason God brings them into your life is because they are going to help you to accomplish your vision. You may help them get theirs accomplished too.

What about the books that you read? If you love books then your shelves will be full of writings that reflect your vision in some way; I know that mine are. If you aren't much of a reader, you will be able to trace your vision somewhere in the few books you do possess. If your vision is to be a man or woman of prayer, you'll read books on prayer. If you want to be a Bible teacher, you will probably read Bible commentaries and theological tomes as other people read novels – you just devour them. Theology – you love it!

It will be the same with your bank account. Jesus said in Matthew 6:21, "Where your treasure is, there your heart will be also" (and notably, let me remind you, he did not say this the other way round). You can always tell what people care about by the way they spend their money. If you want to know what your vision is, check your bank or credit card statements and take note of where your money went that wasn't spent on pure necessities.

Many wise teachers have understood that, whatever we focus on, the area of our life that grows, develops and blossoms is wherever we put our attention, time and money. So vision is self-fulfilling in many ways. Because it's a big thing in our lives we tend to concentrate on it, read about it, spend money on it, think about it and pray about it – until it gets even bigger in our lives. Vision starts as a seed of thought and grows. If you ever eat pine nuts (the seeds that come from pine cones), you will find that if you carefully bite one in two, at the heart of that little seed is a tiny thing that looks just like a pine tree. It's the tree's vision, the seed thought, the dream at the heart of the forest, the thing that will grow one day into a beautiful, tall, fragrant tree. In the same way, there is a seed of thought that defines you, that can't help growing because it's at the heart of you and you nourish it constantly. *That's your vision.*

Vision is internal and personal before it becomes externalized and public knowledge. Nehemiah spoke of it in this way: it's what "my God had put in my heart to do for Jerusalem" (Nehemiah 2:12). Your vision is the thing you want to see happen before you die, and would make your life worthwhile if it did. What do you so want to see before *you* die? *That's your vision.*

Vision Defines Past, Present and Future

Vision is sometimes described as *"foresight* with *insight* based upon *hindsight"*. Vision has to do with my past, my present, and God's long-term dealings with me in the future. Here are some questions to help us enquire into those three key areas of our unfolding life experience.

1. What has God done in your past?

This is how to understand what God has planned for you. What abilities has God given to you by birth – intellectual abilities, manual skills and dexterity, talents, the experience you have gained, and hobbies that you have pursued? What desires have been stirring inside you for quite a while now, that you don't feel worthy of and may have never told a soul about but, nevertheless, they are still there? What learning path have you been on, so that when you look back you think, "That was what I was really interested in; those were special times doing what I really wanted to do and learning things that I really wanted to know about", and such thoughts still awaken unfulfilled yearnings in you? You may have qualifications in this subject, even a degree or post-graduate study. Why? Is it all going to be wasted, and are you never going to use it?

When you look back along the path you have walked, are there certain memories that stand out as really significant; experiences that even now still energize and define you? As you have matured and developed, are there particular areas of skill, or projects you have undertaken, which have called forth comment from others: "You're really good at that!" As we look into our past, noticing how our hopes blossomed into experience, and how the things we thought about and cared about determined the shape of our developing lives, we can start to understand what motivates us, what we are called to, and form a clear picture of our God-given vision.

The astronaut James Irwin tells of how, when he was six years of age, he sat on the porch of his parent's home, on a rocking chair next to his mother. As the evening sun went down, the stars came out and the bright moon began to shine. He leaned over to his mother: "Mum, you see that?" "Yes," she replied, "that's the moon, son." Young James declared confidently, "One day I'm going to walk on that." *And he did!* He was only six years old, but a longing, a dream of what could be, grew and lingered within him until it changed his life. Our seed thoughts are with us from the beginning.

2. What is God doing right now in your life?

Is it time now for you to grow beyond what you have always been? Maybe you have lost your contentment; you are no longer happy with the way things are; you are dissatisfied. This is how change comes about, how caterpillars get to become butterflies! Smith Wigglesworth, the Pentecostal healing evangelist in the early twentieth century, once said, "The only thing that I am satisfied with is the fact that I am dissatisfied." God puts those longings in us and, while other people seem to remain content and think everything is just fine, the stirrings of vision within us create restlessness, an instinct for something more than this. Where do your heart's longings lead you? Do you have a compassionate heart that is outraged for the poor and rejected:

"Why doesn't somebody do something about the homeless?" or "Why doesn't somebody do something about the drug and alcohol problems in our neighbourhood?"

Are you a practical person? Is there nothing you like better than working with wood, or painting and drawing? God gave you those desires. What fulfils and excites you? What activities absorb your heart and soul? In what situations do you feel fully alive, so that you wake up and burn to share what you know, what you see and feel, with others? What keeps you awake at night as you plan and dream and think things over? These are all probably connected with your life vision. What makes you cry? What makes you angry? What are you consistently passionate about? These are all good indicators that you are meant to act on your longings and do something about situations that move you.

3. What has God indicated about your future?

Sometimes this is conceived in a flash; at other times it grows and gestates over a longer period of time, but the Lord is pointing out your future in this. It may require hours of reflection, study, prayer and conversation with trusted men and women of God whose guidance you value, before it finally takes shape in your mind. Vision often seems to come in stages rather than in a fully developed form. It comes in increments; it grows. We see a little bit of the picture, and know that we are in the right ballpark. Then, as we begin to get a handle on what God is saying, he says, "Here's some more", and a further unveiling of the big picture comes to us. What prophetic words have you already had from others that confirm this in your heart? These are also divine indications or confirmations of your future.

Perhaps you have no idea which road God is opening for you to walk along, but your past, your present and your future all belong to each other; they are held together by how you see things – by your vision. What you chose and believed in the past made you what you are now. What you choose and believe now will determine what you become. What will you choose? What do you believe? What do you want to be?

Only you can answer these questions about your past, present and future in a way that will become the key to unlock your understanding: "Yes, this is who I am; who God called me to be – and this is what I came here to do."

As we explore further into the quest to identify a personal calling, a personal vision, here are five questions that have helped others to gain a degree of clarity about their life-calling in God.

a) What do you feel prompted to do?

This prompting is like being gently nudged from behind (or even unceremoniously kicked!) in a certain direction, and it persists; it returns again and again. For example, someone will say to you, "Have you ever considered…" or "I've been watching you for a while and I can't help but think that God may be wanting you to…" At other times it is just a still, small voice in your own heart, but it comes so frequently and so insistently that you can't help but know it's the whisper of God. What do you feel prompted to do?

b) What do you experience pleasure in doing?

As we noted before, this is what "rings your bell", what makes you tick, and it acts as a wake-up call or indicator for the course God is calling you to follow. God's will for your life usually corresponds with what you most enjoy doing; your highest good will also be your deepest happiness. This is not to say that your vision, your calling, will not entail sacrifice or pain – it most certainly will – but it will also bring you most of your greatest pleasures.

c) What do you experience power in doing?

This is where the supernatural enabling of God's anointing comes in. You know that you are somehow empowered to do this. This is not restricted to activities connected with church meetings and worship alone – it's for God's world, all of it. You can be an anointed businessman, banker, teacher, cricketer or footballer (David Beckham looks like an anointed footballer to me, but I wouldn't want to go so far as to assert that the

Holy Spirit is directly connected with the outcome of World Cup football competitions, though many fans like to think so). There's a coming alive, a feeling of power; and other people notice it.

d) What do you receive praise for doing?

When you pursue a genuine calling from God, he will see that others will confirm this to you. This is what you receive the most personal positive feedback and encouragement about. This is what people compliment you for. This is what they regularly commend your ability in. Human agents tell you, "You've really got something there! This is from God." Sometimes, though, we are called to walk a lonely path in service of our vision, especially if it is countercultural or ahead of the times in which we live. Others may laugh at us or ignore us; we may become unpopular for what we know, deep in our hearts, to be true, but others simply have not seen this yet, and resist us. Even so, it is wise to listen to what others feed back to us, and helpful to note when they respond positively. Jeremiah was recognized as a prophet even when nobody wanted to hear what he had to say. This is where it can be sensible to seek the more impartial perspective of a trusted church leader or mentor, to help us distinguish when it is right to persevere in the face of discouragement, or how to persevere in an area where we are not yet confident.

e) What has led to your personal promotion by God?

God will open all kinds of doors and prominent platforms for his servants to achieve what he has gifted and called them to do (Revelation 3:7). What positions of prominence and influence has God already opened up for you, opportunities which are beginning to happen even if the door is only slightly ajar at the moment?

These five questions will lead us to identify our God-given gifts and graces, our areas of strength, and then to work with them as we gain confidence in discerning our calling.

We are feeling our way towards clarity with regard to our personal vision and direction in life. We are looking for the signs God has already given. We are looking for indicators or markers that he has set out in sequence ahead of us to tell us: "Look, read these, and see my personal dealings with you."

It can also be helpful to look beyond our own lives, into the Scriptures and the unfolding life of the church through the ages, looking for the lives that have particular resonance for us – the stories that call to our hearts. With this in mind, here are three simple exercises to help you identify and establish your vision, God's calling on your life. Write down your thoughts about them. It will help you.

• Which Bible characters do you most identify with?
Whom do you especially admire and enjoy reading about? Whose writings do you delight in most, as you spend time with the Scriptures? Whose biography and spirit touches you especially? For me it would be Jeremiah, the apostle Paul, Gideon, Elijah and Moses. How about you?

_____

_____

• Which three people do you most respect?
This could include people you have met or great heroes you have read about in church history or world history. We are thinking now of people from the past or those still living today, not characters included in the Bible: people who are an inspiration to you. For me it would be preachers like C.H. Spurgeon, Martyn Lloyd-Jones and Terry Virgo. They are the three men who have had the most impact upon my life. There are others whom I would regard as close runners, but these are the top three: two now gone to glory, and one from the church of today. Spurgeon was before my time, Dr Lloyd-Jones I was privileged to meet briefly and I treasure his recordings and writings, and Terry Virgo I believe is one of the greatest church leaders of the present time. Who would be on your list?

i. _____

ii. _____

iii. _____

Why?

_____

_____

_____

As you think about your heroes from the Bible and church history, it will help you clarify your own particular and major areas of passion and concern too. You may discover that you share many of their highest aspirations, and live to achieve some of them in your life also.

Finally, to give further focus to your dream, try filling in the gaps in the paragraph that follows. Nobody need ever read this but you, so you can be entirely honest and reach for the stars!

If I had:

_____

(e.g. time, money, information, training, opportunity, freedom from responsibility)
then I would:

_____

If I could accomplish one thing before I die, it would be:

_____

_____

Now write your own VISION STATEMENT (it could be, personal, corporate or both).

_____

_____

_____

_____

_____

If you find this difficult, you may find inspiration in the following summary of Habakkuk 2:2–4. Habakkuk was a man full of questions, notably about God's dealings with his nation, and when he asked God about anything, he anticipated a reply. Take time to ask the Lord all the right questions and wait for a full answer from the Almighty. Habakkuk had resolved, "I will stand at my watch... I will look to see what [God] will say to me" (Habakkuk 2:1). The Lord replied in terms very specifically for him, saying: "Write down the revelation and make it plain on tablets so that a herald may run with it. For the revelation awaits an appointed time; it speaks of the end and will not prove false. Though it linger, wait for it; it will certainly come and will not delay... the righteous will live by his faith."

A God-given vision statement is marked by several features. Use them as a framework as you write a vision statement for your life and, if you are responsible for other people's lives as well, take time to discover one for the company of people that you lead.

1) It is a picture as yet only in your mind's eye – it is a "revelation" from God. So this revelation isn't wishful thinking or daydreaming to enhance your image: it's something God discloses to you, whether it's in pictures or through words.

2) It can be articulated in words – so that even if it is a picture there will come a point where you will be able to

"write it down". You can say, "This is God's vision for my life, for our church, for my business."

3) It is clear and not confused – "...make it plain". It is not a muddled array of confused ingredients that is unclear, approximate or vague. It is a mixture of integrated ingredients that can be described clearly.

4) It is succinct – concise enough "so that whoever reads it may run with it". People are readily able to grasp it, remember and recall it. If you are a visionary pastor of a church, everyone in the church should eventually be able to describe the vision of the church if asked to do so. You will have spoken about it often enough. They've heard you pray, preach and worship God on the basis of that vision often enough, so that it is now in their very bloodstream. It's like a stick of peppermint Blackpool rock confectionery: wherever you slice it, it has "BLACKPOOL ROCK" written all through it. The people have similarly "got it" too, because it's now inscribed in their spirit. It's in their system and they are now running with it. Everybody knows what they are here for. They are all "going for it".

5) It is the future of your life's work or ministry – "...the revelation awaits an appointed time". So you know that there may be a time gap between here and there, now and then. But that is not going to deter you because you are convinced that God is in this and, because God is a sovereign God, nothing can thwart his will. God appoints things and when people fulfil the conditions for that appointed time, it will surely come to pass.

6) It can be – if you are in faith for it.

7) It must be – if God imparts hope for it. "The righteous will live by his faith" or "his faithfulness" (NIV). Faithfulness is sticking to something. Faithfulness is believing for it even when everything is crying out, "It will never happen, you

haven't got enough time to realize this, it's not possible." You can say, "Not so. God has given me hope and it will come to pass. I am going to stick with that, I am going to work to see that vision realized. And even if I don't personally live to see this, someone else will."

Our vision statement is our statement of purpose in the new body of Christ. It helps to define our particular niche or contribution in the marketplace. It's a major part of the real reason for our existence, for our creation by God. What, then, is yours?

Obviously you will not have decided all of that while reading this chapter. Your homework now is to go and seek God about this matter, because these clues will help you hear from the Lord with greater clarity. But be careful, because vision has implications for your life in terms of total obedience to God. Paul said, "I was not disobedient to the vision from heaven" (Acts 26:19). That needs to be our resolve also.

Be Aware of Some Myths About Vision

1. "Vision is a result of a consensus between the church's leaders"

No. Vision is not usually designed by committee, though it results in consensus. People own a leader's vision: they do not create it. Leaders find the vision, and then the people run with it. All the Bible characters we thought about earlier – Noah, Abraham, Moses, Joseph... and I could have added others like Joshua, Gideon, Nehemiah, Paul or Peter – heard individually and clearly from God, and caught others up with that vision. So vision is not arrived at by consensus. It brings such agreement about, where it didn't exist before.

2. "Vision is just another name for 'pie-in-the-sky' daydreaming"

No. Vision is an indicator of what God declares to be possible. He doesn't indulge us in idle fantasies or mere daydreaming. God is serious about vision because it seeds coming reality. This does not preclude thought, prayer, planning, persuasion and research into the difficulties and how to overcome them, and a thorough knowledge of all the facts. Somebody is going to have to do some hard thinking about how to change this situation, and formulate the plans needed and the steps to be taken in order to make it happen, but the underlying factor that will bring it into being is the fact that God has spoken to us.

3. "Vision is the same as our mission for God"

No. Business corporations, like churches, have mission statements. The mission of a fast-food chain might be "to serve the best-quality burgers and outdo all our rivals". A church may take as its mission statement, "To know Christ and make him known". This is certainly biblical and outlines the broad direction we are meant to pursue, but it's not a vision statement. A vision statement details the specifics. It has focus and prevents "bendy-toy" manipulation by others who want to shape it as they like. It helps you to say "No" to certain legitimate opportunities irrelevant to your vision. A vision may also relate to a particular project within the overall mission of the church, so may be defined by a specific time-frame, and it is always, by its nature, very concrete and specific.

4. "With vision we just let-go and let-God, relaxing in the future he has for us"

No. With vision we become co-labourers with God, experiencing his power enabling us to create the future he has planned. Your vision will ask everything of you, and its outworking may prove to be the hardest time of your life in terms of the work demanded of you and others connected with you.

5. "Real vision will insulate us against fear, apprehension and risk"

No. Vision is scary. Visionaries usually invite trouble. Visionaries are often seen as stirrers and a provocation to others. They are therefore targeted by Satan and wicked people. They may be threatened; nasty letters may arrive through their door, or poisonous emails turn up in their inbox. Be prepared. You are going to get into trouble. Things will never be the same again. Joseph, Moses, Noah, David, Nehemiah and Paul got into trouble. You will too.

6. "With vision we will grow numerically and become famous"

Not necessarily. Sometimes vision entails shrinkage and notoriety. Jeremiah's ministry was not enormously successful, at least in his lifetime – he never attracted numerous followers or became famous. He ended up in a cesspit, up to his waste in human excrement, asking God to take this ministry away from him, declaring, "I will not... speak any more in his name" (Jeremiah 20:9). The ultimate goal is the glory of God, who is best glorified through committed people (often a minority) who live the truth (sometimes an unpopular course to take).

7. "Vision will get you to your desired goals in no time"

No. Very often it takes a long time to develop. Time constraints cannot be imposed upon a God-given vision. The Lord alone knows all the factors involved – you and I don't. You may be in it for the long haul. Brace yourself!

8. "Vision is a matter of cobbling together the best ideas around today"

Definitely not! You need to hear from God for yourself. You can't just say, "Let's try this here because it worked over there."

9. "Other churches in the same area must come to share our vision"

Not necessarily. They may share your overall mission (e.g. reach the lost, make disciples, become a worshipping community) but you will have a unique contribution to play as a company of God's people, and so will they. We are not competitive but complementary units in the body of Christ in each town, borough or city. We are all doing what God told us to do for the achievement of the overall picture and the welfare of that community.

10. "Because the senior leader gets the vision first, others have no role in developing it"

No. It is vital that others are consulted and act as a healthy sounding board, because they will perhaps be able to think and strategize better than the visionary himself. They will be able to see how this can become a reality because God has equipped them with the skills to formulate a project. "Many advisors make victory sure" (Proverbs 11:14).

11. "The one who has the vision must see it through"

Not necessarily. A vision may outlast the visionary (e.g. David *saw* the temple, but his son Solomon *built* it). God buries the workers but the work goes on. A vision is usually long-lasting. A big vision may last a generation or more, but it must pass from the visionary to the people, and then be personally owned by them.

12. "If you have vision it will spare you trouble and difficulty as you go forward"

It may spare you some troubles, but it will invite many others. It will save you from experiencing hopelessness, going nowhere, and gathering to you only miserable, depressed and difficult people. But it will bring many trials. Trials are God's vote of confidence in you. They refine faith, mature patience, develop character, fuel perseverance and confirm hope (Romans 5:1–5). Your ability to lead is bound to be tested. Each test is an opportunity to grow, and a stepping-stone to higher things. Every vision comes with a price tag.

Seven Demands of a God-Given Vision

In closing these two chapters about finding God's prophetic vision and direction for our lives, here is a summary of the seven requirements for receiving and implementing vision:

1. *Nurture* – Incubation, a gestation period of shaping hidden and secret information through meditation and prayer.

2. *Faith* – It may seem that you cannot do it. The fact is you can't. But God can! He is calling you to believe him for this vision.

3. *Obedience* – Paul's model is ours: "I was not disobedient to the vision from heaven" (Acts 26:19).

4. *Impartation* – Share it with others so that they can own it and catch something of your anointing in order to make this vision a reality.

5. *Planning* – "In his heart a man plans his course, but the Lord determines his steps" (Proverbs 16:9). "By wisdom a house is built, and through understanding it is established; through knowledge its rooms are filled with rare and beautiful treasures" (Proverbs 24:3–4). See also Proverbs 13:16 and 16:1.

6. *Sacrifice* – "It'll cost ya!" It always does.

7. Perseverance – We are human after all and, though God has given us a glimpse into his plans, we cannot always see or understand the whole. Sometimes, from our perspective, God's timing seems to run with more delays than the UK train network!

Chapter Eleven

Paul on the Prophetic – Healthy Relationships

One of our most valuable resources for understanding and developing prophetic ministry is the material found in the New Testament in the Pauline epistles. Some of these are powerfully relevant to our understanding of church life and practice today and offer an authoritative voice to resolve controversy, and a corrective to the mistakes and confusions we sometimes stray into. Paul was no stranger to controversy, confusion and misunderstanding on these matters since they arose frequently in the churches he founded! Though he was a mighty apostle with a travelling ministry, he also had a pastor's heart and much of his writing addresses the conflicts and differences of tradition and perspective that characterized the church congregations of his day as much as our own. We have a number of key passages to consider, beginning with some words of exhortation from what is probably one of the earliest of Paul's letters, if not his very first, and so one of the most significant documents of the church: 1 Thessalonians.

Church – Meeting God or Meeting People?

Now we ask you, brothers, to respect those who work hard among you, who are over you in the Lord and who admonish you. Hold them in the highest regard in love because of their work. Live in peace with each other. And we urge you, brothers, warn those who are idle, encourage the timid, help the weak, be patient with everyone. Make sure that nobody pays back wrong for wrong, but always try to be kind to each other and to everyone else.

Be joyful always; pray continually; give thanks in all circumstances, for this is God's will for you in Christ Jesus.

Do not put out the Spirit's fire; do not treat prophecies with contempt. Test everything. Hold on to the good. Avoid every kind of evil.

May God himself, the God of peace, sanctify you through and through. May your whole spirit, soul and body be kept blameless at the coming of our Lord Jesus Christ. The one who calls you is faithful and he will do it.

Brothers, pray for us. Greet all the brothers with a holy kiss. I charge you before the Lord to have this letter read to all the brothers.

The grace of our Lord Jesus Christ be with you.

1 Thessalonians 5:12–28

Paul never writes about prophecy in isolation, but addresses it in the context of the whole life of the church. In the same way, even when our discussion is focused on the ministry of prophecy in particular, we achieve a better quality of understanding, and a healthier all-round ministry, if we do not consider it in isolation from the realities of actual church life and daily living, but as we experience them, for this is not a theoretical issue and Paul himself never addresses it in isolation.

We first read about the founding of the church in Thessalonica in the book of Acts (Acts 17:1–10). Paul seems to have spent little more than three weeks establishing the new church congregation in this city before pressure of circumstances, and particularly active persecution from Jewish agitators, eventually drove him out. In the fifth chapter of 1 Thessalonians, Paul contrasts the order and peace of the life of the church built upon God's truth, with the world and its decaying moral values leading inevitably to the disintegration of the fabric of its social order and spiritual life. The world is drunk on its own self-worship, escapist and out of touch with ultimate reality, and is found frequently spouting gibberish while indulging its own imaginative fantasies as substitutes for truth.

Good Foundations

In this cultural context of social decadence and moral confusion, Paul is concerned that the church should be built well, fully alive and completely alert, well-informed and battle-ready, if not yet battle-hardened. In short, fit for action. In a social context that had lost its cohesion, the Thessalonian Christians were to model what it truly means to be fully human and living as God's family. This was no small goal to accomplish, since their founding apostle had taught and worked with them for only three weeks before he was gone, barely enough time to build anything. Yet amazing things had already happened.

What is particularly interesting for us to note, as we read this letter, is that the gift of prophecy was already under way even among these very immature believers – mere spiritual infants who hardly knew anything. Yet it is fascinating to note that, even in that short time, Paul made sure that the gift of prophecy was welcomed and operating significantly among them. We can only conclude that he saw prophecy as a foundational gift for healthy Christian communities and integral to their edification, building and establishment as full-blown churches. Prophecy was not an optional extra or add-on, nor a distant achievement for a spiritually mature élite when they finally emerged.

This offers us insight into one of Paul's priorities among new converts. He wanted fully functioning, Spirit-filled communities, operating in all of the gifts of the Spirit and especially the gift of prophecy. If the Thessalonians were ready for the ministry of prophecy, young in the faith as they were, then so are we. If it was a vital element in building the church then, it is a vital element in building the church now. Isn't it strange that this has not been a priority for many pastors, church planters and builders down the running centuries?

Strange, that those who honour the New Testament in terms of its inspiration, authority and sufficiency to guide and shape the lives of authentic churches, have consigned this particular gift to the dustbin of history as if it was no longer relevant and important to the church. How did we ever come to depart from the New Testament model? Paul considered prophecy vital to the life of the church at Thessalonica, knowing that it was already operating there because he had deliberately ensured that it was. "Do not treat prophecies with contempt," he writes, knowing that this was a reminder of his foundational instruction to the Thessalonians, something he had built into the basic principles of the life of a new church. Why then is prophecy so widely disregarded today?

God's Family – The Church

This letter addresses many important issues that lie at the heart of what it means to be a New Testament church, and particularly its sustained emphasis upon the theme of the church as a family. The last section of the letter reiterates and refocuses once again on the corporate life of the church; on what it means to be a community, indeed to be a true family in Christ. We have a number of models enabling us to conceptualize aspects of what the church is meant to be, all drawn from the imagery of the New Testament. We sometimes describe it as an army, equipped for spiritual warfare; sometimes as a flock of vulnerable but well-fed and protected sheep, trusting their under-shepherds, following their lead, nourished by and dependent on the Good Shepherd who sent them. Elsewhere, Paul speaks of it as a body, a temple and a city-state. But there are still other models of church that we may deduce from watching the early church in action.

We might think of it as a hospital for the walking wounded – a place to be healed. Less helpfully, and less flattering to some Christians, it could be seen as a crèche, full of babies not yet fully weaned from their milk, not yet on solid food (1 Corinthians 3:1–2; Hebrews 5:11–14). Some leaders need to be needed, and may behave as though the church was a crèche or pre-school day-care centre, whose members require interminable nurturing and are never allowed to mature into youth and adulthood. Again, we sometimes run the risk of creating an entertainment model – the church as a lecture theatre or concert hall, where the audience commutes in every Sunday to sit passively watching the stage performances in order to be amused for an hour and a half by a stirring speaker, choir and first-rate band, video screens, lights and smoke machines, and then home again for lunch and a snooze – until next week's rousing performance.

Such a model can result in a cold impersonalism in church life, a bunch of strangers together for an hour or so a week, but Paul wants us to think of the church as a family, a community of people whose lives are interlaced and interconnected with each other, where everyone has a contribution to make and a part to play, a family who gather to encounter God and to experience the Father's love – no passengers, no spectators, nobody's growth arrested at the baby stage for ever. As we embrace Paul's model of the church as family, what are the implications for us as we gather for friendship and fellowship, for work and witness and worship together?

1. Church is a time to honour your leaders (verses 12–13)

"Now we ask you, brothers, to respect those who work hard among you, who are over you in the Lord and who admonish you. Hold them in the highest regard in love because of their work. Live in peace with each other."

Some churches are so resistant to change, especially in connection with the work of the Holy Spirit, that a new minister coming to them is like a man climbing on board a moving train. He can get on, or he can get off, and possibly he can hold on through some tough bends until he's eventually thrown off and nearly killed in the process, but one thing he cannot seem to do is turn that church around in its loyal pursuit of God. This has been the experience of countless pastors in recent times, as it has been throughout church history. Paul is therefore laying the emphasis upon leadership first of all.

There has been an historical problem in the churches that looks like a kind of pendulum swing, as attitudes towards leadership swing back and forth from clericalism to anti-clericalism. We rush alternately back and forth to the two extremes of either placing our leaders on a pedestal, or rubbishing their role and significance altogether. Paul is seeking to set the balance correctly. He urges upon us three responsibilities:

a) We are to respect them (verse 12)

This is for two reasons. Firstly, it is because of their consistent hard work in caring for people. I remember a man once asked me, "Are you full time in Christian ministry or do you *work* for a living?"! Similarly, I've noticed that ministers are often on the receiving end of well-meant, chatty observations such as, "Ah yes, Christmas; that's your busy time, isn't it?" or "What a job! It's like fifty-two weeks of paid holiday a year, isn't it?". A surprising number of people genuinely suppose that ministers work only on Sundays and get paid "double time" for that. Speaking personally, I have never worked as hard in my life as I have since I became a pastor, and this has never let up in twenty-nine years. Paul expects pastors to "work hard". It is the norm. He uses a Greek word here that connotes the idea of tightened muscles, outpoured sweat and great expenditure of effort and energy. And so we are to appreciate such leaders. Secondly, we are to respect them because of the authority the Lord has given to them. They are "over you in the Lord and… admonish you" (verse 12b). They bear responsibility, to some degree, for our very lives. To honour them is therefore to honour God who appointed them.

b) We are also urged to hold them in the highest regard (verse 13)

God appoints them to take his people to places they have never been before in his will. Leaders, therefore, are not only people who know the way and go the way, they can also show the way and take others with them. When you have leaders like this they are worthy of high respect and esteem; they are worth following. But sadly, many congregations find themselves at odds with their leaders almost continuously. We are obsessed with the notion of Greek democracy in the Western world (though in ancient Greek society that excluded women, youths and slaves) and, though democracy may be the safest form of government for state governments today, the ancient Hebrews thought differently when it came to their community life together, and the Bible consistently reflects this. God leads by anointing and appointing leaders for his people, from lawgivers, judges, prophets and kings within Israel, to apostles, prophets, pastors, teachers, elders and deacons in the church of Jesus Christ – leaders through whom God spoke, and gave direction and guidance to his people. The church is a theocracy and not a democracy, it is ruled by God through his appointed leaders and not the people as a whole, and it is the business of people who give their allegiance to such leaders that they should also respect and esteem them and cheerfully follow their lead under Christ.

The Greek word translated "who are over you", *proistemenoi*, was used of a child's guardian with delegated authority from the parents, or a manager of a landowner's estate; sometimes it referred to a chieftain over a force of men. The idea is that the leaders of the church are to be esteemed both verbally and practically, honoured both by our words and also blessed and rewarded by material benefits from those they lead and serve (see also Galatians 6:6; 1 Corinthians 9:7–11; 1 Timothy 5:17), simply because of the role God has called them to exercise for the church's welfare.

c) We are also called to live at peace with them (verse 13b)

This may well have been added because Paul had noted that the primary role of church leaders is to teach and admonish Christ's people. They don't lead by bullying, nagging or by frightening outbursts and angry temper tantrums if they don't get their way. That would be abusive. But they do plainly and directly tell the truth for our benefit. Good leaders are meant to do that; when they do, we are to praise God for them, because there are so many compromisers in leadership today – in politics, in industry, in the world's institutions in general and, sadly, even in God's church. Paul is urging us to expect a quality of leadership that is worthy of our honour. John Stott sums it up like this: "You are not to despise them as if they were dispensable, or flatter them as if they were popes; instead, you are to follow them." Strong but gracious leadership, respected by the people of God, is the best context in which prophetic ministry can truly flourish.

2. Church is a time for serious fellowship with one another (verses 13b–15)

"Live in peace with each other. And we urge you, brothers, warn those who are idle, encourage the timid, help the weak, be patient with everyone. Make sure that nobody pays back wrong for wrong, but always try to be kind to each other and to everyone else."

Paul continues to prescribe the kind of church life in which prophecy can function well. It is to be characterized by peace (Greek: *eirene*; Hebrew: *shalom*). The word "peace" speaks of a situation where everything is in harmony in all of our relationships – vertically in our contacts with God and horizontally in our relationships with one another and the rest of creation around us. Leaders work hard to build this kind of family feel of harmony and peace, because that's the context in which the gifts of the Spirit operate best. When we join a church, we are to be motivated by covenant love, not convenient love. Convenient love says, "I'll hang around here until someone else or something better comes along" – an attitude that, sadly, characterizes all too many relationships in the wider world generally. By contrast, covenant love is a commitment to people you may not necessarily like, at least initially, but whom you will serve faithfully and eventually grow to truly love for who they are in Christ and what they will yet become in him. Indeed, they will also play an important part in helping you to become what you are destined to be in Christ also.

So Paul not only urges us to be at peace with our leaders, but to pursue harmony and authenticity with one another. Fellowship is living in unbroken reality with one another. This will demand of us great effort, and there is no magic wand or possibility of a sudden sprinkling with a bag of "fellowship dust" bought at the annual Christian Resources Exhibition, that can instantly accelerate the challenging process of transformation in our relationships with no effort on our part. Hence, the apostle's strong directives here.

Paul offers a series of practical exhortations, encouraging us to help those who are in need, and to warn the idle (verses 14–15). The Greek word for "the idle" is *ataktoi*, that is "truants" or "shirkers" who, in the context of both letters to the Thessalonians, were people who saw no need to bother with work any more since they believed that Christ was returning imminently (see 1 Thessalonians 4:11–12; 2 Thessalonians 3:6–13). "Warn those who are idle," says Paul. The church is a battleship not a cruise liner. No one on board is on vacation, simply there to enjoy the voyage to heaven while living a life of leisure as the hard work is done by a small number of paid staff, employed to meet our every need. On a battleship every person on board is a member of the crew and therefore has a job to do in both their daily work and ministry to their fellow crew members. There can be no idleness. This balance of supporting the weak and warning the idle is entirely appropriate for a family, where the tasks of the household are shared, and each person, from toddlers to grey-heads, is deserving of love and personally responsible for active cooperation together

Paul encourages us to speak the truth to one other, urging us to be honest, authentic and direct in our communication. Often, we settle for "close encounters of the evangelical kind" on a Sunday morning: "Good morning dear brother, how are you?" "Oh, splendid, thank you. God bless you. See you later." So we often retreat behind cheerful façades, constructed to maintain appearances and keep others out. That's not Paul's idea of church life. Rather, we are to speak the truth in love to one another, and so not only "warn the idle" but also "encourage the timid". The "timid" (Greek: *oligopsuchos*) are literally the "small-souled", those of a "nervous disposition". Churches have their fair share of "small-souled" people. They are always dithering with self-doubt, anxiously biting their nails and worrying about various problems and difficulties. They are no sooner lifted up one week, than they are down in the pits just days later. But we can put courage back into "small-souled" people, and timid mice can eventually become roaring lions by the power of the Spirit of God.

Paul also mentions "the weak" who, within the context of this epistle, are the morally weak, those who are prey and susceptible to sexual temptations from the surrounding culture (1 Thessalonians 4:1–8). He asks, in effect, Will you judge them, or will you help them? Paul's heart was to help them, as we can see from his earlier instructions on sexual immorality in chapter 4:1–8. Our preaching is to fortify believers, young and old, against an over-eroticized culture, and the weak in that particular area can be strengthened to make a stand and cultivate purity and self-control until such time as they are married and sex becomes appropriate for them. In a loving fellowship, where the commitment is so unconditional that the church becomes a family, this direct, honest, authentic expression of love is part of our prophetic ministry: lifting the fallen, supporting the weak, encouraging the faint-hearted.

3. Church is a time to encounter God (verses 16–17).

"Be joyful always; pray continually; give thanks in all circumstances, for this is God's will for you in Christ Jesus."

Some Christians look like they were baptised in vinegar or lemon juice, if they were ever baptised at all. And that may be the root of so many of their problems. They are so miserable. Yet Paul offers us the challenge of a way of life that doesn't wait for circumstances to change in order to make us happy, but rather promotes a strong view of God and his sovereign control of all things; this is the help we need to create the conditions whereby we feel we are "over the circumstances" rather than "under" them.

Worship is so much more than what we do on Sundays. What we do on Sundays is like the tip of the iceberg. Nine-tenths of our worship of God occurs elsewhere, and the rest of the week is meant to be the cultivation of a God-centred life. What we begin on Sunday in the gathering of the people of God overflows in God-centred living marked by a joy and gratitude that energises our work and play in the everyday. Our attitude of gratitude is itself partly what it means to worship, and this kind of constant awareness of God in the way we live our lives is the vital ingredient in leavening the atmosphere of a community or town, bringing the subversive and transformative effects of the kingdom of Christ to it; and if we Christians are not engaged in doing that, who will be? Archbishop William Temple once underlined the importance of worship in this way: "The world can be saved from political chaos and collapse by only one thing, and that is worship." No wonder that joy, prayer and thanksgiving are uppermost in Paul's mind here.

God has to move from the circumference to the centre of church life once again, no longer edged out by tradition, financial concerns, buildings and property or the-way-we-do-things-here. When God is the focus of everything, we will discover a new awe for him and excitement in him. If we are to return to the New Testament standard of saving the lost, healing the sick and delivering the demonized, then it will be because we have once again become "a house of prayer for all nations", a place and a community where Christ is gospelling the community through the words and works of his people again. Our God is willing; our God is able; the question is, are we?

Joy-filled Christian communities like this celebrate together regularly and always have much to celebrate. Every service or fellowship gathering will radiate the positive confidence – the *knowledge* – that God is real, God is gracious, and is pouring out his gifts upon us so that we can have existential, day-to-day encounters with him by the week. John Stott sums it up like this: "Every worship service should be a joyful celebration, a joyful rehearsal of what God has done for us through Jesus Christ. So let there be organs, trumpets and guitars and singing and let us make a joyful noise!" Amen!

4. Church is a time to really listen to God (verses 19–21, 27)

"Do not put out the Spirit's fire; do not treat prophecies with contempt. Test everything. Hold on to the good. Avoid every kind of evil... I charge you before the Lord to have this letter read to all the brothers."

Here, Paul speaks of both the prophetic word and the preached word, and we need both if we are to grow into the kind of churches God meant us to be. Paul's apostolic mandate for the churches he founded includes both sound preaching and substantial prophetic input. Paul's teaching follows the Old Testament model of the prophet being first called into the presence of God to listen, then sent forth to act and speak. Paul is eager to caution us against thoughtless dismissal or disrespectful contempt of such prophetic ministry in the churches today. We have no business rescinding these instructions as if they were no longer relevant. Paul in effect is saying, "Listen carefully to the Spirit's voice, discern his activity and do not extinguish his incandescent flame" (see verses 19–21). In other words, don't douse prophetic fire.

We can extinguish prophetic fire with our cold looks of discouragement when someone steps to the microphone to prophesy, or by responding to prophetic words with cynicism and sardonic comments. We "treat prophecies with contempt" when we are critical and picky about the way they are expressed, or when we freeze out prophetic ministry by receiving it in sullen silence. There are so many subtle ways to douse the flame of prophetic fire, leaving us room to pretend we said nothing and did nothing to block the development of ministries and gifts, and therefore hold God responsible for the absence of prophetic ministry in our midst.

As I made my preparations to write this book, I came across a recording of a sermon on 1 Corinthians 14, preached by a prominent evangelical pastor. I purchased it and listened to it eagerly, expecting to find fresh pointers and insights for my book. The more I listened, the more disappointment overwhelmed me. The pastor warned his hearers to be wary of charismatic renewal because of the confusion it causes. He told us that miraculous gifts have ceased and are only demonic counterfeits today, not to be sought or desired because they cause such havoc in the body of Christ – though if they had indeed ceased, as he strongly asserted, there would presumably be no need to warn people not to desire or practise them since they are unavailable anyway. This is something like warning people not to collect counterfeit £7 notes. No one would be tempted to do this, for none of them are actually in circulation. Counterfeiters only imitate real denominations of £10, £20 and £50 notes.

If demonic counterfeits of spiritual gifts exist, and they do, then the devil must know the real thing actually exists. There was no mention in this taped sermon I heard, of Paul's urging us to "eagerly desire spiritual gifts, especially the gift of prophecy" from that very chapter (1 Corinthians 14:1), nor of his instruction in the same context to both move in the gifts and ensure peaceable order in the way they are practised: "Therefore, my brothers, be eager to prophesy, and do not forbid speaking in tongues. But everything should be done in a fitting and orderly way" (1 Corinthians 14:39–40).

I have no way of knowing what unfortunate experiences may have influenced this preacher to become so disillusioned and distrustful in his attitude towards charismatic renewal: but I do know that I, personally, in many years of pastoral experience, have seen nothing but good flow from the gifts of the Holy Spirit, even in the imperfect context of day-to-day church life as they are manifested in the lives of weak, flawed and sometimes sinful human beings. I also count it a very grave thing to discard and discredit so lightly the wisdom, authority and teaching of the Scriptures in this way.

Paul makes it plain beyond mistake that we are not merely to avoid resisting the Holy Spirit's work in prophesying, but to actively and eagerly promote it as well as responsibly weigh and test it. The word used in the Greek for this weighing or testing means "to test with a view to its approval". Its primary intent is not faultfinding, but rather confirmation and positive approval. Though, occasionally, as we consider a prophecy, we may not be satisfied that this is an authentic word from

God, our mindset as we approach prophetic ministry is to be positive and enthusiastic about it and not suspicious and hostile towards it. We are testing the word in order to discover what the Lord is saying to us through it; to filter out the fish from the bones, not the bones from the fish. We are testing with a view to approval. That's how goldsmiths test gold; that's how merchants test diamonds and silversmiths test silver. We would never discard precious metals because they were mined with dirt and base minerals attached to them. Instead, we refine the raw material or cut and polish it to show it to its best advantage so that the precious bullion or jewel may shine forth. This is an entirely different way of viewing things: the aim is to honour the gifts of the Holy Spirit so that the church will become less like a fridge and more like a furnace, because the Spirit's fire is burning there and part of his work is to refine the gift of prophecy also.

But it is also vital that we note the importance that this passage attaches to the public reading and preaching of God's Word in the Scriptures (verse 27). We must be exposed regularly to whole chunks of the Bible, along with a detailed explanation of their true meaning and application to our lives, conducted by those gifted and called to do this. We need both the written Word of God in Scripture and the *rhema* or spoken Word of God in prophecy. It is the written Word of God that is finally authoritative for all the people of God, in all places and at all times, but prophecy can also contribute the more local, specific and present-day application of the timeless word for a particular people group. The Word of God is always pertinent and relevant to our life as a church of Jesus Christ, and our first calling as a prophetic people is to be summoned into the presence of God in order to listen to what he is saying to his church, both in the eternal truths of the Scriptures and in his still, small voice in the hearts of those who are able to hear him.

5. Church is a time to really experience God (verses 23–28)

"May God himself, the God of peace, sanctify you through and through. May your whole spirit, soul and body be kept blameless at the coming of our Lord Jesus Christ. The one who calls you is faithful and he will do it" (verses 23–24).

How do we experience God? Well, I suppose in some ways it is "better felt that telt" (as we say in Lancashire), but sometimes we have a direct, first-hand experience of the presence of God, and other times we are touched by him through human encounters. As Paul speaks of the Spirit's touch in verses 23 and 24, "May *God himself* sanctify you through and through" – intimate phraseology that speaks of God's direct dealings with us and a very intimate drawing near of the holy to us, both as individuals and as a gathered church. As we make room for these encounters in our worship and fellowship meetings, as well as in our personal daily lives, God comes to impart a transforming touch to the whole person – spirit, soul and body. He is there to illuminate our intellects, speaking to us and informing us. He is there to affect our emotions and move us deeply. He is there to engage our wills and lead us to significant choices and decisions. He is there to heal our bodies and disturbed minds of fears, sickness and suffering. We need to experience God personally and directly through the Spirit's touch.

But, of course, there is also human agency that mediates the presence of God to us. Paul writes, "Brothers, pray for us. Greet all the brothers with a holy kiss" (verses 25–26). God doesn't just lob his blessings to us over the Milky Way! He blesses you through the people you stand or sit with as the church gathers. So, as well as encouraging our direct communion with God: "Pray for us" (verse 25), Paul also encourages positive, demonstrative love in the church family as well: "Greet [one another] with a holy kiss" (verse 26). A "kiss" or "physical demonstration of affection" varies from culture to culture. It may be common to shake hands, rub noses, kiss cheeks or simply hug one another depending on the country or location. But whatever the appropriate cultural expression might be, Paul says, "Let it be holy". A "holy kiss" is an expression of loving affection and not an incitement to lust, and implies an embrace characterized by modesty, pure intention and respect. Serious damage can result from exploiting the opportunity for a "holy kiss", the sign of God's *shalom*, as a covert means of romantic expression and inappropriate, stolen intimacy in church.

When we gather as God's church, we are meant to meet both with God and one another as brothers and sisters in his family. The charismatic gifts serve these purposes admirably. There are many churches you visit which feel kindly and welcoming – like a nice, friendly social club – but where the movement of the Holy Spirit is never felt in power and never really expected. There are also great preaching centres where you can go to hear the word of God proclaimed with power; you learn a lot, but you never feel that you belong; you've attended a successful event in an auditorium full of visitors, but you were not welcomed into a family.

The vision Paul holds out to us, in this wonderful epistle, is of a fellowship of believers whose closeness is as honest, direct, authentic, comforting, encouraging and nourishing as a family; and where God's power and glory is the heart and soul of the worship. A healthy church is a place where we meet with God *and* with people in life-changing preaching, authentic prophecy, and healing of body, mind and spirit. And God isn't jealous about that at all, because he has commanded that this should be the case.

Chapter Twelve

Paul on the Prophetic –
Men and Women Together

The next passage we shall consider raises issues of spiritual authority, role relationships between men and women, and what has sometimes become known as the ecclesiastical version of the "battle of the sexes". It is found within a notoriously difficult and controversial section of 1 Corinthians.

> I praise you for remembering me in everything and for holding to the teachings, just as I passed them on to you.
>
> Now I want you to realise that the head of every man is Christ, and the head of the woman is man, and the head of Christ is God. Every man who prays or prophesies with his head covered dishonours his head. And every woman who prays or prophesies with her head uncovered dishonours her head – it is just as though her head were shaved. If a woman does not cover her head, she should have her hair cut off; and if it is a disgrace for a woman to have her hair cut or shaved off, she should cover her head. A man ought not to cover his head, since he is the image and glory of God; but the woman is the glory of man. For man did not come from woman, but woman from man; neither was man created for woman, but woman for man. For this reason, and because of the angels, the woman ought to have a sign of authority on her head.
>
> In the Lord, however, woman is not independent

of man, nor is man independent of woman. For as woman came from man, so also man is born of woman. But everything comes from God. Judge for yourselves: Is it proper for a woman to pray to God with her head uncovered? Does not the very nature of things teach you that if a man has long hair, it is a disgrace to him, but that if a woman has long hair, it is her glory? For long hair is given to her as a covering. If anyone wants to be contentious about this, we have no other practice – nor do the churches of God.

1 Corinthians 11:1–16

Some allege that when Paul wrote these words in 1 Corinthians 11, he was unwittingly betraying the cultural bias of his training as a Jewish rabbi and, further to that, he was influenced also by his own personal psychological history that had resulted in a morbid fear and dislike of women. Such objections are well-meant as support for women in their struggle against oppression, but they are misguided and inaccurate as representations of the true facts. Paul was no misogynist, and he is actually giving the Corinthians, and therefore us also, instruction concerning the context in which prophecy best functions. Elsewhere, he has a great deal to say about women which is utterly liberating, truly honouring and full of appreciation for the part many had played in his own mission and ministry as partners and team-members alongside men (see, for example, Romans 16:1–16; Philippians 4:2–3; Colossians 4:10–15).

Prophecy functions best not only in an environment of family love and fellowship such as 1 Thessalonians 5 depicts, but also where God's will for men and women in their created gender distinctions and role relationships is truly honoured. This is an issue of enormous controversy in the body of Christ today, reflecting the turbulent currents of thought in the wider world regarding sexuality and gender. There, men and women are considered interchangeable and there is a progressive denial of the gender distinctions God has designed and created between men and women. There has been a blurring of these created differences and a move towards unisexuality, homosexuality, bisexuality and such practices as cross-dressing, same-sex partnerships and surgical sex-changes. 1 Corinthians 11 is a crucial passage expounding the timeless and unchanging biblical treatment of gender differences and role relationships between men and women in creation and in the church. We are paying attention to it here because it has great relevance to the functioning of prophecy in the local church.

In the Beginning

God launched the flow of authentic spirituality in his world as far back as Eden, before the Fall. This state is now being progressively recovered in Christ in order to assist and facilitate the movement, once again, of his divine power among us, his redeemed people. Sin must not be permanently allowed to vandalize God's original intentions for humankind. It is sin that stops the flow of God's power and, biblically speaking, sin is any denial of or departure from the revealed will of God.

The primary issue here in 1 Corinthians 11 is the flow of divine *power* and *authority* in the church. It is helpful to think of the distinctions and overlap between these two words. Imagine an Indian *mahout* with an elephant. The road is blocked by a fallen tree. The mahout wants to travel along the road to the next village but has nothing like the physical power needed to move the tree. The elephant has the power to move the tree but has no plans in mind, and waits patiently to obey the instructions the mahout gives. The mahout is the one in authority. When the mahout uses his authority in telling the elephant what to do, and the elephant uses his power in moving the fallen tree, then the way forward is cleared and the journey can go on. Power with authority behind it makes things happen.

In Greek, *dunamis* ("power") means "working strength to accomplish a task". How we need power in the church of Christ today! Without this, what changes can we effect? We can change the lightbulbs or the colour of the paintwork but little more. In the New Testament, authority (Greek: *exousia*) is "the right or permission to act on behalf of another". So we need both "might" *and* "right", because might is not always right!

Imagine an unarmed but uniformed policeman encountering a gang of heavily armed thieves robbing a bank. The policeman has the badge (authority) but no power (a gun). The robbers have power (guns) but no authority (permission to use them). God's plan is that his people have both authority and power. God wants to give us power to change both people and circumstances in line with the will of God, and also grants us full permission to use it. You need power to face opposition and unfavourable circumstances and yet still be able to win the day. And authority is official permission from God to use his power to achieve those ends.

The Bible understands authority, not as freedom to do whatever you like, but as freedom under control and fully accountable, seeing all human communities and institutions as ultimately rooted in God's kingdom order and therefore answerable to God. The norm is power with God-given authority to back it up. The former is given to us by the Spirit, the latter from the Father and the Son. So, in the Old Testament, the prophets, judges and kings were figures of authority not because of who they were, but because of who God is, and how his kingdom works. God called and ordained them to their service and status, and their authority was exercised with accountability to him. Because it was God himself who gave them their orders, this accountability did not *lessen* their authority and power but rendered it *far greater*.

In the New Testament, in the story of Jesus' healing of the centurion's servant, Jesus marvels at the faith of the Roman soldier who responds to Christ's offer to visit his servant at home with the insightful words, "I do not deserve to have you come under my roof. But just say the word, and my servant will be healed. For I myself am a man under authority, with soldiers under me. I tell this one, 'Go,' and he goes; and that one, 'Come,' and he comes. I say to my servant, 'Do this,' and he does it" (Matthew 8:5–10).

What is interesting here is that the centurion describes himself not as a man of authority or in authority, but *under* authority. It is his submission to a greater authority (that of Rome) that gives his commands the whole weight and force of the empire behind them. The centurion recognized that Christ's Word would go forth with power, because his life was submitted in total obedience to the will and authority of God. God would heal through Jesus, at a remote distance, without the need for Christ to be personally present. To exercise authority we have to be under authority, the authority of God.

This is delegated responsibility because it is the right to command changes in people's beliefs and behaviour, and nobody has that right inherently – it has to be authorized by God. We would refuse to listen to anyone who wants to impose their will upon us without proper authority to do so. No church leaders or community will be spiritually effective and authoritative unless they are in full submission to the Word of God and rightly aligned with his will. Therefore, for example, it is right to ask the question of anyone in leadership in a church, "Who put them there?" If they are there by human appointment alone, then there's going to be trouble. If they received 75 percent of the vote in the church meeting and that's the only reason they are there, it isn't a good enough reason. The question is, "Did God put them there? Has God authorized them? Has God given them responsibility?", because if he has then he will also give them the power to back up his appointment, and things will change for the better, provided such leaders are seeking to carry out his will.

Our contemporary society places a high value on freedom, independence, human rights and equality, which has to be good news – if God himself is allowed to define all of those terms and not rebellious human beings. Yet, at the same time, prizing those values highly runs the risk that sin will cause us to despise and reject authority, and become increasingly autonomous and anarchic in conduct, pursuing individualism and lawlessness. Such people eventually turn into serious losers. Clean power leaks away from them, and unclean power replaces it. They become lost, lonely, dangerous and bewildered. As the Bible puts it, "God sets the lonely in families, he leads forth the prisoners with singing; but the rebellious live in a sun-scorched land" (Psalm 68:6). God's will for human beings is the loving, respectful, traditional structure of a caring family, and those who reject his ways eventually experience emotional aridity and spiritual drought.

In the home, as in the church, there is a God-ordained authority structure which, just as in the healing of the centurion's servant, permits the flow of life-changing power for the benefit of others. In order to exercise this authority you have to be voluntarily under authority, and that's why this is so pertinent an issue in the home and the church in connection with the matter of positive and mutually beneficial male–female role relations. The submission and authority that Paul is addressing here is an essential component of these relationships both in the home and in the church.

The submission of women to male authority in home and church is paradoxically in order to elevate them. This often comes as a surprise to some who have only experienced the abuse of authority before, since this is not about the *loss* of a woman's authority but rather its *increase* and *enhancement*. This is real "girl power"! The disputed key passages where Paul discusses role relationships between men and women are 1 Corinthians 11:3–10, 1 Timothy 2:11–15 and Ephesians 5:22–24. In each case we see that Paul consistently focuses his understanding of the distinct roles of men and women on the thesis that women prosper best under the primary leadership of men.

In the home this will be under the headship of their husbands, and in the church it will be in ministering as part of mixed teams of men and women, under the authority of duly appointed godly men who encourage others to function fully according to their God-given gifts. Paul grounds his reasons for stating this position with such clarity and insight upon three fundamental factors. None of them are culturally conditioned by the climate of his times nor by his pre-Christian background of an anti-women bias within rabbinical Judaism, for Christ had set Paul free from this heritage and taught him to value and help women to enjoy their newfound privileges in Christ. Nor is his teaching some kind of weak concession to the customs of the wider culture of the Greco-Roman world, for here Paul was just as countercultural as his master Jesus was. Instead, he founds his theology on three timeless and unchanging realities:

1. The nature of the Godhead

"Now I want you to realize that the head of every man is Christ, and the head of the woman is man, and the head of Christ is God" (1 Corinthians 11:3).

There is a correlation between male–female relationships and those that subsist within the Holy Trinity, an eternal flow of mutual submission and authority even within the Godhead itself, among the mutually indwelling persons of the Trinity, and this is part of the eternal being of God and not just a new arrangement between the Persons of the Trinity in the economy of creation and salvation. There are distinctions of authority and responsibility within the Trinity itself and these are ontological (to do with the very nature of the Godhead or "Godness" of God). Therefore the different roles exercised economically among the Trinity of divine Persons in terms of creation and redemption are true to their eternal nature as God, and this is reflected in men and women made in God's image.

Consider the term "head" (Greek: kephalē). Some argue that this word simply means "source" and carries no idea whatsoever of authority within it, only the concept of origin. But lexical studies have shown that out of 2,336 uses of this word in the Greek literature of the time, nearly all carry this sense of possessing or having authority, with only a few disputed exceptions that could possibly convey the idea of a "source" in a small minority of instances. So in verse 3 (of our passage from 1 Corinthians 11), we are told that "the head of Christ is God" and this means that Christ submits to the Father's headship and that this relationship is non-reversible. The Father doesn't submit to the Son, but the Son submits to the Father. It's irreversible, as it should be also in the role relationships we have been talking about between men and women.

But further, because of the nature of the Trinity, headship and submission do not necessarily imply superiority, inferiority or inequality, for they do not do so in the Godhead. Therefore, women are not inferior to men, any more than Jesus is inferior to the Father, or the Holy Spirit is to the Father and the Son. But there is an order that God wants us to maintain so that his power can flow cleanly through families and into the church. The members of the Trinity are all equal in power, dignity, status and Godhead but, alongside this fact, there is also mutual submission and servanthood within the Trinity, and has been from all eternity. This should be reflected also in our homes and churches as we who are made in God's image cheerfully accept submission and servanthood towards one another in the Lord – differentiation of roles, yes, but not inequality of persons, nor diminishment of being. The Father is equal to the Son and both are equal to the Holy Spirit, but the Father is the begetter and director of the Son, and the Father and Son are the senders of the Holy Spirit, who proceeds from them (John 14:26, 16:7). This beautiful, generous interrelationship of submission and servanthood within the Trinity is the pattern that will release power and joy in our domestic relationships within marriage and the family at home and in our gathered life together with others in the church.

2. The created order of Adam and Eve (1 Corinthians 11:3, 8)

Paul's consistent position was that God's original creation, narrated in Genesis 1–2, revealed his perpetual arrangements and will for men and women in their future relationships together. Genesis 1–2 is absolutely foundational to Paul's thinking, as it should be for ours, on just about every important issue we face today. Many assert that Genesis teaches distorted myths about history, origins, science, time, space, sin, death, men and women, sexuality and the family – leaving us free to reject them for more "enlightened" views such as naturalism and evolution. Everything we find there, we are told, is pre-scientific, pre-historic and culturally outmoded. We can experiment with new models and paradigms for all of these institutions and activities, as if God had not spoken and told us the "flaming truth" or "true-capital-T-truth" at all (the late Francis Schaeffer's graphic way of denying the alleged mythological nature of these narratives). Actually, because Genesis 1–3 is foundational to all that the Bible says elsewhere on these issues, we have to come to terms with that and take these chapters very seriously indeed, taking great care to expound them correctly. The creation order affects both the domestic and ecclesiastical situation for men and women.

"The head of every man is Christ, and the head of the woman is man" (verse 3 of our passage from 1 Corinthians 11). Here, the Greek word *aner* (man) and *gunaikos* (woman), can mean either "man" and "woman" or "husband" and "wife". It is not clear if Paul has one or both meanings in mind. He does not state that all the women in the church are to be submitted to all the men; it is a submission only to the men who have positions of responsibility respective to those women in each particular active sphere. A husband has responsibility in his home, and the elders of the church hold final responsibility in the church. The women are only to be submitted to the particular men who have a legitimate God-given authority in that sphere and not to all of the men in general.

Again, in verses 8–10 of 1 Corinthians 11 we read, "For man did not come from woman, but woman from man; neither was man created for woman, but woman for man. For this reason, and because of the angels, the woman ought to have a sign of authority on her head." Similarly, 1 Timothy 2:11–15 reads:

> A woman should learn in quietness and full submission.
> I do not permit a woman to teach or to have authority over a man; she must be silent. For Adam was formed first, then Eve. And Adam was not the one deceived; it was the woman who was deceived and became a sinner. But women will be saved through childbearing – if they continue in faith, love and holiness with propriety.

Paul sets out clearly for us here the creation order in which God made Adam and Eve in the beginning, and this is the origin of linear, hierarchical distinctions in human relationships, in order that clean power and authority may flow in a context of mutual service and submission without becoming contaminated by human misunderstanding, distortion and sin. Paul makes clear that the Lord gave Adam primary responsibility in his marriage by reason of the fact of his primogeniture, or "firstborn" status. Adam was made first in time. This was a divinely planned and created order implying hierarchy, and designed to safeguard God's perfect paradise from the encroachment of uncleanness and the invasion of the powers of darkness, as long as God's arrangements and personal authority were respected by Adam and Eve (Genesis: 1:26-28; 2:15-17). If this authority structure – God, the man, then the woman – was respected and observed in their joint task of dominion over the animals (including the serpent) and the rest of the created order in God's world, then the evils that have invaded our planet like the demonic squatters of rebellion, sickness, suffering and death would never have been allowed to enter. They are all a result of the Fall, the "great thud" or bottom-up reversal that their rebellion ignited (Genesis 3; Romans 5:12ff). Paul argues his case from the clear record of the Genesis narrative (Genesis 1–3). These chapters are the ethical and theological foundation for the rest of the Bible. Everything else that the Bible teaches on men, women, marriage, sex, family, government, nationhood, ethnic diversity, business, work, scientific discovery and technology, human authority etc. flows in a continuous, connected trajectory from the norms of the creation narrative. No wonder these chapters have been subject to continuous assault, misinterpretation, denial and rejection. They really are that important. And the relevant facts are these:

> a) The woman was made after the man – "For Adam was formed first, then Eve" (1 Timothy 2:13)

We called this his "firstborn" status, sometimes termed primogeniture. In the Hebrew household the firstborn son had a peculiar degree of responsibility. He would inherit a double portion of his father's inheritance because he would have a greater responsibility for the running of the family than his brothers upon the death of their father. Here, Paul is telling us that Adam was the firstborn. He was made at a different *time* from Eve. I have heard people ridicule Paul's statements here as if they were utterly irrelevant, but Paul wrote them for a reason. Eve was made after the man, not simultaneously with him and certainly not before him, signifying the divine intention to initiate an order and authority structure that God has ordained for all men and women.

> b) Eve had a different origin from the man – "For man did not come from woman, but woman from man…" (1 Corinthians 11:8)

Hers was a derived origin. He was her source, in a very real sense, but one which simultaneously underlines his headship in Paul's theology. She was made *from* the man. God took living tissue from Adam's side, a mass of flesh, bone, skin, blood vessels and fat, in probably the first "cloning" experiment in history – and it worked! Matthew Henry, the Puritan Bible commentator, observes astutely that this was, "Not out of his head to rule over him, nor from his feet to be trampled on by him, but from out of his side to be near to him, from under his arm to be protected by him and from near his heart to be loved by him." He is right. This is not about domination and oppression. A man's headship is there to release the full potential of all those God has placed under his authority, especially his wife and his children (and if it doesn't result in that, it is not godly authority).

> c) Each had a different purpose and role in their creation – Eve was to function as Adam's partner or helpmeet/helper; his closest companion, serving alongside him in the task of dominion (Genesis 1:26–28; 2:18–22)

She was made *for* the man. Adam's role was primary, for he was the initiator. Eve's role was that of his closest ally and partner in this global task. Woman is designed both physically and psychologically to act as the nurturer and carer of life and order, in total support of the man in his role as initiator, chief executive officer, director, inspirer and visionary. His wife is his full partner in the wide range of tasks that God calls them both to accomplish together. Proverbs 31 indicates that she, too, legitimately carries a wide range of authority and initiative in the exercise of her role, domestically, economically, in business, and in shared honour and rewards for their achievements together.

Wherever these divinely ordained authority structures are denied or overturned, the emasculation of men and the unseemly domination of women over men is the result. Masculine power atrophies as women become stronger and more masculinised than truly feminine, giving room for dark demonic forces to enter and damage God's order and plan for human relationships. Witchcraft, control, intimidation and manipulation begin to distort male/female encounters, creating ugly caricatures of God's beautiful initial design in their first creation. The best biblical illustration of this is the narrative of Ahab and Jezebel (1 Kings 17–21).

The creation ordinance goes to the very roots of our instincts. Paul speaks about the witness of nature (1 Corinthians 11:13-15), the inner sense of propriety that tells us instinctively when something is wrong, and is uneasy if men are not acting like men, and women are not behaving like women. Grace does not obliterate nature, but rather it enhances and endorses it. When we observe that something is not natural, it is a valid biblical way to approach and judge what is morally right or wrong, particularly in sexual behaviour. Homosexuality and lesbianism are not natural (Romans 1:21–27). They are unnatural because the term "natural" essentially means "the way God the creator designed and made things to be in the first place". And even though our perspective may have been distorted through sin, we still instinctively know when a situation is not right. We may be too cowardly to say so; we may keep quiet about it; we may even choose to just suffer in silence. But it is time the church spoke up and said, "This is not the way it's meant to be. God did not design us this way."

Many warped behavioural and immoral practices today are causing great difficulties to both individuals and whole societies, simply because they are unnatural. This is particularly true of sexual practices like paedophilia, bestiality, homosexuality, fornication, adultery and solo-sex. Thomas Aquinas affirms, "Grace does not scrap nature; it brings it to perfection."

3. The redemptive pattern established in Christ (see 1 Corinthians 11:3–4, 11; Ephesians 5:22–24)

Paul now locates his instructions with regard to male–female role relationships within the perspectives offered by the newer situation of our redemption and recreation in Christ, something he develops more fully in his letter to the Ephesians. 1 Corinthians 11:11 alludes to the great recovery of divine order in Christ: "In the Lord, however, woman is not independent of man, nor is man independent of woman." This statement enforces our mutual interdependence upon one another as men and women, a theme we shall develop later. But this mutually beneficial arrangement does not eliminate the fact that we are different by design, something that Paul makes clear in Ephesians 5. Here Paul addresses husbands and wives directly, explaining the creation ordinance of gender roles and distinctions: "Wives, submit to your husbands as to the Lord. For the husband is the head of the wife as Christ is the head of the church, his body, of which he is the Saviour. Now as the church submits to Christ, so also wives should submit to their husbands in everything" (Ephesians 5:22–24).

The fall into sin of both Adam and Eve, and the entrance of sin into the world as a consequence, distorted the nature and respective roles of them both, and of their offspring. However, due to God's grace to us in Christ, through the redemption and reconciliation accomplished by him, God does not render these roles and distinctions redundant, but restores them. Paul's instructions to Spirit-filled married couples are in keeping with all the timeless principles that we have seen so far, and create the foundation for the healthiest and happiest of marriages, which are now possible for us through the gospel.

Our generation stands in need of hearing and heeding this wisdom again and again, because there is a leakage of power in marriages and families everywhere. Many women in the world have been used, abused and oppressed by men; and women in the church have sometimes been neglected, sidelined and devalued to such a degree that they have been kept merely "hushed and hatted", their gifts and potential crushed in a misguided attempt to implement these very scriptures. They have lost the power God would have channelled through them, and the way to recover it is to reinstate loving leadership in the home and the church, honouring God's authority, and understanding how human authority depends on a true alignment with the will and Word of God. Women are to flourish and reach fully their divinely given power and potential under God, in the home and in the church, under the blessing of the primary leadership of godly men who have their best interests at heart. Such leadership is designed to facilitate the equipping and releasing of women's potential, just as Christ himself does.

Galatians 3:28 is sometimes quoted in support of a different viewpoint on these matters. It reads, "There is neither Jew nor Greek, slave nor free, male nor female, for you are all one in Christ Jesus", and has been called the "Magna Carta of Christian feminism" by those who interpret it as a mandate for total egalitarianism and interchangeability between the sexes. But, while it is right to celebrate the equal dignity and worth of redeemed men and women in Christ that this passage upholds, it is also essential to hold in mind that the same apostle who wrote Galatians 3:28 also wrote the passages we have considered above. Galatians 3:28 does not address the issue of the respective *roles* of men and women in the church and domestic scene, but upholds their equal status as justified and adopted children of God, with access to full "sonship" (used inclusively for men and women) through faith in the gospel of Christ, within the family of God.

The context makes this plain. The preceding two verses, as well as the discussion in the epistle as a whole, are concerned with the matter of justification and the saving effects of union with Christ by faith alone. This makes us completely equal in status, worth and dignity before God and in his kingdom, without obliterating the divinely created differences between us. Regardless of race, sex or social standing, we are "all one in Christ Jesus". This is the theme of Galatians. The epistle does not discuss role relationships within the church, but the separate but related issue of salvation in Christ. Paul discusses the vexed question of role relationships elsewhere in his other epistles. It would be quite wrong to countermand Paul's writings on the issue of gender differences, roles and male–female complementarity, on the basis of Galatians 3:28 taken out of context.

God's Pattern for All Time

These three principles, then, the nature of the Godhead, the created order of Adam and Eve, and the redemptive pattern established in Christ, are to be normative for the cultural expression and characteristics of Christian life and witness, whether in the privacy of individual households or in the public gathering of the household of faith.

In our present age, just as in the times when the epistles of Paul were written, we are called to be truly countercultural where that culture has been warped by sin. In the words of Samuel Rayan, "A candle light is a protest at midnight. It is a nonconformist. It says to the darkness: 'I beg to differ.'"

The Greek background of 1 Corinthians 11 is very interesting and relevant for us as we look around at today's world. Prevalent at Corinth, particularly, but in many other Greek cities as well, were the mystery religions – alternative spiritualities developed for those who either had no access at all to the state-sponsored, official religious cultus of the time (slaves, women, foreigners) or who were bored or disillusioned with the formal civic and religious ceremonies and paraphernalia of the Greco-Roman world. These cults appealed enormously to marginalized people, because they appeared to offer certain moral and spiritual freedoms, as well as escape from the drudgery and repression of their daily lives. Sexual licence, liberal consumption of alcohol, and cathartic release of emotions through dance and drugs, were intrinsic elements of worship in the cults of Dionysus and Cybele, especially during the various festival meals eaten to cement spiritual union with the deities. Religious rites were noisy, uninhibited affairs where the women danced like whirling dervishes, with noisy and wild ululations to the gods. Sex, seen as a means of bringing fruitfulness and productivity to the land, was a regular feature of religious observance, often resulting in the grossest forms of sexual excess. Released from the social constraints of daily life, and frequently very drunk, people's sexual exploration ventured into very experimental territory, reversing sexual roles between men and women or dominance roles between highborn and slave. Cross-dressing, bisexuality and homosexuality – no taboos were left untouched. To the twenty-first century citizen, this scenario may seem all too familiar, reminding us of the clubbing scene and the lifestyles of famous celebrities. Excess, decadence and debauchery were all as much a feature of Paul's cultural environment as they are of ours.

Keep Your Hat On?

Many of Paul's converts at Corinth came from just such a cultural milieu, and you will know that these are the kinds of issues he addresses in the two letters to the Corinthian church because he was dealing with the remnants of habits and expectations derived from their former days in the pagan cultic worship they had previously known. The issue, as it were, "came to a head" in Corinth over the question of head coverings (1 Corinthians 11:1–16). Whether or not Paul is referring to a literal veil or some kind of headdress here, a scarf, or perhaps even a feminine hairstyle, is not the central point at issue, though it has been the focus of much controversy.

"If a woman does not cover her head, she should have her hair cut off; and if it is a disgrace for a woman to have her hair cut or shaved off, she should cover her head," writes the apostle (1 Corinthians 11:6). Many church leaders have interpreted this to mean that a woman should both wear her hair long and wear a head covering also. On the other hand Paul says (verse 15), "For long hair is given to her as a covering", which would suggest that the long hair of the woman is itself the form of covering that Paul had in mind. Either way, his point is that "the woman ought to have a sign of authority on her head" (verse 10). The crux of the matter is not whether she does or does not wear a hat or veil, but whether she dresses distinctively as a woman and is easily identified as such, and thus makes apparent her cheerful affirmation of God's created order in male–female relationships.

My own view is that Paul is telling us that a woman's hair is given to her for her covering, and that he is talking about a long, feminine hairstyle here, then asking, "Does not the very nature of things teach you that if a man has long hair, it is a disgrace to him, but that if a woman has long hair it is her glory?" (verses 14–15a).

His instructions amount to the conclusion that men should look like men and women like women, and that the clear, God-created distinction of male and female should be made unmistakeably apparent in their style of dress and especially in the way that they wore their hair, perhaps because this would be the aspect of their appearance most evident in a public gathering, and also because in a mixed community of Greeks and Jews the wrong signals could inadvertently be given by loose, unbound, uncovered hair, which amounted to a sexual invitation. So Paul's instructions cover the two points of gender distinctiveness and modesty in dress.

He sees this detail of dress and presentation as of great significance, because the covering, he says, is a "sign of authority on her head" (verse 10). In the context of the argument as a whole, this can only mean a sign of the male authority that she willingly acknowledges and cheerfully submits to, and also a sign of the authority that she therefore exercises for God as a consequence of her willingness to minister under this same flow of authority. Covering her head signals her gladness at being a woman with no desire to usurp or adopt a masculine role or appearance. She is delighted with the way God has made her. To be cheerfully under authority is also to be able powerfully to exercise it. This, as we have already seen, is how biblical authority works.

The church, in living counterculturally to its sociological environment, establishes a very distinctive and recognisable culture of its own. Therefore Paul also appeals to the value of custom, the recognisable shape of church tradition as it formed its stance towards the conflicting norms of the surrounding pagan world. Surprisingly, church tradition is used in support of his argument (verse 16): "If anyone wants to be contentious about this, we have no other practice – nor do the churches of God." Paul is here alluding to the consistency of practice between the apostolic churches that he and others had planted everywhere, in their beliefs and conduct on these issues: they had no other custom. And so, if we aspire to become truly apostolic in both belief and behaviour in our churches, and thus conformed to New Testament norms, then we must listen to what the apostle tells us that church life should look like. This is what it means to be an apostolic church; it means that we are gladly submitted to the apostolic authority of Paul and the New Testament epistles in their directions to both churches and individuals.

In all that we have said in this matter it is important to stay with the thought that propriety, modesty and gender distinctiveness, while both necessary and important, are secondary issues to the main focus of our study, which is about moving in the prophetic and allowing ourselves to becomes channels of the power and grace of God's Holy Spirit.

The purpose of men looking like men and women looking like women is not that the church might become unimpeachably respectable, but that we may be so truly aligned with God's intention and will for our lives that our community can become a lightning rod for his glory.

This is why, in verse 7, Paul says, "A man ought not to cover his head, since he is the image and glory of God; but the woman is the glory of man." The man is not to cover his head because he is the reflector of God's glory, and a woman covers hers because she is a reflector of man's glory. What does it mean to reflect glory? It means there is a channel or flow of God's anointing and power operating upon them both in a linear flow downwards to bless the earth. The fact that the man is the initial reflector of the glory of God means that he must not wear a feminine hairstyle, because it would mean he would not recognize the true origin of his God-ordained role and responsibilities directly under Christ. He is a reflector; he reflects back to the source of his authority, namely God himself, by wearing the appropriate hairstyle. And a woman wearing a feminine hairstyle is reflecting that she acknowledges that there is a cascade or flow of power from God, that is partly, at least, conveyed through her connection with male leadership in the home and in the church. By means of her willing submission to the authority of her godly husband and also that of godly leaders in the church, she experiences increased manifestations of God's power at work in her life and ministry.

Entertaining Angels Unaware

"For this reason, and because of the angels, the woman ought to have a sign of authority on her head," Paul concludes (verse 10). A "sign of authority" is to be a conspicuous feature of her personal appearance that displays her respect for herself as a woman and for the men around her, as men. In Paul's day this sign was clearly long hair: a feminine hairstyle, a sign of both the authority she was under, and also of the authority she now exercised. And the angels are said to take notice of this, both good angels and bad angels.

Angels are present when we worship together on Sunday mornings, both the good and the bad. Good angels are the guardians of the created order and are delighted when they see men acting like men and women acting like women. Evil angels are now cosmic vandals, demons of destruction who work for the disruption of the created order, and are therefore delighted when they see rebellious hearts and bad attitudes, even when this rebellion shows up in freaky displays of subversive and rebellious modes of fashion! Unisex outfits, or cross-dressing between men and women, are invitations for demons to infiltrate. Wearing rebellious styles in fashion frequently demonstrates that someone has a problem with authority, and this then becomes a landing strip for the demonic to gain a foothold in his or her life. We ought to be aware that both un-fallen and fallen angels take note of what goes on when we gather for worship, either to seek an opportunity to protect us or, in the latter case, to harm us.

The parenthesis of verses 11–12, underlining our mutual value as men and women in Christ, is there to prevent abuse of the concept of male headship: "In the Lord, however, woman is not independent of man, nor is man independent of woman. For as woman came from man, so also man is born of woman. But everything comes from God." Notwithstanding the primary role of male leadership in the church and in the home, men and women are mutually interdependent upon one another by God's design. They need each other, and cannot survive or thrive without one another. Like every man that ever lived, I was born from a woman; I have no independent existence apart from my mother, and I thank God for her. That makes men and women not only equal, but also indispensable to one another. This is seen most powerfully in the partnership of Christian marriage. Women are not second-class citizens. Paul wants women to be honoured, elevated, trained, taught, released, deployed and fulfilled. He wants all of their gifts flourishing in the life of the church and especially the gift of prophecy. But such prophecy is to be spoken by a woman with her head "covered" (verse 5) in the sense we have discussed, that is, as an expression of personal modesty and a cheerful acknowledgement of how that "sign of authority" operates beneficially within her.

So, here in 1 Corinthians 11:3–16, Paul is teaching the proper submission of women to male authority both in the home and in the church because the church is seen as an extension of the family. It is anomalous, even contradictory, for the church to allow spiritual conflict and confusion to develop by fostering a situation where a woman is directed to submit to her husband as her head at home, and then is appointed to act as an authority over him if she holds the office of an elder or bishop in the church! It is clear that in Paul's thinking about male–female relationships, their roles are essentially non-reversible.

Our conclusion then is this: women are neither to be "hushed" nor "hatted" but cheerfully submitted to the Lord, content to be women, and increasingly released to operate in their God-ordained ministries and become all they were meant to be in God's kingdom, truly honouring his order for men and women working at their common task of witness and worship together. Prophecy is itself affected by this requirement: "Every man who prays or prophesies with his head covered dishonours his head. And every woman who prays or prophesies with her head uncovered dishonours her head – it is just as though her head were shaved" (1 Corinthians 11:5–6).

So let's make sure we're all properly covered.

Chapter Thirteen

Paul on the Prophetic – Love Changes Everything

We come now to what Paul describes as "the best way of all": love as a prophetic lifestyle. The prophet is first called into the presence of God, then sent out to share what was glimpsed, felt, seen and heard in that holy presence with both God's people and on occasions, also, with those who guide the nation. Since God is love, and the hallmark of Christ's disciples is love, it follows that a life of love is the apex of prophetic ministry. Paul's rightly famous, lyrical, beautiful passage on the nature of love is heard almost always out of context: at weddings and funerals it is a favourite choice. But of the millions who have heard it, how many would know, if you asked them, what its context is, and how it fits into the teaching of the apostle on the life of the church?

It is almost impossible to understand biblical teaching correctly without reference to its immediate scriptural context, and this passage, however inspiring it may be when read alone, is no exception. Paul's famous Corinthians passage on love was designed to be read in the context of teaching about spiritual gifts (especially prophecy and speaking in tongues). It makes clear for us the crucial importance of the unified life, the drawing together of worship and witness, until all that we are outpours all that God is, for the world that needs his rescue and salvage plan in Christ.

The purpose of the great passage on love in 1 Corinthians 13 is not to offer an alternative to using spiritual gifts in life and worship, or to suggest that as long as disciples are loving it doesn't really matter whether they move in the gifts or not. Several chapters of this epistle are given wholly to careful dissertation and instruction on the use of the charismata in public worship. It has never crossed the apostle's mind that his readers would take him to mean that the gifts are to be left behind and forgotten because the only thing that matters is love. He is writing into a situation where jealousy and wrangling, impatience and exclusion, have marred the common life as much as unseemly disorder, indiscipline and chatter have marred their acts of worship.

The passage on love is intended to offer not an alternative to spiritual gifts but the best context for the effective ministry of the gifts of God's Holy Spirit: love is to be the activating grace which will cause the flow of spiritual power to be channelled into a healing, converting, convicting, encouraging experience of the presence of God. When the gifts of the Holy Spirit arrive as they should, namely, marinaded in the redeeming, forgiving love of God, then lives are transformed, minds are changed, people are reconciled, and the witness of the church is faithful to the heart as well as the mind of the God who is love.

As love is to be both the context and the activating ingredient of all that we prepare and present in public worship, as well as the inspiration of the way we live at home, it is worth thinking about what this may mean in practice. The choice is not gifts *or* love in Paul's mind, but gifts *without* love or gifts *with* love. There is no other alternative. Love *without* gifts is a concept that would make no sense to the apostle. For Paul, this was never a valid possibility to him for the church of the future.

1. The necessity of biblical love (1 Corinthians 13:1–3)

To Paul, love is not just a "nice feeling" or a "warm puppy" or a "feeling you get when you feel like you have never felt before". Love is very practical. It is not *philia*, the Greek word that describes affection for someone you like and who likes you – a friend, for example. Nor is it *storgē* (family affection) or *eros* (sexual attraction). It is *agape* that the apostle is talking about here, the love which enables us to give ourselves unreservedly to people who are utterly different, with whom there is nothing in common to attract us. Such love is essential for the proper operation of the gifts, including prophecy. The gift of tongues, used without love for self-promotion and effect, is just a rerun of the confusion that occurred at the Tower of Babel – confused and alienating babbling (Genesis 11:1–9)! Prophecy, knowledge and faith without love are seriously disabled for their divine purpose, since God is love. The German reformer Martin Luther once said, "I'd rather obey than work miracles." It seems that the church at Corinth preferred to work miracles rather than obey. Paul said, in effect, that a fireworks display of miracles without love would prove ephemeral and empty, because the gifts are not complete without love.

What about faith, giving and martyrdom without love (verse 3)? Time was that we would have found it hard to see how such a thing could be, but now we have televangelists with crocodile tears pleading for money, an impersonal welfare system that treats people like numbers, and homicidal suicide bombers aiming to bribe God into giving them access to paradise through murderous violence, and we can therefore see all too well where "faith", "giving", and "martyrdom" without love can take us. Those in the church who give money in order to ease their consciences, or because people are watching and it may prove to be a canny business move to be generous – well, such giving has lost its prophetic content, and its power to heal, encourage and empathize. It's not so much a gift, but an advertisement. At best it is "cold" charity.

2. The nature of biblical love (1 Corinthians 13:4–7)

The loveless use of the gifts of the Spirit had become common place at Corinth, and Paul now underlines the necessity of love for two reasons: (i) the way I am by nature, and (ii) the way other people are. Paul illustrates this in many ways. The congregation at Corinth had become careless and heartless in their attitude towards one another, even though they were rich in the charismata. Paul reminds them of the mainspring of their Christian faith, and sets out before them again how love in action will look and feel.

a) Love deals with the darkness I find in myself (verses 4–5a)

"Love is patient." Do you know that it took the Italian artist Leonardo da Vinci four years to paint the smile on the face of the Mona Lisa? How long does it take to turn a church of awkward and difficult people around until it becomes a vibrant, joyous community? As long as love directs it should take. The Greek word *macrothumia* (translated "patience" here) denotes an ability to wait, to cut people slack, to adjust the pace, to slow down and wait for the latecomers. "Love is kind," Paul continues. Our dealings with people are to display a generous heart that will invest in their progress and allow them to become all that they have the potential to become.

Next, Paul gives us a list of the things that love is *not* – indicating how love is to outshine the darkness. All of us struggle with temptation and sin, and we need love both for our own healing, and to bring healing to others. I'm naturally envious, I want to be prominent, I would like to be a hand or an eye, not a foot or a nose, in Christ's body. And you might quite like to become the next John Stott, John Wimber or Reinhard Bonnke, along with having their international ministries and fame. And so you become envious when you see these ministries effectively at work. You not only regret that you don't have these gifts, you're also sorry that someone else has them instead!

"Love does not envy, it does not boast", not even in the form of the exaggerated reports we sometimes call "evangelastics", as we expand the number of converts made in a recent mission, or casually mention having had several visions while immersed in our regular three-hour prayer session at four o'clock this morning.

Love "is not proud"; the word *physao* that Paul uses here means "to be puffed up with wind", like an inflated balloon – just as colourful, but just as empty. It describes someone full of hot air.

Love "is not rude". How many impatient, insensitive outbursts and interruptions this covers! "I've got to get this word into the proceedings... *right now!*" – with words like these some Christians reveal a pushy "look at me, I've got this gift, take notice of me right now" mentality. Others express anger to get their own way, behaving in a bullying, disrespectful and discourteous way. "These new choruses are rubbish!" "Either she goes or I go!" "God has moved on from this church and I'm moving too!" Love "is not rude, it is not self-seeking". It isn't manipulative and domineering.

b) Love deals with the darkness I encounter in others (verses 5b–7)

Because there is darkness in all of us, we each battle with carnal ambitions that strive to be fulfilled. But then, we also have to deal with the darkness we encounter in others. Love "is not easily angered". People sometimes rub me up the wrong way with trite prophecies, ostentatious and noisy tongues, flaunted abilities and so on. God himself will often see that such incidents happen to test us – but love has a long fuse and reacts with self-control. It is not easily angered.

Love "keeps no records of wrongs". Some people will add reams to our file of "bad things that have been done to me". God tells us to put that file through the shredder and totally forgive them.

"Love does not delight in evil..." Do you ever gloat when others have been found out in some immoral behaviour? "I knew that all along," you say. "I knew that his theology was suspect, and now here's the proof! Serves him right!" How easily we fall into criticizing the way another church or denomination orders their life and worship – *ours* is always such an improvement on theirs! How quick we can be to think the worst when we hear of misdemeanours in another fellowship than our own. Every Christian group, even those with the purest theology, have times when people stumble and fall. Why would we want to gloat over a fallen brother and the disgrace he has brought to the body of Christ and to the

Lord himself, thinking that it makes our own denomination look purer? Instead, we should weep.

Having looked at how love deals with the darkness, Paul turns his gaze again to the light: Love "always protects, always trusts, always hopes, always perseveres. Love never fails". Therefore, we will attempt to guard each other's reputations. We are resolved to believe the best of one another. We are to remain in faith for positive change within people. We continue trying to help them, because the Lord has told us to do just that. We don't give up on one another; we nurture, we encourage – we are in this for the long haul.

3. Biblical love motivates us to desire spiritual gifts (1 Corinthians 14:1–5)

Desiring and eagerly pursing spiritual gifts is not only to be in the context of a loving attitude, it may also be one of the best expressions of that love, for the gifts of the Holy Spirit are the Lord's provision of essential tools and equipment to bless others, and to build the church in strength for its task of extending God's kingdom. "Follow the way of love and eagerly desire spiritual gifts, especially the gift of prophecy" (14:1). It is ineffective to feel love for people without practically helping, encouraging and supporting them. And the gifts are God's instruments or power tools to bring healing, hope and vision to others. We dare not neglect them.

Here, the gift of tongues is very important: it is a "starter" gift, helping believers who are just beginning in the use of God's gifts to make progress quickly, helping us to grow in intimacy with the Father, and thence to encourage the movement of spiritual power in a worship gathering and help to accelerate healing and transformation in the lives of people who are struggling (see the life and work of Jackie Pullinger). But our special focus here is prophecy, and Paul is especially keen that we should prophesy. We cannot manage without these gifts.

We should never have allowed them to be neglected, let alone made redundant or left to die out. We discern four particular characteristics in the highly desirable gift of prophecy, when we compare it with the gift of tongues.

a) Tongues are God-ward, while prophecy is man-ward (verses 2a, 3a)

Tongues are for prayer and praise – both God-ward activities. "Anyone who speaks in a tongue does not speak to men but to God." This has implications for how we interpret them. Sometimes tongues are interpreted at a meeting as if they were prophecies. There may be either of two reasons for this: firstly, the tongue may be the kind of prayer which declares or proclaims God's wonderful nature (as some of the psalms do, e.g. Psalm 19:1, "The heavens declare the glory of God..."). Secondly, what seems to be an interpretation may actually be a prophecy stimulated by the "starter" effect of tongues. As a general principle, we should expect to hear praise or a prayer when tongues are interpreted, because tongues are God-ward utterances, albeit spoken in languages unknown to the speaker. Prophecy is directed outwards from God to people, is readily understood by the hearers for whom it is intended, and so is especially valuable in building up the body of Christ. Tongues bring human needs to God; prophecy brings God's answers to humanity (verse 3). Prophecy is a gift that really effects visible changes in people's lives, often immediately, and regularly occurs as the immediate answer to our prayers in tongues. Prophecy is often God's response to the requests voiced by others in prayer or praise directed toward him in tongues. Love desires to bless others and will pursue such an edifying gift.

b) Tongues are incomprehensible to us; prophecy isn't (verses 2b, 3)

"He utters mysteries," says Paul, concerning the tongue speaker. As they are understood only by God in the first instance, tongues are usually for private devotions, and should only be heard in public at the Holy Spirit's direct prompting, and when those who have the gift of interpreting tongues are present so that all may be edified and benefited maximally (1 Corinthians 14:27–28). The spoken utterances of prayers in tongues, though they move and spiritually edify us as we feel their power, and encourage God's work of transformation in our lives, are something that even the speaker does not understand, whereas prophecy is immediately accessible to people when they hear it in their own native tongue.

    c) Tongues, unless interpreted, only edify the speaker; prophecy edifies all (verse 4)

So, when the church gathers, the question needs to be asked, "Is it going to be just for my own personal edification that I will be concerned with, or am I here for everybody's else's edification?" Love is preoccupied with the latter concern.

    d) Tongues are a means to an end, but prophecy is the end (verse 5)

"I would like every one of you to speak in tongues," says Paul (he means this seriously – we should prize highly the gift of tongues), "but I would rather have you prophesy." The Greek word *hina*, translated "rather have" in the NIV, usually carries the idea "in order that". There is a hint of the instrumental purpose of tongues – "in order that you may prophesy". The charism of tongues is a wonderful gift of God, never to be underestimated in its value and power, but it is in a sense a subordinate gift, useful for stimulating and accelerating the movement of other gifts such as prophecy and healing. Tongues are often the key to moving in the other gifts of the Spirit, including words of knowledge and wisdom as well as healing and prophecy because, as we pray in tongues, we are fine-tuning, as with an FM radio, into the divine wavelength in the Holy Spirit and facilitating access to many other gifts of the Holy Spirit that can flow through us. "I would like everyone of you to speak in tongues, in order that you may prophesy."

4. Biblical love makes us desirous to be understood by others (1 Corinthians 14:6–19)

As we continue through this section on order in public worship that follows on from Paul's famous passage on love, we keep in mind that juxtaposition of these passages that are so often considered separately. What is said here about tongues and prophecy in public worship has immediate relevance to creating a community that is characterized by a loving attitude. Here, as Paul writes about the prioritizing of prophecy over tongues in public worship, it is not because the gift of tongues is trivial or unhelpful, but because *in the context of public worship* our primary concern is to make ourselves understandable and accessible. "If the trumpet does not sound a clear call, who will get ready for battle?" asks Paul (verse 8).

If the worship session is full of individuals speaking uninterpreted tongues, the effect would be like an inexperienced military bugler making a hash of the required tune to be played, while all of the troops, armed and ready for battle, were shrugging their shoulders in bewilderment and looking at each other saying, "What is he signalling? What's the command he's playing? We can't understand his directions, they're so unclear." People cannot respond to something they do not understand. It would be nonsense to our hearers (verse 9). We may as well talk to the birds. We would sound like a foreigner, not a friend. As meaningful as a prayer spoken in Russian, Croatian or Swahili might be to God in one of our meetings, the rest of us would not understand (though it is possible that one or two foreign nationals might be present who speak those languages). And of course, we could never say an enthusiastic "Yes!" to such a prayer. There's enough to battle with already in our gatherings that might hinder the total engagement of all of the people without the additional hindrance of unclear and incomprehensible spoken utterances. We need to be able to understand all that is said, and respond with a resounding "Amen!"

At all times, people need to be able to count us as a friend, and not as an alien or stranger to them (verses 10–11). Their minds need to be engaged with the worship, for we often use our minds little enough as it is (verses 14–15). And therefore the public use of tongues must be interpreted into our native dialect in mixed gatherings, and the twin gift of "interpretation of tongues" is also a special manifestation of the Holy Spirit, which we can call on in this ministry. What is true of tongues is also true of relevance and accessibility in the preached message: love promotes understanding. If the preacher's address is complex, abstruse and difficult, he might as well be speaking in tongues for all the good it will do. To make ourselves understood, to speak in the language of our hearers, is part of our demonstration of genuine love toward others.

5. Biblical love makes us sensitive to the presence of unbelievers (1 Corinthians 14:20–25)

Paul continues to expound his rationale of love in ordering public worship, by explaining that where there are large gatherings with many unbelievers present, it is probably not always helpful for tongues to be used publicly because we should put ourselves in their place, by cultivating an understanding of their point of view. Unbelievers will just think you are mad. Tongues are most edifying in private prayer meetings with believers, and then only if they are interpreted. Prophecy has the potential for tremendous evidential and evangelistic impact upon unbelievers, demonstrating the reality of God and unmasking their suppressed need of him. This sensitivity to outsiders extends to the clarity needed in all we do. Explain what we are doing in worship and why. Set people at ease. Appoint a really friendly hosting team to greet and help newcomers, and to offer them attractive bulletins or literature if required. We should always avoid becoming introspective, assuming that only the in-crowd who are familiar with our proceedings will be attending.

6. Biblical love promotes good order and peace (1 Corinthians 14:26–35)

The presence of love promotes accessible order and harmony in what we do. It creates a generosity and humility that gives way and allows others to be heard. Our worship gatherings should never be carnally ostentatious, chaotic or competitive. No gift should monopolize the meeting to the detriment of the other gifts of the Spirit and several other essential ingredients of public worship (verses 26–27). Those who have something to contribute should not be so preoccupied with their input as to forget that the input of others is of equal worth (maybe even more). The number of contributions of tongues and prophecy should be sensitively limited and, in the case of tongues, always interpreted (verse 28).

> a) With regard to prophecy, this means prophetic contributions should flow in order, without interruption or hasty overlap (verses 29–32)

"Two or three prophets should speak," the apostle says. Then time should be given to assimilate the meaning of what was said, by proper discernment of the weight and content of those prophecies (verses 29–33). Paul doesn't mean that only two or three prophecies are allowed in any one meeting. He means that only two or three should be contributed in unbroken sequence before a suitable pause is allowed in order to weigh their significance. Otherwise, we might forget what the first speaker said by the time we've arrived at prophecy number nine! We need to cultivate a spirit or attitude that truly values and esteems prophecy, and refuses to allow it to be lost in the mêlée of gifts on display in a lively, Spirit-directed meeting. If there are weighty words being uttered, then we're directed to consider what the Lord has been saying every time there are two or three prophecies in a row. We may need to act upon them there and then, and cannot afford to simply pass them by. Instead, let us test them with a view to sifting the gold from the dross, and acting obediently upon what we have heard. This is the loving thing to do.

> b) Also in connection with the orderly use of prophecy, Paul gives some direction concerning the conduct of women in the weighing of prophecy (1 Corinthians 14:29–35)

This is in keeping with what Paul has written elsewhere about the roles of men and women: "As in all the congregations of the saints, women should remain silent in the churches. They are not allowed to speak, but must be in submission, as the Law says", urges Paul (verses 33–34). This is not to be read as an absolute prohibition on women making vocal contributions in mixed meetings of men and women together, as it has often been interpreted to mean, for Paul earlier encouraged women to make such vocal contributions (1 Corinthians 11:5). This statement occurs in the context of instruction about judging and weighing prophecy. "If they want to enquire about something, they should ask their own husbands at home; for it is disgraceful for a woman to speak in the church" (verse 35). Paul regards it to be unseemly for a woman publicly to assume authority and to challenge the content of prophecy while there are authorised men present to do this. He is cautioning: Don't let the women do this, don't let the women be found standing up, arguing about whether a prophecy was of God or not – it's unseemly and it wouldn't look or feel right to outsiders or to us.

But of course, the women can prophesy personally in public, because 1 Corinthians 11 has already told us that they can. Provided their attitude is right and godly, they can prophesy, lead off in prayer, and contribute many other vocal and powerful contributions (1 Corinthians11:5). All Paul desires, here, is that the creative design of headship and submission should be properly observed, and it can be seen that the women are respecting the authority of their husbands and other leaders in the church.

Our aim must be to foster a "fitting" and "orderly" style of meeting (verse 40): "…everything should be done in a fitting and orderly way". When scriptural instruction and direction is observed, everything goes well. And notice something else. We have a tendency in mainstream evangelicalism today to read this text with the emphasis placed on the wrong command. Conservatives rebuke charismatics by highlighting the latter part of the exhortation, "…everything should be done in a *fitting and orderly way*", as if proper protocol and decorum was all that mattered. And so they prohibit anything unusual from happening, forbidding anything that takes them by surprise or interrupts their set liturgy, so that everything is performed in a way that's predictable and safe. But their charismatic friends read it as saying: "... *everything should be done* in a fitting and orderly way", in their desire to see all heaven break loose every time they gather, so that a kind of divine chaos is the result. The text actually says, "...everything should be done in a fitting and orderly way". God wants both the whole spectrum of the charismata on display in all of his churches, and a divine order that helps to keep the church *faithful*! So we must grow in the prophetic.

We can summarise how Paul expected worship to be conducted in terms of its flow and content. Worship should be:

1. *Vocal* – A wide variety of spoken and sung contributions should be present when we gather in small groups and even in large congregations.

2. *Intelligible* – Everything should be clearly understood by the majority of the people present.

3. *Balanced* – No one manifestation of the Spirit is to dominate the proceedings, but rather there should be an orchestrated display of everything that God wants to do, as the Holy Spirit directs and leads.

4. *Orderly* – Worship should be truly spontaneous, but also prepared and not chaotic. All must work together in much the same way as the performance of a musical symphony does, only in this case the Holy Spirit himself is the composer and conductor.

5. *Shared* – As many people as possible should be able to take part as the Spirit prompts them.

6. *Scriptural* – The scriptures – read, taught, believed and obeyed – lie at the heart of every Christian gathering, and everything that occurs is submitted to and tested by its conformity to scripture.

7. *Real* – All that happens is pervaded by God's loving presence, so that even unbelievers and other visitors exclaim, "God is really among you!" (1 Corinthians 14:24–25).

Chapter Fourteen

Growing in the Prophetic (Part 1)

Alec Motyer once made the observation, "In their own day the prophets were headline makers and pace-setters in the national news. So if we find their words tedious, unclear, less than exciting the fault does not lie with them."[16] Motyer is absolutely right. We can be so dull of hearing sometimes that we ignore the voices that spoke so powerfully centuries ago in God's Word, and that still speak powerfully all down the centuries to shape the lives of God's people today. These were men who were forced into hiding for years, as Elijah was when he fled to the Kerith Ravine, in order to escape the consequences of his prophetic words to the corrupt King Ahab. They were men who had hit squads – both human and demonic – sent out to assassinate them, as Elisha had when he was holed up in the city of Samaria under violent siege from royal assassins.

Sometimes, like Amos, they had deportation orders served upon them demanding that they recross the border from whence they came, and were absolutely forbidden to prophesy any longer in the place God had directed them to target with his truth. Jeremiah was buried alive in a cesspool and eventually (according to tradition) was stoned to death. Isaiah met martyrdom by being sawn in two. These men were perceived as highly dangerous: red-hot pyromaniacs who would burn down whatever stood in their way with their flaming words – not the harmless cranks or bearded poets some people today imagine the prophets to have been. Poets are not usually hounded for their productions unless they have the courage to produce politically sensitive work in the context of a cruel and intolerant regime. Prophets often draw a price on their heads. And plenty of people are willing to collect it.

Authentic prophecy that is extremely influential, stirring and challenging can even overturn governments and turn nations back to God. It is highly provocative. It will inevitably invite opposition. How we need this kind of ministry today both in the church, and if God so wishes, in national life also. Just as the cry goes up, "Is there a doctor in the house?" when there is an emergency and someone is taken ill, so the church should be calling, "Is there a prophet in the house?" We live in gravely disturbing and troubled times, and the soul of humanity everywhere is incurably sick. The prophetic ministry is rare and even frequently discounted among the people of God who, of all people, should love and listen to the voice of the living God.

Wanted: Prophecy Today

Yet, I am more and more convinced of the vital necessity of prophetic ministry today. The earth cries out for prophets with something of the calibre of the men and women of old, the seers, sayers, reformers, restorers and agents of renewal who were electrified by God's Spirit and spoke accordingly, and certainly not with the mild and innocuous utterances that regularly pass for prophecy in some quarters today. We are looking for the kind of prophecy that has been mentored by long exposure to the study of the canonical prophets of Scripture and thus steeped in their courage, wisdom and passion for truth and justice. The earth languishes and waits for fresh winds of the Spirit of God to blow, and for the recovery of a renewed and expanded vision of God arising from the prophetic books of Scripture that reveal an awesome picture of God in his transcendence and absolute control of all things – a picture that can still resonate with power and hope for us in our fear and need, if the writings of those now dead are loosed once again to speak to our hungry hearts.

Abraham Heschel, Jewish philosopher and biblical scholar, commented concerning the prophets of the Old Testament: "The situation of a person immersed in the prophets' words is one of being exposed to a ceaseless shattering of indifference; and one needs a skull of stone to remain callous at such blows." When was the last time that exposure to the writings of one of the canonical prophets had a similar effect to that of a violent blow to the head with a blunt instrument, so that it struck with such force that it shattered your indifference and meek resignation to the often appalling situation of the *status quo*? Yet this ought to be the kind of experience that happens to us regularly if the light of reality is to shine in.

I am convinced that the primary task of prophetic ministry is to dynamite all that blockades the way for a move of God's Holy Spirit to break out among his people, and to promote all the right conditions preparatory and conducive to such a move of God among us again. The church always stands in need of a mighty move of God's Spirit, reviving and quickening our life once again, and perhaps never more so than right now. We have lost so much ground and influence in our nation, and nearly all of our credibility. We are sidelined and counted as irrelevant. We need to recover our prophetic voice. Dr Kenneth Kaunda, president and leader of the first African Christian nation of Zambia, once declared his conviction that "what a nation needs is not so much a Christian king on the throne, as a Christian prophet in the palace". It is almost beyond our imagination to think that such a voice could be raised up today to speak with penetrating power into the hearts and minds of prime ministers, cabinet members, parliamentarians and other government leaders and society shapers at the heart of our nation. Yet maybe it is on God's heart to raise up such voices even now. We should aspire to develop ministries of stature in the realm of the prophetic to tell both the church and the world what neither of them is truly willing to hear as yet. Nevertheless, only an authentic word from God can save us. In a word, this message is the gospel declared with a powerful prophetic edge.

What is it That Prophets Actually Do?

1. Prophetic men and women have supernatural access to both God and other people

It is God who calls and anoints prophets to stand in his presence and hear his voice. Therefore, he is the one who will open the doors of opportunity for that voice to be heard. We must believe that God can open such doors for us. He can open doors into the life of the church – into its many streams and denominations, many of whom are stone deaf or resistant to God speaking to them. He can address the ears of individuals who really need to hear from God. He can open doors into the homes of millions by means of the media – through radio, the press and television. God can open doors into high places, making a way of access to the lives of the most prominent people in the land, so that his faithful people and messengers may befriend, draw near, win confidence and convey faithfully God's restoring word to them, daring to say exactly what God wants said into those people's lives. Prophets, because they are listening, regularly hear what others don't hear regularly at all. And because they know who has spoken to them, they dare to voice what others would be afraid to say, undeterred by the possible negative consequences.

Jeremiah once described such prophetic men and women as those who have "stood in the council of the Lord" and added that, because they have seen and heard his word in that holy place, they are now compelled to proclaim that same word "to my people" – the people of God. Prophets have access to both God and other people (Jeremiah 23: 18, 22).

2. They are men and women of strong passion and emotion, as well as strong conviction and insight

They are not mere dictation machines, reporters or secretaries, dispassionately and impassively noting the things they have overheard from the Almighty – by no means! In authentic prophecy, the messenger's whole personality is caught up with God and with the immensity of the task at hand. The nearer we get to God, the more truly human we become, and the more every part of our redeemed humanity is activated and released, including our emotions, until we fully recover our true God-given identity again and become the people God meant us to be. That is why prophetic people are commonly not easy people to live with.

There is nothing casual, trivial or petty-minded about them. They see the big issues and, under God's hand, they are able to set in motion huge movements of change, and often stir significant numbers of men and women into action for the Lord. As a result, huge directional changes start to occur in the churches, for such is the presence of God upon such individuals that they can effect very unusual and unexpected outcomes. Prophets bring the fear of God to otherwise hostile or indifferent people, and arrest their attention to heed what God is saying, until they are at last compelled to recognize what he is like and who he really is, amid the bedlam of confusing and contradictory religious voices clamouring for our faith and allegiance.

3. Prophets carry enormous responsibility

Sometimes, like Jeremiah, the burden is so great that they cry out to God in complaint. They may even angrily declare, as beleaguered Jeremiah eventually did, "I will not... speak any more in his name!" (Jeremiah 20:9). He felt so low that he exclaimed: "Cursed be the day I was born!" (Jeremiah 20:14). Even today, out of sheer frustration and desperation, prophets occasionally attempt to shake off the burdens that God is laying upon them, or plead like Moses, "O Lord, please send someone else..." (Exodus 4:13). But they simply cannot succeed at this. God is very persistent and, with Jeremiah, they declare, " ... his word is in my heart like a fire, a fire shut up in my bones, and I am weary of holding it in" (Jeremiah 20:9). For prophets, God's Word is like a serious case of heartburn that will not subside with a dose of the antacid of personal complaint towards the Lord and requests to let them off the hook. They must speak, even if it kills them!

Would that we had many more preachers and prophetic voices that could no longer suppress the call to speak the whole counsel of God, so that it would not remain under wraps any longer than necessary. Such preachers speak out exactly what God wants said into every situation he calls them to speak it, because truly prophetic people hate plastic piety, and the lies and pretence that can characterize even the church. Such prophets are not like the court prophets in the pay of the king, proclaiming peace where there is no peace; they tell the unvarnished truth, whatever it may cost them.

4. The role of a prophet is therefore a gutsy and courageous one

We have seen that their call is the twofold task of afflicting the comfortable and comforting the afflicted, and it will probably prove dangerous to exercise this ministry. It will certainly not always prove popular. Not only the prophets of old, but those who speak out Christ's truth today, may find themselves arrested, imprisoned, beaten, stoned, silenced and even killed. Called upon to mediate God's direction and word to the people and circumstances that cry out to him for intervention, prophets courageously provoke resistance, opposition and, sometimes, repentance and change in those situations.

Walter Brueggemann writes, "The role of the prophet is to nurture, nourish and evoke a consciousness and perception alternative to the consciousness and perception of the dominant culture around us." Brueggemann touches upon the disturbing reality that the church is so often in danger of being slowly assimilated by the mindset and dominant consciousness of the culture around us. We run the risk of being *of* the world as well as *in* the world, in conflict with Christ's explicit intention for us (John 17:14–17), and that is why we need prophets so much. They are part of the protection Christ provides for his vulnerable people. It is their job to shape a totally new mindset and God-centred, biblical worldview in the minds, consciousness, thinking, choices and lifestyle of the people of God.

Prophetic ministries are one of God's instruments in dismantling a godless culture and rebuilding it in line with the Architect's blueprint, found in the scriptural vision of holiness, justice and peace that marks the kingdom of God. They clear the ground of rubbish so that a seemingly remote and impossible dream can begin to be realized in its place. Prophets are men and women not only of the present, but of the future. They are future-orientated people, and the gift they hold out to a lost world is, quite simply, hope.

A hopeless believer is an anomaly, a contradiction in terms. But it is only the Word of God that can impart authentic hope, in contrast to the world's make-believe or wishful thinking. According to the apostle Paul, sinful societies are "without hope and without God in the world" (Ephesians 2:12). Prophetic ministry exists to change that; to act as God's instrument in fostering a renewed awareness of the Spirit in even the most godless situations, and so herald a springtime of real hope.

How Do Prophets Hear from God?

Prophets linger deliberately in God's presence, attentively devouring the Scriptures and cultivating intimacy with God so that they can hear the Spirit's voice speaking to them. They inevitably return to bring back to us something of the numinous, transcendent dimension of God's holiness, character and greatness – a touch of magnificence to spill into our shabby world. Preacher Jerry Savelle, speaking about the presence of God that rests upon certain individuals, observed, "As followers of Jesus you and I are supposed to be carriers of hope and carriers of faith, so that every time we walk into a hopeless situation our very presence ought to change the atmosphere around us. I have been in a room when Oral Roberts walked in and everyone there would sense his presence. When he enters something else comes in with him and there is an air about him that is sensed by everyone present. Although I have never met Billy Graham personally, I have been told it is true of him also."

I met Billy Graham once, in 1975 at the centenary of the Keswick convention in Cumbria, and along with millions of others I can vouch for the fact that there really is something special, even startling, about him. Secular observers pick it up, too. The well-known British broadcaster Sir David Frost has interviewed him on several occasions, and has always been fascinated by a sense of the divine presence that accompanies Billy Graham. Others agree. "When he enters a room, a hush falls on the place," Jerry Savelle continued, "because everyone in attendance recognizes a holy presence in their midst." That's it. It is the afterglow of a God who still speaks to and anoints his servants.

Even if there are no prophets of the stature of the scriptural prophets today, nevertheless, we still have prophetic people who are able to hear from God and to speak for him and reflect something of his hope, glory and presence into the lives of those who are eager to encounter and hear from him. Yet, though the afterglow of God's *shekinah* glory shines about them, as all believers are meant to experience this and to be transformed progressively by it (2 Corinthians 3:18), prophets live with many human limitations just like everybody else. The immutable power of God's eternal truth works in and with the ordinary, imperfect human reality of those who are called to proclaim it.

We see something of this in the story of the call of Moses (Exodus 4), when the fallen prince of Egypt, now a humble desert shepherd, attempts to argue with God about his personal unsuitability for this appointment to become God's deliverer, conscious of his inability to complete this daunting task. God refutes and demolishes every one of his arguments until Moses finally tries one last shot to change God's mind. "O Lord, I have never been eloquent, neither in the past nor since you have spoken to your servant. I am slow of speech and tongue," he pleads, wretchedly contemplating the prospect of proclaiming the oracles of God to Pharaoh's face with a chronic speech impediment that jars against the background of the sophisticated courts of Pharaoh's palace and his articulate courtiers. He protests that not even the encounter with God has succeeded in transforming him into an outstanding orator.

God listens to his plea and allows Moses to rely on his brother Aaron as the mouthpiece of the message, in much the same way as a prophet speaks for God: "You shall speak to him and put words in his mouth; I will help both of you speak and will teach you what to do. He will speak to the people for you, and it will be as if he were your mouth and as if you were God to him. But take this staff in your hand so you can perform miraculous signs with it" (Exodus 4:15–17).

So it is with all of God's defective and flawed prophets of ancient times, and also among prophetic ministry today. God knows and understands our limitations and gives us one another to help compensate for them. Together we must consent to bear his message to our contemporary society and together face the consequences that this task may bring. Prophets are more concerned about God's feelings than they are about the emotional reactions of their hearers to the things they have to say. They don't make things up or steal words from others. They don't court favour or trade in "political correctness", so it's important for them to really hear from God, or they simply have nothing to say.

When he speaks to us, God has no shortage of ways to convey messages to his people. He has a diversity of means at his disposal. We talk of "seeing things with our mind's eye". We call it imagination, but God can put things into our mind's eye. He can put things into our "spirit's eye", so that we are seeing something highly unusual that we didn't imagine, and then begin asking questions about it in order to discover its significance: "What is this? What does it mean? Who is it for?" If this happens when we're asleep we call it a dream. If it happens when we're awake we call it a vision. God can bring both verbal and visual data directly into our minds, bypassing the usual route of a background of sensory input and experience to shape our understanding. Let's reiterate and expand something we noted in an earlier chapter so that we can become more aware of God's varied approaches to us.

1. Mind → Mouth

As a teacher of the Bible I use my mind to plan the things I am going to say when I preach. I may be imparting simply factual information, perhaps about the history or textual origins of a biblical book, or the cultural context of some scriptural teaching. I may not be thinking of this aspect of preparation as an opportunity for God's transformative touch to enter someone else's life, but God sometimes surprises me by using that mental preparation and cognitive process to bring something of his life-giving word to others, through the thoughts and voice and work of the prophet.

2. Spirit → Mind → Mouth

As I prepare, a third layer of my humanity is involved when I consciously immerse myself in God's presence in prayer, opening my spirit as well as my intellect to his influence. In my daily quiet time with God, and in seeking his will as I prepare for worship, preaching, teaching and pastoral engagements, I invite the light of God's Spirit to irradiate and direct me, chasing out any lurking shadows, and then pouring forth in truth, healing, wisdom, knowledge, faith, and prophecy if he wishes, for those who need God's intervention and touch.

3. Spirit → Mouth

Sometimes, the Spirit's influence goes straight past my mind without stopping! Paul noted that when he prayed in tongues "my spirit prays, but my mind is unfruitful" (1 Corinthians 14:14). Bypassing the mind and rational thought, God enabled him to pray by a stream of inspiration from the Holy Spirit in his spirit, expressing God-given thoughts in God-given words. When this happens to me, I am not choosing the words – I don't even understand what I am saying; God's Spirit uses me as a mouthpiece directly. This can even be true when I am speaking in my own language to others; it doesn't apply solely to speaking in tongues. Sometimes, in preaching, I will use a phrase or image

or analogy that I hadn't intended, without really knowing why
– it just seems right. Sometimes in conversation, an image or
idea will press upon me so forcibly that I share it with the other
person. Often, this is the Spirit of God taking up my offer to be
his mouthpiece, used by him as a channel of grace; though my
mind has no part in the planning of this message (it's as much
a surprise to me as it might be to my hearer), God is using me
to communicate his life-changing word.

4. Body ➜ Mouth

God can use everything he has made to speak for him. He has
created all things, and his breath is what gives all creation life.
Everything that is, is made by him and for him, and continually
tells the story of his power and love and grace – as Psalm 19:1
puts it, "The heavens declare the glory of God." Therefore we
have records of the occasional extraordinary instance, such
as the story of Balaam's donkey (Numbers 22:28), where the
Holy Spirit will find a way for his voice to speak even through
an animal.

We can deepen our understanding of how prophets hear
from God, what they do and how their ministry is shaped, by
earthing the principles of prophetic ministry that we have been
looking at in the life narrative of a particular biblical prophet.

Habakkuk – the Experience of a Biblical Prophet

Habakkuk is especially interesting to us because he lived during
very troubled times, in his nation and the wider international
scene, that were not dissimilar from our own, and he struggled
intellectually and emotionally with the same problems as those
that disturb us today. He also typifies for us the characteristic
focus of all the biblical prophets, for Habakkuk's burden was
the spiritual and moral state of his people. Judah was full of
violence, lawlessness and injustice: God's people had lost faith,
and so had also lost spiritual ground in their walk with God.
They had reached a state where they couldn't stop the rot, let
alone reverse it.

Habakkuk's contemporaries no longer honoured the Law of Moses or the rest of Scripture. They trivialized the worship of God and lived as if their teaching and belief were an irrelevancy to normal, day-to-day living. Instead of summoning the nation back to obedience and authentic dealings with God, their political and religious leaders were among the worst apostates, playing fast and loose with their faith tradition and indulging in the same kind of "live for today" greed, exploitative dishonesty and sensual decadence we see everywhere around us today. The meaning of life was the pursuit of gold, girls and glory. Modern-day news headlines such as, "Police Bust Up Mayor's Drunken Party" or "Minister's Secret Affair With Parliamentary Secretary" would have come as no surprise to Habakkuk. Then as now, if those in the public eye have few scruples about such self-indulgence and the flouting of biblical moral standards, we can be certain this will be the norm at the grass-root level in society as a whole.

For the prophet Habakkuk, Judah was becoming an increasingly unsafe and violent society. This rings bells for us. Just recently in London, the Metropolitan Police commissioner received crime reports and statistics for many of the city's largest estates and boroughs and said openly that a huge crime wave is gathering among young people – those in their teens and twenties. He added: "It scares me, because we are incapable of halting this crime wave at this time." It's no wonder London's streets are becoming more and more dangerous in certain places. There is a situation of disparity as there was in Habakkuk's day, with the gap between the wealthy and the poor ever widening. Habakkuk also knew that these conditions foster envy, and spell danger and discontent. So he decided to do several things under a sense of divine compulsion.

1. He rose up early (1:2)

"How long, O Lord, must I call for help, but you do not listen? Or cry out to you, 'Violence!' but you do not save?" He determined to pray, to take counsel with his God before he prophesied to his community. He began to call out to the Lord about the state of the nation.

2. He began to take note, and care deeply (1:3)

"Why do you make me look at injustice? Why do you tolerate wrong? Destruction and violence are before me; there is strife, and conflict abounds." He refused to remain aloof and ignorant concerning the state of the faith community and of the nation. He got involved. He began to observe first-hand the mess that people's lives were in: the marital strife, child abuse, drunken brawling, the killings, rape and child abduction, assaults and robberies. Back in the world of today, British television recently featured a disturbing, award-winning documentary series, part three bearing the title, *Hunting the Paedophiles.* Paedophilia has been with us in every age, but an increasingly mobile and anonymous society, the breakdown of family life, and the new possibilities afforded by electronic communication, have all contributed to the vulnerability of our children. Watching the programme made me feel the same mixture of anger and disgust that Habakkuk felt as he confronted the decadence and moral disintegration of his times.

Worst of all, God did not seem to be answering Habakkuk's prayers; in fact, it seemed God wasn't even listening to him. I think that in large quarters of the church today, there is a gnawing suspicion that God is not listening to us or our prayers for mercy and revival either. Far from being able to come up with the keys to success and the faith to turn this situation around, some leaders and churches seem to have given up on spiritual warfare altogether. They have resigned themselves to inevitable defeat and the triumph of evil.

Likewise, Habakkuk was sinking deeper and deeper into doubt and fear, so that two negative convictions become more and more entrenched within his mind: (i) prayer seems pointless and (ii) God seems powerless. He had prayed so much, but God hadn't intervened. Habakkuk had cried out to God, but the Lord kept silent. Habakkuk dialled 999/911, but all he heard was a busy signal – no one lifted the receiver at the other end. He cried all the louder, but all he could hear was the echo of his own voice. How easy it is for us to identify with his sense of despair.

3. He started to complain, precisely because prayer seemed pointless and God seemed powerless (1:3–4)

We ache as we hear his pleading tone, "Why do you make me look at injustice? Why do you tolerate wrong? Destruction and violence are before me; there is strife, and conflict abounds. Therefore the law is paralysed, and justice never prevails. The wicked hem in the righteous, so that justice is perverted." Tormented by these preoccupations, Habakkuk complained bitterly to God, his feelings of frustration erupting in two fundamental questions. The first was "How long, O Lord?" Have you ever thought that? He is basically saying, "I have my limits. I cannot keep faithfully bringing the burden of a nation to you in this way, with no answer at all from you." The second complaint was "Why?..." He needed some answers! He begged God for explanations to help him make sense of what was evolving in history, right before his eyes: "Why don't you stop this? What's holding you back, Lord?"

But God had not forgotten him. The Lord did speak to Habakkuk. There came, in the end, an answer to the prophet's longing for a word from God. God unveils to Habakkuk the divine plan that is about to unfold:

> Look at the nations and watch – and be utterly amazed. For I am going to do something in your days that you would not believe, even if you were told. I am raising up the Babylonians, that ruthless and impetuous people, who sweep across the whole earth to seize dwelling places not their own. They are a feared and dreaded people; they are a law to themselves and promote their own honour... They fly like a vulture swooping to devour; they all come bent on violence... Then they sweep past like the wind and go on – guilty men, whose own strength is their god".
>
> Habakkuk 1:5–11

If the prophet's complaints had been noisy up to now, here was the trigger for the loudest complaints of all! God is, in effect, telling him that he is indeed about to act concerning the state of the nation and its apostasy and departure from God, but not in the way that the prophet either expected or wanted. God is raising up the notoriously cruel and viscous Babylonians as his rod of chastizement for his rebellious children, and they are about to invade Judah in a *Blitzkrieg* of overwhelming force and numbers.

Habakkuk was so shocked that God would use a godless people to punish his holy nation that he erupted immediately into his third complaint: "How *could* you?" That's really the gist of Habakkuk 1:12ff:

> O Lord, are you not from everlasting? My God, my Holy One, we will not die. O Lord, you have appointed them to execute judgment; O Rock, you have ordained them to punish. Your eyes are too pure to look on evil; you cannot tolerate wrong. Why then do you tolerate the treacherous? Why are you silent while the wicked swallow up those more righteous than themselves?

As we today look upon our modern world with all its unrest and warfare, noting the violence of extremist terrorist attacks in busy shopping streets and restaurants, we see that much of the aggression is motivated by religious conviction and a desire to supplant what the perpetrators judge to be failed faith-systems with one that they see as more authentic and beneficial to societies everywhere. Some suicide bombers and terrorists have made it very clear that they are disgusted by the decadence, moral decay and secularism of the West, and regard any attack upon Western society as legitimate holy war.

As we consider this, just like Habakkuk we are thrown into a confused state of mind. On the one hand, we cry out to God to save us, shocked and horrified at terrorist violence, convinced that terrorism is wrong and must be stopped at all costs. On the other hand, we cannot help but see that the terrorists, in their critique of our seemingly powerless religion and political philosophies, do have a point in their outspoken contempt for formerly "Christian" societies. Our secular Western lifestyle has indeed become decadent, unfaithful to the call of God upon our lives and to our spiritual history and its legacy of godly order, intellectual advance and spiritual freedom, as we shamelessly serve Mammon and leave God's poor to fend for themselves in the gutter. Like Habakkuk, we feel both that to be violently overwhelmed is not right, and cannot be God's will, and that to some extent we may have brought this upon ourselves by our own moral choices and arrogant apostasy. None of us likes to hear this, and therefore we can sympathize with Habakkuk's bewilderment.

In Habakkuk's case, his questions seemed to him as appropriate as they were urgent. How can a pure God use such impure and cruel agents of retribution, a people who where more wicked than Israel was? Surely, the so-called cure for the nation's ills, namely, the Babylonian invasion, was worse than the disease of Judean sin? Yet, Habakkuk had to see that it was the all-wise God who was declaring this punishment, and he was not about to adjust his thinking on account of Habakkuk's inadequate assessment of the need for such action. Instead, Habakkuk's thinking had to line up with God's. Yahweh wanted his prophet to see things as he sees them, and Judah's sin was gross and totally self-destructive. It is all too common for us to minimize our sins and maximize God's perceived injustice in dealing with those same sins. We hastily conclude, along with Habakkuk, that God's punishment is unfair, unjust and "over the top" – for we are not that bad, really – therefore, God is unjust!

The Bible is always taking us by surprise in its relevance and power for contemporary application; this is what it means to exercise the spirit of prophecy – even texts written thousands of years ago are still speaking to today's world with the urgent voice of truth. The God of the Bible still surprises us, challenges us and, often, even offends us.

A.W. Tozer once analysed the malaise of the church in the 1950s in this way: "The glory of God has departed from the church and another God whom our fathers knew not is making himself at home among us. This God, we have made. And because we have made him, we can understand him.

Because we have created him, he can never surprise us, never overwhelm us, nor astonish us, nor transcend us." Given our apathy, complacency and addiction to the goal of "personal peace and affluence" (Francis Schaeffer's succinct summary of our major preoccupation in the West), I think the God of many contemporary believers in Britain today is that kind of God. He doesn't do anything shocking; he doesn't surprise us; he never overwhelms us in this way. In many cases, we don't even fear him.

Yet the God of the Bible is not a nervous, ingratiating deity, cautiously trying to win some scraps of faith and allegiance to himself from an aloof and indifferent public while desperately pleading, "If only somebody would just believe in me!" He is not eager to win human favour at all. He is not a down-and-out bum on the streets, in dire need of our pity. It is we who are the down-and-outs. God is the dispenser of charity, not the recipient of it. It is we who are in desperate need of his intervention and invasive, radical action. We need his mercy. He doesn't need ours. And so, although Habakkuk still found grounds for complaint, he nevertheless needed to listen carefully to God's considered reply to those complaints. There is a big difference between the boldness with which Habakkuk cried out to God, and the cynical battering some unbelievers try to give the Almighty. Habakkuk was genuinely looking for divine help to strengthen his shaken faith.

Similarly with us today, there's a big difference between the way a child of God sometimes calls out in outrage and confusion to God, and the way an unbeliever berates and pours scorn upon him whenever things go wrong. As David Prior puts it, "One is a denial that refuses to believe, and the other is a belief that refuses to deny." One way to honestly get our faith and genuine doubts sorted for real is to complain sincerely to God, and then listen to what he has to say in response. John B. Taylor, Old Testament scholar and former bishop of St Albans, wisely observes that, "The abiding value of the book of Habakkuk is that it presents a picture of a man who believes and yet questions." It is alright to question God. You may gain valuable insights from him that you would never have obtained in any other way.

When we are puzzled or find our faith stumbling as we think about the present state of the world and the church, it helps to have truly prophetic people around who feel things deeply and ask the questions other people will not voice, so that there is the real possibility of hearing from God about those concerns. Prophets are often among the first to feel the strongest of negative emotions triggered by appalling situations arising within their nation, and to feel them deeply and then confront God directly with the questions that will alone enable them to obtain some helpful answers. But such dialogue with God requires a degree of mature insight and prophetic sensitivity. This is why we need to grow in the prophetic.

And so we come to this pivotal section in Habakkuk 2:1–4, verses encapsulating most of what we need to know about maturing and growing in our ability to receive and transmit prophetic words from God.

Receiving the Prophetic Word

Habakkuk complained *in faith* – we have already noted that. He did not merely "dump" his grievances on God and walk away in a petulant huff. He expected an answer from God. He knew God to be a speaking, communicative God. God speaks to his people in similar ways today. Habakkuk described his receptivity to God not as a passive state, but as an eager, active state, using the terms "stand at my watch" and "look to see".

He said, "I will stand at my watch and station myself on the ramparts; I will look to see what he will say to me, and what answer I am to give to this complaint" (Habakkuk 2:1). Watching and waiting are mandatory activities for anyone who wishes to grow in the prophetic. As prophetic people we must learn the art of deliberately looking up, and actively taking our time to hear properly. This is not a *"Que sera, sera"* Doris Day, stoic theology of resigned and passive indifference to fate, but a state of alert and attentive quietness, expecting God himself to speak.

1. Watching implies you possess the faith to see something new

Growing in the prophetic implies that you have a faith expectancy that God speaks and is often ready to transmit an audio-visual presentation of data into your spirit. God will give you a new perspective on the situations that trouble you. He may show you pictures or give you a message, or lead you to a scripture; and when he speaks, his Word is transformative, bringing hope and understanding, then strengthening faith. This doesn't happen to people in a big hurry to sound off and then move on. Instead, we must get on tip-toe and linger.

2. Watching is best done by climbing higher

Habakkuk resolved, "I will... station myself on the ramparts" (2:1). He knew his calling and responsibility. As a signed up member of the human race, and particularly of the people of God, he had first listened to what people had to say; but then he got ready to watch and wait for what God had to say. We, too, are summoned to listen to the human analysis of our situations – we can hardly help doing so. We read the daily newspapers; we catch current affairs broadcasts on the TV and listen to regular bulletins throughout the day. We read informed analysis of the state of the nation. We know what the psychologists, sociologists, politicians, economists, philosophers, journalists, pundits, neighbours and our family members all think. But the primary calling of a prophet is to listen to God on behalf of others, and discover a higher divine perspective, which may be startlingly different from the analysis of human reason alone. So the prophet goes higher, standing on the ramparts above the clamour and cacophony of human voices.

Prophetic people watch the opinion polls or canvas their constituencies in order to find out what would be perceived to be the safest or most popular course of action to take, at any given time; but they are more interested in what God has to say than they are about human guesswork, opinion or speculation.

Prophetic people are called to offer alternative perspectives to those currently prevalent in society around us. They go to God in order to obtain them. As we grow in the prophetic, we become known for our countercultural and often angular pronouncements – for though we listen to the crowd, it is not the voice of the crowd we are following.

3. Watching is often a solitary business

Prophetic listening is a private and intimate activity, involving an unusual level of solitude and silence. We have to shut out the noise and static coming from competing sources, and become focused and centred upon God. He is a God who speaks, and a God who surprises us. Sometimes in a busy railway station or at a party we are taken by surprise as a word from God arrives in our hearts. Prophetic people acquire the habit of always listening, always watching, keeping a detachment in their hearts whatever they are about, because God doesn't always wait for the silence. Yet sometimes finding a place of silence and solitude is part of the preparation of our hearts. Just as God called Abraham his friend into the desert, Moses his prophet and Jesus his Son, so he calls us into wilderness silence and solitude, to wait, watch and listen for his revelation. Moving in the prophetic was never about instant fixes; it takes time, and it takes self-discipline.

4. Watching implies waiting, for it may take time for God to speak

The necessary time should not be begrudged. And therefore, Habakkuk was prepared to wait. We have to "drop out, turn off and tune in", though not in the way of Dr Timothy Leary who advised 1970s hippies to go on a "psychedelic trip" with hallucinatory drugs like LSD. The Holy Spirit himself, not dangerous narcotics, is the only one who can really open the doors of perception to us, and he doesn't mess with our heads in the way dangerous drugs do. His Word is not delusional; it is clear-sighted, sane and real. Though God may surprise us wherever we are, it may require hours or even days of silent meditation and prayer to quieten our hearts to receive his living word. Prophetic people must have the self-discipline to wait as well as to be solitary. God is always ready, but we are waiting for the *kairos* moment, the seasonal or "now" moment when his time is ripe to speak. Our watchword is "wait and see": God does nothing in a hurry. Daniel waited three full weeks before his answer came (Daniel 10). Jeremiah was put in a vaulted cell where he "remained a long time", before the word for King Zedekiah came to him (Jeremiah 37:16).

5. Watching and waiting is a very responsible role

Hosea affirmed, "The prophet, along with my God, is the watchman over Ephraim" (Hosea 9:8). We are familiar with the concept of a watchman. We regularly see armed soldiers, policemen, Group 4 security guards and other uniformed men stationed near public buildings, gates and doors. Walking past Buckingham Palace at about 10 o'clock one evening with my wife, I looked out for the famous grey-coated, Busby-bearskin-hat-wearing guards – they weren't there! I asked one of the two policemen outside the railings, "Where are the guards in the bearskin hats?" They replied, "They're all safely tucked up in bed!" I looked at these unarmed policemen and inquired, "What would happen if there was a raid on the palace right now? What if armed gunmen stormed these fences and gates?" One replied, "Well, I think they'd probably come out and give us a little assistance if that happened." I'm sure that they would! And just as the queen of England always has a watchman, even an unarmed policeman, to raise the alarm, so too the Lord of all has his watchmen. They may be few, they may look unimpressive, but there are mighty unseen forces ready to respond when they sound the alarm.

Prophetic people carry responsibility, not just for their own wellbeing, comfort and safety, but also for that of hundreds and perhaps thousands of other people also. The watchman's task is to be alert to spiritual reality – and that means looking out for danger and deception as well as for God's Word of truth. Every congregation needs watchmen whose eyes and ears are open, who can read the signs of the times and also hear the Word of God.

When Habakkuk says, "I will look to see what he will say to me" (2:1), he is playing a vital part in the God-appointed defence of his nation, acting as its early-warning system detecting enemy activity as early as possible. Prophetic people are called by God to listen to information from him concerning the heavenlies, the natural realm and hell itself – above us, around us and beneath us. They act as watchmen for both church and nation. We need such sentries on constant duty, and that is why we aspire to grow in the prophetic. What others call "peace and quiet" isn't always seen that way by the prophet.

6. Watching and waiting require obedience

Habakkuk's receptivity is not merely for private consumption. The prophet's word must be trustworthy and honest; we have to know we can rely on prophetic people to see truly and report faithfully. When God speaks, the prophet's pledge is to convey accurately what God said, resisting the temptation to edit it, modify it, add to it, soften it, distort it or simply remain silent. Total obedience is essential.

This is what it means to receive the prophetic word.

Transmitting the Prophetic Word

Habakkuk's tortured enquiries as he cried out to God for answers, and his time of watching and waiting as he climbed onto the ramparts as a watchman to wait for God's Word, were about to bear fruit in two further revelations from the Lord. Habakkuk was to discover that there are times when God displays zero tolerance for evil. God gives people space and freedom to make decisions and learn life's lessons by facing its challenges. He allows us to live with the consequences of our actions, but he also hears our prayers, rescues us in mercy and does not tolerate evil. It is important that we listen to God, watching carefully what he is doing, so that, like Jesus, we can be sure to do nothing but what we see the Father do. Too often we fall into the temptation to offer what Rick Joyner calls "unsanctified mercy" – the desire to show mercy to those situations and people that God has already placed under judgement. We are guilty of widespread theological resistance towards, even denial of, the biblical doctrines of God's justice, holy wrath against sin, and the realities of hell and eternal punishment for sinners. This causes us to fail to appreciate the necessity for the penal and substitutionary aspects of Christ's atonement on the cross. If we have not yet seen the radical depths of the human problem in terms of our sin, we are in no place to accurately assess the radical nature of God's gracious solution to it, in Christ and his cross. Sometimes we attempt to be kinder than God, and feel repelled by his apparent unkindness to sinners in allowing the consequences of their actions to return into their lives. Unsanctified mercy is mistaken tolerance; an attitude that is not true compassion but, often, indulgence of sin. Unsanctified mercy is a failure to answer our Christian calling to be God's prophetic people in the world of today.

As he watches and waits, Habakkuk now receives information from God about the punishment that God had in mind to afflict upon his people. As we move on to read Habakkuk 2:4–20, we shall come to understand more fully, along with the prophet, some of the reasons why God sent the Babylonians to chasten his people. Then, in chapter 3, God lifts Habakkuk's eyes to the long-term and more hopeful future, offering Israel new hope of revival and restoration. But first, let's dwell on Habakkuk 2:1–4 where God underlines some of the principles we have considered before as we saw what it means to move in the prophetic.

1. Prophecy involves seeing and transmitting vision from God

"I will look to see what he will say to me" (verse 1). God has access to our imagination. This can seem dangerous to many Christians, knowing how hypnotherapists and psychologists can do this also, sometimes for purpose of public entertainment or behavioural analysis and change, maybe even for dubious personal control and advantage over us. The language of "visions and dreams" has become associated with human exploitation, manipulation and careerism and made many believers become wary and suspicious. Though it is right to be on our guard, we must also learn to trust God, and open our visionary capacity to receive the Holy Spirit's perspective upon how things can and should be. The gift of prophecy is not one more party trick or mind game; it is God's authentic anointing, beside which even the most elegant sophistry of the world begins to look like a third-rate hallucination.

2. Prophecy should often be recorded and written down

"Write down the revelation and make it plain on tablets so that a herald may run with it" (verse 2). This preserves the details so that they are not forgotten or mislaid somewhere on the long journey from reception to fulfilment. It also prevents distortion in the retelling from one person to another. Get into the habit of recording your dreams. Get into the habit of writing up your prophecies too, perhaps by first recording them on tape and then transcribing them, especially the kind of prophecies that trusted leaders have judged to be weighty and urged us to heed and implement. Recording them also helps us to keep faith alive in our hearts for what God has said to us over the years, perhaps many years beforehand.

When the church I formerly pastored finally moved into the Middlebrook Centre that we acquired at such great expense for a meeting place, on the day the building was opened our guest preacher was a close prophetic friend called Rodney Kingstone. He preached as requested, but he also gave a lengthy prophecy of what God would do among us in the years ahead, not only in this building and through the agency of the church in the rest of Hampshire, but also with a sister church in Bournemouth. It was such a weighty prophecy. He predicted what God would do amongst students and young people in that city in coming visitations of the Holy Spirit, along with many other things. It was so important that we decided to print it in full and enlarge and frame the script for public display. In panels where cinema posters and bingo announcements once hung, in a back-lit, brightly illuminated screen, we displayed that prophecy. It hung there for at least five years and fuelled countless requests to God in daily early-morning prayer meetings, because prophecy keeps faith alive when faith grows dim. Much fruit came as a result of both that prophecy and those prayers, as we saw events unfold exactly in line with all that God had promised.

Prophecy should be so clear that he who *runs* may read it, and so memorable that he who *reads* may run with it.

3. Prophecy has a deadline for its fulfilment in God's timing

"For the revelation awaits an appointed time; it speaks of the end and will not prove false. Though it linger, wait for it; it will certainly come, and not delay" (verse 3). The language here is not the vocabulary of instant success or quick results. It is the vocabulary of delay: "awaits an appointed time", "wait for it", "though it linger". It may await new generations yet to be born. This, again, is the tension between the "already" and the "not yet". There may be only partial fulfilment, with much more still to come. One preacher expressed our frequent frustration in waiting for God like this: "The problem is, I'm in a hurry ... and God is *not!*"

4. Prophecy must be mixed with faith if its hearers are to benefit

"See, he is puffed up; his desires are not upright – but the righteous will live by his faith" (verse 4). Most predictive prophecy is conditional in its fulfilment. It is not guaranteed unless certain conditions are fulfilled on the part of those who hear it. It requires both faith to receive it, and obedience to act on it. Prophecy not only clarifies our confusion, it also galvanizes us into action, whether by giving, preaching, praying, witnessing, reforming the church, writing or simply persevering in what God has said. So verse 4 tells us two very important results that prophetic ministry is meant to effect in our lives:

a) Faithfulness – "The righteous will live by... faith".

True faith is not a temporary persuasion for a few moments or weeks. It is to be equated with fidelity or faithfulness. It means perseverance in believing what God has said. God is looking for faithful, not fickle, people.

b) Life – "The righteous will live..."

Prophecy is an invitation to live, not just survive or barely get by, but truly experience life in the fullness of God's love. Since the faith God is speaking of here is no temporary persuasion in the flush of sudden emotions stirred during a meeting and just as quickly abandoned and forgotten, it will transform our whole lives. Christ offers us life in all of its fullness, along with freedom from fear and discontentment, and much else that may blight and diminish life.

Prophecy helps to keep the church *faithful*! Prophecy helps to keep the church *alive*! That's why it's worth all the watching and the waiting, and that's why we must grow in the prophetic.

Chapter Fifteen

Growing in the Prophetic (Part 2)

God showed Habakkuk all of these things to summon the people of God to awaken and become a praying community again, seeking God's face and the outpouring of his Holy Spirit.

In an earlier chapter I told how, two years before the 11 September 2001 terrorist attacks on the twin towers of the World Trade Centre in New York, a friend of mine with an outstanding prophetic ministry saw vivid mental pictures of those terrible scenes that shocked the whole world. What she saw did not enable her to specify time, place and event, but she was able to say that a major city would experience some kind of fire in the sky with so great an outcome that people would be forced to search their hearts and seek God, asking, "Why?" Aware of such disaster looming, she began to plead with God, as Abraham did for Sodom. She came into God's presence and called out to him, interceding persistently until his Word came to her to stop praying, because the judgement could not be averted. She then asked him what he was saying and doing in so momentous a visitation, and he told her, "It will be a summons to the believers in every nation on the planet to pray for revival in their nation, so that mercy may triumph over judgement."

The church should be at the forefront of asking questions. The church should be praying for revival in every nation too. The prophetic helps us to do both things more urgently.

In the modern world we are tempted to believe there must be a formula or "quick fix" solution for everything; we are impatient to see fast growth and accelerated outcomes. We research ways to make cattle, chickens and orchards grow faster and produce bigger yields – often at the price of cruelty or future degradation of land quality. But in prophetic ministry there is no fast track to maturity. Nor is prophetic ministry a knack to be acquired. The issue is not about "Seven simple ways to prophesy effectively", but rather developing firm convictions about "before whom we stand" and "in whom we minister". Prophecy is a relational ministry and there is nothing mechanical about a good and healthy relationship, especially with God. There are no shortcuts and no techniques, but there are some principles that apply. In considering those principles here, we shall also look back and summarize the material of earlier chapters.

1. Say and do whatever he tells you

If faithfulness to God and to the human community is required of us, then let us resolve to be faithful. Jesus said, "Whoever can be trusted with very little can also be trusted with much, and whoever is dishonest with very little will also be dishonest with much. So if you have not been trustworthy in handling worldly wealth, who will trust you with true riches? And if you have not been trustworthy with someone else's property, who will give you property of your own?" (Luke 16:10). The Lord spells out true faithfulness in three main areas. We must prove ourselves faithful with seemingly unimportant issues before bigger matters will be entrusted to us. How you manage material things and everyday situations is the test of your ability to be trusted with spiritual responsibilities. Finally, the demonstration of a good track record, with delegated responsibilities passed down to us from others, can alone reveal if we're ready for a God-given call to leadership responsibilities of our own. Similarly, God trains prophetic ministry by watching how we handle "little" words of apparently small significance; our daily lives which we sometimes call "secular" and see as of no consequence; and our lessons in learning real accountability to those over us in the Lord.

If we long to grow in prophetic ministry, we have to make progress in faithfulness, after duly testing the validity of what we think God has asked us to do. If it is truly from God, we can throw caution to the wind, refusing to give in to the fear of other people, though genuine uncertainty and doubts are never totally avoidable. The best advice is, "Feel the fear, but do it anyway." Forgiveness is often easier to obtain than permission!

Knowing this, and conscious of his responsibility to a much higher authority, Elijah confronted King Ahab (now completely under the control of his Phoenician wife Jezebel): "As the Lord, the God of Israel lives, whom I serve..." (1 Kings 17:1). That is the key to treading on the fear of opinion – knowing whom you serve. As the apostle Paul said, "If I were still trying to please men, I would not be a servant of Christ" (Galatians 1:10). In Tozer's words, "The man or woman who is intimate with God cannot be intimidated by man."

2. Get into the habit of obeying and acting on God's word

If we fail to take note of genuine prophecies that the Lord has given to us and refuse to deliver them, record them, respond to them, and act upon the words that God has already been giving to us – why would he give us any more? Determine to plot a course of total obedience to God if you are both the recipient of a prophetic word, or the hearer of a prophetic word. God means business, and so should we.

3. Remove the most common obstacles to listening

What kind of things distract and prevent God's people hearing from the Lord?

a) Sinful attitudes

These include anger, envy and bitterness. When these things are seated in our spirits, they colour and distort all our listening and speaking. They cause interference on our spiritual airwaves, making us insensitive to God even when we desperately need to hear from him. We will not see what he is showing us if we are facing in the opposite direction; we need to change our attitude, turn around – repent. Then we will see and hear clearly again.

b) Unhelpful sensory or emotional input

This can produce "static" and prevent us from hearing from God. What we expose our mind to must come under the discipline of faith, including the things we watch and listen to for entertainment. These can pollute the mind. Some television, movies, music, news reports and magazines can leave a nasty taste behind. Every New Year it can take a long time to recover from the Christmas "blahs", after up to ten days or more of overeating, drinking, sleeping late and watching endless hours of TV. It may take up to a fortnight to get back to the right spiritual temperature again. Now imagine that self-indulgence lasting throughout the whole year. It takes thirty to sixty minutes for some individuals to even begin to tune in, during church on Sunday morning. If that's becoming typical for you, then think about what you regularly engage in on most Saturday nights, and how long you stay up, where you go out to and who you were with, and what kind of things went on when you got there. Don't look for any "mysterious" explanations or say, "The devil's really attacking us this morning – did you feel the oppression in the air?" Sometimes it is as practical as this: there's too much static crackling in our minds, so that our spirits are no longer tuned in to the Holy Spirit's wavelength.

c) Prophetic trivia and vulgarity

We may be tempted to trifle and play games with prophetic ministry – God help us! We are not like clairvoyants, palmists and fortunetellers, paid for a performance on demand. We can't set up a booth in the entrance hall with a sign reading, "Hands and Hearts Read", "Scriptures on Request" or "Get your Words of Knowledge Here!" It doesn't work like that. The prophetic ministry can be a lot of fun and very exciting, but it is fundamentally very serious and not meant to be just plain silly. A friend told me that, in the stream of churches to which he belongs, at a recent gathering of prophets one of the prophetic men turned up with his hair dyed blonde, wearing a long, black duster coat, black T-shirt, black trousers and black, shiny leather boots, like a figure from the film *The Matrix*. His prophetic status had clearly gone to his head. Somebody nearby jokingly quipped, "He's been too close to the *Shekinah* – he's got spiritual sunstroke!" Another man at the same event moved around the gathering carrying a sink plunger in his hands and saying, "The Lord wants to get rid of the spiritual blockages in your life, brother." Memorable, but silly. Unlike clairvoyants and palmists, we cannot prophesy to order, nor should we play around with this gifting for the entertainment of others. Don't trivialize it; don't make it appear vulgar or ridiculous. This may only serve to bring authentic prophecy under suspicion, or even into disrepute.

d) Daydreaming and fantasizing

This distracts us from our real purpose, particularly as we fantasize about ourselves, our future ambitions or self-importance, rather than focusing upon God and his deserved glory. Prophecy is concerned with big dreams about God's great kingdom, not little fantasies about our own personal empire. Let's place the focus where it rightly belongs, not upon you and me, but upon God and his kingdom. Then we are likely to hear more accurately from God.

e) Over-indulgence in food, sensual pleasures and intoxicants

These make you sleepy, sluggish or in some ways may even alter your consciousness and lead to ruin, especially over-indulgence with drugs or alcohol rather than being filled with the Holy Spirit (Ephesians 5:18). In the 1940s in the USA, God moved incredibly powerfully in the wake of the Pentecostal movement in what became known as "The Healing Revival", in which tens of thousands of people were healed of astonishing and incurable conditions, leading to hundreds of thousands of conversions. But this level of power was hard to handle with integrity and, when you read the biographies of the leading figures of that movement, it is tragic to find out how many of them were taken out through selfish indulgence and a manipulative exploitation of the advantages that God gave to them. Major ministries collapsed in the midst of great scandal just about everywhere. So beware of pursuing this ministry of prophecy for personal profit, pornography or the praise of other people. Beware of excess and over-indulgence, for they ruin our ability to hear God.

4. Rekindle your dulled imagination

Take time out to be free enough for wonder, for meditation and serious thought. We live in what often appears to be a flat, prosaic and two-dimensional world – everything cynically subjected to the "bottom line" of facts and figures, or suffering from the absence of God who is deemed to be non-existent. But God's world is glorious, vibrant with colour, creativity and joy. In prophecy we traffic with God's transcendence and the magnificence of God's presence, and also discover his down-to-earth immanence in even the smallest details of our daily lives. To grow in prophetic ministry we must observe a Sabbath principle of taking time out with God. Old Testament scholar Walter Brueggemann explains, "Our commitments of all kinds hold us tightly, and keep us so constrained that we have little room for change. Sabbath is an invitation to imagine our life differently. In risking Sabbath, we can discover life can be lived without the control that reduces us and leaves us fatigued." As we step aside from a busy week to be with God's people and to hear from God, we find our imagination cleaned out and sanctified through his word, rekindled through new kinds of images, and stimulated by the power and wisdom of the Bible's Big Story in all of its parts. In God's presence we move into the realm of the real, finding exhilaration and insight.

Millions spend half of their waking lives watching soap operas on TV when they could be caught up in the wonders of forgiveness, healing, transformation and miracles – the work of God that fulfils and satisfies us instead of leaving us empty and purposeless. We owe it to ourselves, as well as to God, to engage wholeheartedly with the Bible story, recovering our sense of mystery, wonder and awe once again.

Prophetic people are meant to be emotionally alive, and not stone-dead. The Greek verb word for "to feel compassion" – *splagchnoiomai* – means to have the experience of such emotion that you feel it in your stomach, liver and intestines – it is a "gut-level" love. St John Chrysostom said, "The glory of God is a human being who is fully alive", and Jesus said, "I have come that they may have life, and have it to the full" (John 10:10). God wants to give us the ability to reach the heights and the depths, to explore new horizons, to cry real tears again and, for that to happen, we need our feelings to be reawakened. As well as allowing the drama and power of the biblical story to touch and move us, it is part of our prophetic discipline to read novels and poetry and to watch films that depict heroism, love, tragedy, courage and vision. So why not let some past and present masters of observation like Shakespeare, John Donne, Fyodor Dostoevsky, Anne Tyler, Annie Dillard, William Trevor, John Steinbeck, Alexander Solzhenitsyn and Charles Dickens fire some of your emotions deeply? Read the short stories of Raymond Carver, Carol Shields and Alice Munro who all portray the hopelessness of American life in the 1950s and 60s and right up to contemporary times, and they may help to move you again as you gain insight into the secularism of recent generations. Let them get to you so that you feel what they feel about lost humanity.

Take time to listen to a wide variety of musical genres – especially live concerts when we can feel the atmosphere and watch the musicians play. This often rekindles the spark of a sanctified imagination and a profound empathy for the human condition. So does spending time with new babies and young children, or those whose lives are ending, and those who are culturally very different from us.

Then tune your imagination to hear from God himself. God feels things too. Walter Brueggemann writes, "The prophet is a voice that shatters present reality and evokes a new possibility in the listening assembly", adding the words of Hans Urs von Balthasar who said, "God needs prophets in order to make himself known and all prophets are necessarily artistic. What a prophet has to say can never be said in mere prose." Think about that, and allow it to help you gain permission to rekindle your emotions and take you on a genuine "mystery tour" beyond the reduced, "nothing buttery", mechanistic and naturalistic worldviews of our secular contemporaries, to a place where your imagination is once again quickened in the same way as the imagination of Abraham was, as he gazed at the stars above the desert, or as Moses felt as he wept over the plight of the Hebrew slaves, or as Elijah was lifted in his spirit as he stood on the mountainside – listening, always listening, beyond the earthquake, the wind and the fire, for the "gentle whisper", the "deep calling to deep" hush of the voice of our tender God.

5. Marinade yourself in the Old Testament, in particular, the prophets

When was the last time you read the minor prophets in their entirety, or waded through bigger books like Isaiah or Jeremiah? To advance in prophetic ministry it is essential to become completely immersed in the prophetic literature of the Bible. Most of the Old Testament is prophetic. When we refer to the books of the prophets in the Bible, we often leave out some scriptures that the ancient Hebrews would have included. For the Hebrews, the history of the people of God was "prophetic history", so they included Joshua, Judges, 1 and 2 Samuel, and 1 and 2 Kings in the category of "The Prophets". How those historical narratives come to life when we see their inspiration in that way! The more we meditate on Scripture, the more our thinking and speaking will absorb and reflect the Word of God, so it is important for us to get to know the key biblical events, the major Bible characters and the overall development and themes of this great story of God and his people.

From 1997 onwards, my home church in Winchester held prayer meetings at six o'clock in the morning, and for the first two years we held these for five mornings a week. I led most of them, beginning each one with a short talk. During the years that we ran those prayer meetings, I gave over 300 ten-minute messages, many of which drew upon the Old Testament narratives and prophetic writings. To prepare for them, I spent a long time in Old Testament books that I had hardly ever ventured into during twenty years of ministry, and I can honestly say that it changed my life. You can't do that morning after morning, as an incentive to help people to pray, and not have it affect you profoundly. Try it.

I understand better, now, the major burdens and concerns of the Old Testament prophets. I had to notice the variety of ways in which they expressed themselves and I was awed at the vivid reality of the pictures they used, the contemporary imagery that captured their minds. As each day went by, I found myself caught up in their changing moods and emotions. Some mornings we all wept copiously together, overwhelmed by the burden of the Word of the Lord that the prophets so powerfully conveyed. I grew closer to God and felt more deeply in awe of him. I learned to be less intimidated by "big" people and more impressed with a "bigger" God, because I caught a glimpse of our finite littleness in the context of God's majestic greatness and glory, as the Old Testament prophets saw him. I understood the way the psalmists exulted extravagantly in the holiness and majesty of God, and lost their fears: What can man do to me? Of whom should I be afraid? And I ceased to feel frightened of the devil or his demons; they seemed very small compared to our creator God. Once I had grasped something of God in his greatness I understood how reduced Satan is in his final defeat at the cross.

Someone once said, "Mystery is not the absence of meaning, but the presence of more meaning than we can comprehend." Sustained meditation upon the Scriptures leads us back to mystery again. Becoming a little more familiar with mystery, I learned to live at peace with paradox, accepting those things that don't seem to make complete logical sense in the Bible (though I'm sure that they do); those elements of Scripture that I can't quite reconcile or that won't allow us to weave them into a neat theological system. I made friends with the wildness of God and began to delight in his grandeur, a wildness that cannot be packaged or domesticated. I no longer fret over the puzzling loose ends connected with the Trinity, God's eternal foreknowledge and his predestination of all things, as well as Christ's deity and humanity, time and its relationship to eternity, and God's holy justice and yet his tender mercy. And I have learned to live with many unanswered questions: the apparent contradictions in things that God has plainly revealed, and the remaining mysteries in my life that I won't fully understand until I get to heaven – *praise God*! The more familiar we become with the perspectives of the prophets, the more we find our vision of God expands. What greater incentive to study them could I give you? If you are continually amazed by God yourself, there will come a time when he uses you to amaze other people too, by the way that you speak of him or minister for him. They will not be impressed with how good you are, but how great God is.

Prophetic ministry energizes amazement as people rediscover who God is in a world that is increasingly losing its power to feel awed or amazed any more. Every genuine prophet is amazed by God. And where best to begin to wonder at his glory than in a slow, careful reading of the Bible as a whole, and particularly the neglected and rugged terrain of the Old Testament for a while.

Without a thorough grounding in Old Testament studies, we miss seeing the full significance of the resonances from them contained in the writings of the New Testament, and therefore fail to catch a great deal of its meaning. As we read the Bible in its entirety, it comes alive before us. In its pages we find the face of God revealed; and he is majestic; he is glorious; he is beautiful. So let the Old Testament prophets penetrate the numbness and despair you see all around you, by relaying to jaded people all around you something of the prophets' vision of God.

6. Submit your messages cheerfully and trustingly to leaders who are over you in the Lord

It is nothing but our own insecurity that makes us hesitate to offer our prophetic words to be weighed. We fear rebuke and rejection; we are afraid of being ridiculed or dismissed. But 1 John 4:18 states, "There is no fear in love. But perfect love drives out fear, because fear has to do with punishment. The one who fears is not made perfect in love." An essential component of growing in prophetic ministry is learning to rest in God, to trust him, to find our security not in always being right, or even in being respected, but in belonging to him, with nothing to fear, nothing to prove and nothing to hide. Learn to weigh and evaluate prophecy properly and submit to others who can help you to do this well. Ask godly leaders to train you in that process. God will grant you wisdom: as James says, "If any of you lacks wisdom, he should ask God, who gives generously to all without finding fault" (James 1:5).

Ask God for wisdom. Find people around you who are consistently prophesying with accuracy. Ask them to offer you some advice. Ask them questions. Invite their input concerning your recent attempts to prophesy, even if they disagree with you. Any disagreement will only sharpen you more and signal to God that he can trust you with even very unusual messages, because you are not too proud to admit you get it wrong sometimes.

Such people will get up again, move on and inevitably grow. When little children attempt to walk as they grow, they inevitably trip up and fall many times. We pick them up and set them on their feet again. Likewise, as we grow in a prophetic ministry we occasionally stumble, but he lifts us up and sets us on our feet to try again. The Father loves to help us to mature. Don't be afraid of your blunders. We all make mistakes; that's how we learn.

7. "Hang out" with prophetic people

Something happens in your spirit when you are exposed to the company of believers with a great prophetic ministry. I am thinking of people like A. W. Tozer, John G. Lake, Ern Baxter, Arthur Wallis and Derek Prince, all of whom are now with the Lord, but whose prophetic Bible teaching ministry is still available in books, CDs or on tape – "he still speaks, even though he is dead" (Hebrews 11:4). Others I could mention who are our contemporaries include Rick Godwin, Steve Nicholson, Jack Deere, Charles Simpson, John Paul Jackson, David Carr, Mark Stibbe, Michael Eaton, Jeff Lucas and Terry Virgo – prophetic teachers all; and there will be others whose ministry you know that speaks especially to your heart. Spend time with this type of teaching and preaching, listening carefully to what these teachers have to say. Anointing is transferable, and we believe in spiritual impartation, so anointing can spill over from them to you in the will of God. Like the high-voltage current running in high-power electricity overhead cable lines, it can arc from one person to another. It did so for Saul when he drew near to the company of the prophets – *whomph!* – and a prophetic mantle came upon him. He wasn't looking for it; he didn't ask for it; but it came anyway (1 Samuel 10:5–12).

Try to become part of a learning environment with other prophetic people if possible, where you can pray for, instruct, correct, encourage and help one another. In prayer meetings, home groups or cell groups, flow in the prophetic – allow the prophetic to be stirred in you. Whether you receive positive feedback ("How did you know that? That's amazing!") or negative ("What was that all about?"), it's all helpful; it's all part of what God uses to cause us to grow. Attend occasional prophetic gatherings and important retreats if you can. Turn up at special training schools and major conferences where the speakers plan to teach in a concentrated way on these themes. Mix with prophetic people in your movement or denomination. *Learn, learn, learn.*

8. Read all you can on prophetic ministry today

Recommended titles are listed at the back of this book and include works by Wayne Grudem, Graham Cooke, Jack Deere, Cindy Jacobs, Bill Hamon, Jim Paul, Mike Bickle and Rick Joyner, among others. You will find areas of overlap that help us to hear what God is saying to the present age, and you will find each voice also offers a unique perspective on prophetic ministry and gifting. Read with intelligence, not with naïvety, remembering that we prophesy only in part – none of us is infallible, and some are more insightful than others. As you read the works of others in this area of prophetic ministry, sense the prompting of God to weigh and sift what you read, for that skill is also a real dimension of your own gifting in God to test things thoroughly and hold on to divinely revealed truth. Look for excellence; look for the word that inspires and convicts. Jack Deere's books are outstanding, and so are Wayne Grudem's, in my opinion, but you will learn invaluable things from all of these dedicated and insightful authors. Read all the prophetical literature you can get your hands on and, if you liked and benefited from them, encourage the authors themselves and recommend their work to others still learning about this gift. Write a letter saying how much you enjoyed their books. Stay a learner for the rest of your life in this realm and *read, read, read* as much as you can. Serious study imparts wisdom to us and it increases faith, because faith comes by hearing the Word of God, and solid instruction derived from it.

9. Be passionate about the things that Christ is passionate about

Prophetic people are wired for action, all-alive, alert in all of their God-given senses. They truly care and they will notice the very things others seem to miss. They really feel passionately about the very same things Christ himself is passionate about: the state and health of the local and wider church, authentic Christian unity, renewal and revival, reformation and word-centred biblical preaching, justice for the poor, seeking and saving the lost, announcing and demonstrating the kingdom of God, enjoying and experiencing God's grace, exposing legalism, heresy and witchcraft in the church, and declaring the freedom and simplicity of the gospel.

In this connection, I want to underline the fact that prophetic people truly love the church as Christ loves the church, and share his passion for the church's mission to a lost and disintegrating world. The so-called para-church prophetic ministry that has no hands-on involvement with the local church and isn't rooted in, or accountable to, it or its leaders, warts and all, is likely to lose its way and become dangerous to itself and to others. We all need the strength and wisdom of a healthy church around us. When the Lord Jesus prophesied to the seven churches in Asia Minor (Revelation 2–3), he was engaging with local churches as their Lord, prophesying into their common life in a thoroughgoing involvement with them, "walking among the candlesticks" of the specific witness of each Christian community in its particular locale. Christ's messengers have to be as involved as he is involved, in order to earn the right to speak and be heard with some degree of credibility by God's people at home or abroad. The sheep listen to the voice of the shepherd, and they run away from a stranger. In the same way the flock of God's people respond to the voice they know, and are rightly wary of those who are just "passing through". So, if there is an aloofness and a negative, couldn't-care-less withdrawal from the church present within you, in connection with the people for whom Christ couldn't care more – then adjust, change, repent and get into a place where you feel, "I am home, I belong, I should be here, this is my church."

A.W. Tozer once said, "So precious is the church in the eyes of God that it is scarcely possible it should ever become too precious in the eyes of men. 'I love thy church, O God', comes immediately after 'I love thee, O Lord'." He also said, "There are various ministries and departments within the church that may seem necessary and make for smoother running of things. But when any department begins to think of itself as a thing apart, unrelated to the local body, it will become a cancer on the church's life and leads to its final destruction." I personally truly love the wider church of Christ. I love the church that meets at Westminster Chapel where I pastor, because God has knitted my heart to them. I am passionate about building the church well, seeing it working as Jesus meant it to. Above all, I love the times when we see, to a greater or lesser degree, the manifestation of God's glory in the church.

This is why zeal for Christ's church is one of the greatest incentives we have to grow in the prophetic, because this is Christ's passion also. The church was purchased with his life-blood (Acts 20:28). You don't want to become a cancer, draining the life out of the body of Christ. You want to become a cure for those cancers, serving in such a way that you help to restore divine health to its community life and grow in your love for it, become more committed to it and serve its mission in every way you can. Prophetic ministry is like every other aspect of Christian ministry in that it inspires us to care about the things Christ cares for – and basically, Christ cares about people.

10. Remain convinced of the importance and value of prophetic gifting and continually seek God for it

The devil will see to it that you come to a place where you eventually question this gifting and even become cynical about it. From time to time this happens, especially when we see so much nonsense claimed for prophecy, and so many abuses carried out in its name, as well as the "wacko" silliness that often accompanies the practice of this gift. Some prophets indulge a flamboyant style of self-display. Others are blatant money-grubbers and, sometimes, crowd-pleasing, glitzy, ostentatious performances and showmanship mark their ministry. This can have the effect of making you want to distance yourself not only from these abusers, but even from the gift itself at times, saying, "I won't have anything more to do with this!"

Then there is the let-down of major disappointments that we have all experienced at some time, so that you grow cynical about the delay in seeing prophetic announcements come to pass. I once asked Dr R.T. Kendall, my predecessor here at Westminster Chapel, "Have you ever had any prophecies spoken over Westminster Chapel?" Understandably, I was curious about that matter as incoming new pastor. I wanted to know what God had already promised to the church or warned it about.

He said, "Prophecies? We've had so many that they are coming out of our ears. *Amazing prophecies!*" He then proceeded to tell me some of them and they were, indeed, truly amazing. He added, somewhat forlornly, "It's waiting to see them come to pass that's the problem." R.T. Kendall finally retired from his ministry at the chapel in February 2002 after twenty-five faithful and very fruitful and influential years, and left the place feeling that he had not yet seen what he had fully expected and longed for at Westminster Chapel. His autobiography, *In Pursuit of His Glory*, fully documents these longings. The title of the book says it all. He has been in pursuit of revival for all of his ministerial life. But none of us dares lose heart. Instead, let us keep looking and waiting, watching and praying. "Hope deferred makes the heart sick", the Scriptures observe in Proverbs 13:12, but, if so, let us stir up the gift of God that is in us and allow God to refuel all of our genuine hopes and revive our pale spirits.

11. Submit your life to scriptural revelation as a whole

I repeat the central emphasis running through the whole of this book, namely, the foundational importance of confidence in the full inspiration, authority and sufficiency of the Bible in its entirety for our beliefs and practices, especially in connection with this ministry of prophecy, since this ministry is so often targeted for delusion or destruction by the devil. Recent decades have seen all kinds of alien elements, emphases and doctrinal aberrations sweep through the church, often at the instigation of those known as "prophets". These include vivid reports and bestselling books about trips to heaven and hell (a questionable boasting in the light of Paul's reticence to speak of such things himself in 2 Corinthians 12:1–6); inordinate interest in the activities of angels and the encouragement of others to court direct dealings with them (*contra* Colossians 2:18–19); the promotion of novel and unscriptural methods of "strategic-level spiritual warfare" that have subtly undermined confidence in Christ and the gospel itself to pull down city-wide spiritual strongholds (which Paul modelled, for example, in Ephesus, where he made no attempt to attack the goddess Diana directly, yet took the city for the Lord – see Acts 19:1–22, and note verse 37); and distorted teachings about God that deny his Trinitarian nature, his predestination and knowledge of future things (*contra* Ephesians 1; Romans 9–11), and his holy wrath against sin and his punishment of it, which requires substitutionary atonement for God's justice to be satisfied and the sinner to be mercifully saved (*contra* Romans 1:18–3:25).

Neglect of the written word of God will actually incapacitate you for the task of bringing pure and weighty *rhema* words of God. It means you will either run out of steam over time, or you will run off into error. Either way, you will become useless.

We need to know the Word of God.

We need to obey the Word of God.

We need to memorise the Word of God.

We need to get "back to the Bible".

12. Stay natural

It is certainly true that God called and used some very colourful and unusual personalities to prophesy to his people in the Bible, individuals such as Elijah, Amos, Ezekiel and Zechariah. Strange as they were, they were all authentically true to themselves and the way God made them. You also are unique, and God knew what he was doing when he chose you to carry his message to his people. Only God can promote you, and only his promotion is worth anything at all. So, when God is not saying anything, you are not saying anything; and when he is, it is good enough as it is – you don't need to dress it up in special phrases or a sepulchral tone of voice; you just deliver it as naturally as you can.

There are three types of "man" in the Bible: the "old man", the "new man", and the "human". When you were born again, it was only the first one that was put to death in Christ – the "old man". The "new man" and the "human" are still to remain very much alive. You are now a new man in Christ Jesus, for "if anyone is in Christ, he is a new creation; the old has gone, the new has come!" (2 Corinthians 5:17). This means that the "human" is made more fully and authentically human now. Redemption restores us. Grace makes you become more "normal" again. When you are filled with the Spirit you at last begin to see your normal, natural self made whole and set free.

It is insecurity and defensiveness that makes people "pump up" ministry into an attention-seeking sideshow. It isn't necessary. The Word of the Lord is enough, and has what it takes to find its target: "Not by might nor by power, but by my Spirit,' says the Lord Almighty" (Zechariah 4:6). And when we go to worship, we don't need to put on a special, holy persona as we step into the church. We are at home here; these people are our family – we can relax and be ourselves. This is essentially about learning to trust God, and also his people.

13. Stay nervous!

You always have been and you always will be dependent on God for effective prophetic ministry. You cannot turn it on, you cannot work it up, and you cannot produce it to order. So let God know that you need him and that you consider yourself nothing without him. Express your dependence upon him. It was said of C.H. Spurgeon that, whenever he entered the massive pulpit of the Metropolitan Tabernacle in London, as he climbed the large winding staircase to the main platform, he would pray on each step, "I believe in the Holy Ghost, I believe in the Holy Ghost..." He stayed in a dependent and nervous mood in each season of his ministry until his death, and that was one of the secrets of his tremendous power. He needed God. Well, if *he* needed God, spiritual giant that he was, then you and I need God also. Therefore, let us decide to remain utterly dependent upon him.

Prophecy relies utterly upon the work of the Spirit in prompting existential revelation from him, and we must resist any external pressure from others to "perform", for example, when we are urged to prophesy over every single person within a large group. God may help us to receive something significant for each one, but perhaps not. We are to prophesy as the Spirit directs and remain silent when he has not given us anything to say. We are never to become mechanical in this ministry; we are to remain Spirit-led and spontaneous.

14. Grow up yourself, as a person

It takes many years for a man or woman of God to mature in their gifts and ministry. Jesus spent thirty years preparing for three years' ministry, a proportion of 10 to 1. We would like it to be the other way round: three years' training for thirty years of ministry. God is not in that kind of hurry with us. The fact is, we are always training, we are always preparing for future usefulness and effectiveness, and we need to cease being childish and become biblically knowledgeable and mature. That would include such matters as being road-tested through difficult trials. None of us would drive vehicles that had not been thoroughly tested over a million miles by the manufacturer, or buy a washing machine from a firm that never ran tests on their products. Even with machinery, it is through repeated testing that safety, reliability and quality are achieved.

God knows exactly what he is doing. He will not break us. His grace is sufficient for us. We are safe in his hands as he repeatedly tests and strengthens, tests and strengthens us – though we may feel unbearably fragile at times. The apostle James wrote, "Consider it pure joy, my brothers, when you face trials of many kinds, because you know that the testing of your faith develops perseverance. Perseverance must finish its work so that you may be mature and complete, not lacking anything" (James 1:2–4).

Alexander Solzhenitsyn said, "Even nature teaches us that perpetual wellbeing is not good for any living thing." And he should know; his life and destiny were forged in the Soviet gulags during the deep sub-zero freezing winters of Siberia. There is an obvious explanation here as to why that man was able to stand up to the might of Joseph Stalin and the Soviet Communist empire, eventually experiencing expulsion from his own native Russia, only to emerge on the world stage as a powerful voice for truth, and freedom from all human tyranny. Where did such great moral fibre emerge from? In loss, deprivation, suffering and testing.

Maturity is also displayed when we become more socially well-adjusted, so that we actually like people and enjoy their company greatly and, for the most part, they also like us. Mature people are able to bear bitter disappointment and handle gracefully those times when we are passed over and ignored, knowing that God is ultimately for us and that our ministry is under his sovereign control in such a way that we can trust him to do the right thing by us, always. Our maturing in Christ is about our whole life and character; it isn't just a Sunday thing. We must be exemplary in our conduct, gentle, courteous and respectful, absolutely trustworthy in our handling of money (our own and other people's), and scrupulously modest and respectful in our dealings with the opposite sex. Power, money and sex have caused so many to stumble. As we move in the prophetic we should be aware that *God is trusting us*. By his grace, may we never let him down.

15. Let God promote you

Scripture encourages us to seek and desire spiritual gifts, but not the position or influence that they may bring. That's up to God. Rick Joyner says, "…every bit of influence we gain from self-promotion or self-seeking will end up being a stumbling block to us. We will end up falling off every platform that we build for ourselves, and the higher we build it, the farther we fall." The evidence that you are seeking spiritual gifts out of selfish motives often shows up in one thing: *striving*. Striving to be noticed; striving for recognition, for applause and for promotion. This is often rooted in past experiences of rejection. Rejection is frequently the lot of prophetic people. At some point or another people will reject you, and it seems to be a regular experience in the background of nearly every prophetic person I know, that they were rejected painfully and hurt. But dwelling on past rejection can make you self-centred and self-conscious instead of God-conscious and other-orientated. And, of course, it can distort your ability to perceive things accurately. Rejection needs to be healed by renewed experiences of the love of God.

This will also deal with any uncovered and unhealed bitterness. In the Old Testament, one of the requirements of the priests who ministered in the tabernacle was that they were to have no scabs on their body (Leviticus 21:20). Scabs are unhealed wounds. They are ugly and irritating, and they can make us ashamed and over-sensitive, as well as resistant to the touch, gaze and company of others. Time, understanding, wise action and the Father's healing love are what we need here, not shutting ourselves away from others or snapping like a wounded animal when anyone comes near. We don't need to prove anything or fight to create and keep a niche for our ministry. God will open the way when we are ready again. We deal with bitterness of rejection by totally forgiving those who have wronged us.

In regard to promotion, remember that, "No one from the east or the west or from the desert can exalt a man. But it is God who judges..." (Psalm 75:6). It has nothing to do with either the impersonal forces of chance or the personal decisions of other people, ultimately. God is totally in charge of our elevation to places of greater usefulness. Joseph learned that, Daniel learned that, and you and I need to learn it also. It is vital that we leave our promotion to God.

The writer to the Hebrews indicates that this was at the heart of both the priestly ministry of the Old Testament and the priestly ministry of Christ himself. He writes, "No-one takes this honour upon himself; he must be called by God, just as Aaron was. So Christ also did not take upon himself the glory of becoming a high priest. But God said to him, 'You are my Son; today I have become your Father.'" (Hebrews 5:4–5). God put him there, and God will put you exactly where he wants you to be. And that conviction lies at the heart of all confident and effective ministry.

16. Seek to cultivate genuine humility

> Your attitude should be the same as that of Christ Jesus: who, being in very nature God, did not consider equality with God something to be grasped, but made himself nothing, taking the very nature of a servant, being made in human likeness. And being found in appearance as a man, he humbled himself and became obedient to death – even death on a cross! Therefore God exalted him to the highest place and gave him the name that is above every name, that at the name of Jesus every knee should bow, in heaven and on earth and under the earth, and every tongue confess that Jesus Christ is Lord, to the glory of God the Father.
>
> Philippians 2:5–11

The point of being a Christian prophet is to represent faithfully the revelation of God in Jesus Christ, and we cannot properly represent that revelation faithfully without humility (Philippians 2:5–11). To be humble means conducting ourselves without arrogance; never treating others with contempt; being willing to listen. It means God can successfully correct you when you are wrong, and can trust you with power because you will not take any of the glory to yourself; otherwise, prophecy becomes corrupted and the power is lost.

Usually, the greater the anointing, the greater the authority and power needed to accompany it. So, Moses received greater revelation than anyone in the Old Testament, and Numbers 12:6–8 tells us that God spoke to him face to face! Perhaps this is also the reason why he was the most humble man on the face of the earth according to Numbers 12:3. Somehow these great privileges carried with them the responsibility to humble himself before God. Similarly, the apostle Paul, because of the extraordinary revelations that he received from the Lord, was also assigned a demonic tormentor – a "thorn in the flesh" – to keep him humble (2 Corinthians 12:1–10).

So it must mean that extraordinary power, revelation and influence are usually given only to those who possess an unusual degree of godly character, especially displayed in their humility. God says quite bluntly, "I will not give my glory to another" (Isaiah 42:8). Humility was vital to the long-term success of these two mighty ministries, those of Moses and Paul. It will also be vital for your ministry also.

Regular prayer cultivates humility, acknowledging our dependence on God "night and day" and drawing close to him (Isaiah 62:6–7; Luke 2:37; 1 Thessalonians 3:10; 2 Timothy 1:3). This includes our groaning and crying out to God: "Help me, Lord", "Give me wisdom in this situation", "Lord, is there anything you want to say here?" – knowing that holy wisdom, not just bright ideas, is what we need. That dependence upon God is a trademark of humility.

Generous giving also displays humility: giving of yourself and your resources for the welfare of others. This ministry is not about you and your personal gains. It is about others and what they can receive from the Lord through you. Paul holds up the model of Christ's selfless service: "You know the grace of our Lord Jesus Christ, that though he was rich, yet for your sakes he became poor, so that you through his poverty might become rich" (2 Corinthians 8:9). Christ's ministry was a giving ministry. It was all about what he could give, not what he could get.

Unwavering faith indicates humility, especially in the face of personal tragedy, or great resistance and opposition. This is one of the striking characteristics of the two witnesses described in Revelation 11:3–6, who so faithfully prophesied to their contemporaries that they faced a martyr's death and their bodies were eventually abused and abandoned in the streets. They proved faithful unto death. Similarly, in Revelation 12:11, others just like them are said to be able to overcome the "great dragon" "by the blood of the Lamb and by the word of their testimony", and also because "they did not love their lives so much as to shrink from death". That is unwavering faith. This humility is going to mark many of the "Last Days" prophetic people whom God will raise up.

17. Cultivate a growing sympathy with God

This will mean that our lives and the orientation of our minds and hearts synchronize gradually with God's own heartbeat. Zephaniah tells us that God rejoices and sings over his people (Zephaniah 3:17). Do you feel the heartbeat of God? Do you ever feel such delight in God's people? Do you love to be with them? A.W. Tozer once wrote, "The key to spiritual progress is to find out what God wants and then to love it, and to find out what God hates and then to hate it." Do you love the things God loves and hate the things God hates? Prophetic people become angry about the things God is angry about. They are excited about the things that God is excited about.

And one final word. Prophetic people need to draw as close to God as they can possibly be, in order to hear from him as clearly as they can. We need to soak in God's presence. E. Stanley Jones, a missionary to India, stated, "Prayer is time – exposure of the soul to God." Thérèse of Lisieux observed, "Prayer, after all, arises from our incompetence; otherwise there is no need of it." Both the church and the world greatly need the presence and activity of people who are marked in this way, people who are unafraid to listen, unafraid to hear and unafraid to speak exactly what God wants spoken into situations of great jeopardy, discouragement and confusion. And one day, the world and the church will hear them to great effect. Some of the greatest contemporary opponents and critics of authentic prophetic ministry, in the wider church today, will live to thank God for its clear restoration and operation in their churches, communities and nations.

God's timing will eventually arrive for prophetic people everywhere, as this gift matures and deepens. This possibility constitutes, for us all, both a responsibility and a call to prepare and ready ourselves for that time. In the eighth century BC, God called a stunned and spiritually overwhelmed priest, routinely attending to his duties and serving in the temple in Jerusalem. He was summoned to embark upon what would eventually involve decades of outstanding but highly controversial and strongly opposed prophetic ministry, most of which was largely rejected in his lifetime. This call was also a mandate to display incalculable courage and endurance in the face of that opposition. In a shattering encounter with Yahweh in all of his transcendent power and glory, an encounter that involved both the shattering and disintegration, then the repair and reintegration, of Isaiah's inner soul and personality, God asked him: "Whom shall I send? And who will go for us?" (Isaiah 6:8). Isaiah's response to that question changed the whole course of his future ministry and life, as well as the future of his nation. Indeed, it ultimately helped change world history.[17]

Most certainly, God continues to ask the same question of chosen individuals all over the world. Surely, the crucial issue that still remains to be answered must be: *"Is anybody really listening?"*

Recommended Reading

Considering the importance attached to prophetic ministry in both the Old and New Testaments, it is surprising how little reading material is available on the nature, practice and validity of prophecy today, other than works giving an introduction to the Old Testament and to Old Testament prophecy, as well as many significant commentaries on the canonical prophets. At times, even some of this material is lightweight and patchy, and so offers little substantial help. Below are some of my recommendations, all of which contain insightful, thoughtful, practical and frequently scholarly material.

Old Testament Prophecy

Walter Brueggemann, *The Prophetic Imagination*, Philadelphia: Fortress Press, 1978

Walter Brueggemann, *Hopeful Imagination: Prophetic Voices in Exile*, London: SCM Press, 1992

Robert B. Chisholm Jr, *Handbook on the Prophets*, Baker Academic, 2002

Hobart E. Freeman, *An Introduction to the Old Testament Prophets*, Chicago: Moody, 1968

Greg Haslam, Elisha – *A Sign and a Wonder*, Kingsway Publications, 1995

Greg Haslam, *A Radical Encounter With God*, New Wine Ministries, 2007

Abraham Heschel, *The Prophets*, New York: Perennial, 2001

Walter C. Kaiser Jr, *Back Toward the Future*, Grand Rapids, MI: Baker Book House, 1989

Willem A. VanGemeren, *Interpreting the Prophetic Word*, Grand Rapids, MI: Zondervan, 1990

New Testament Prophecy, Yesterday and Today

David Aune, *Prophecy in Early Christianity and the Ancient Mediterranean World*, Grand Rapids, MI: Eerdmans, 1982

John Bevere, *Thus Saith the Lord*, Lake Mory, FL: Creation House, 1999

Mike Bickle, *Growing in the Prophetic*, Eastbourne: Kingsway, 1995

David K. Blomgren, *Prophetic Gatherings in the Church*, Portland, OR: Bible Press, 1979

D.A. Carson, *Showing the Spirit: A Theological Exposition of 1 Corinthians 12–14*, Carlisle: Paternoster, 1995

Graham Cooke, *Developing Your Prophetic Gifting*, Tonbridge: Sovereign World, 1994

William DeArteaga, *Quenching the Spirit: Examining Centuries of Opposition to the Moving of the Holy Spirit*, Lake Mary, FL: Creation House, 1992

Jack Deere, *Surprised by the Power of the Spirit*, Grand Rapids, MI: Zondervan, 1993

Jack Deere, *Surprised by the Voice of God*, Grand Rapids, MI: Zondervan, 1996

Jack Deere, *The Beginner's Guide to The Gift of Prophecy*, Ann Arbor, MI: Servant Publications, 2001

Michael Eaton, *The Gift of Prophetic Teaching*, Tonbridge: Sovereign World, 2008

Gordon D. Fee, *God's Empowering Presence*, Peabody, MA: Hendrickson, 1994

Ernest B. Gentile, *Your Sons and Daughters Shall Prophesy*, Grand Rapids, MI: Chosen Books, 1999

Wayne Grudem, *The Gift of Prophecy in 1 Corinthians*, Washington, DC: University Press of America, 1982

Wayne Grudem, *The Gift of Prophecy in the New Testament and Today*, Eastbourne: Kingsway, 1988

Wayne Grudem (ed.), *Are Miraculous Gifts for Today? Four Views*, Leicester: IVP, 1996

Bill Hamon, *Prophets and Personal Prophecy*, Shippensbury, PA: Destiny Image, 1987

Bill Hamon, *Prophets and the Prophetic Movement*, Shippensbury, PA: Destiny Image, 1990

Bill Hamon, *Prophets, Pitfalls and Principles*, Shippensbury, PA: Destiny Image, 1991

Greg Haslam (General Editor), *Preach the Word*, Tonbridge: Sovereign World, 2006

Clifford Hill, *Prophecy Past and Present*, Eagle, 1989

Graham Houston, *Prophecy Now*, Leicester: IVP, 1989

Cindy Jacobs, *The Voice of God*, Ventura, CA: Regal Books, 1996

Rick Joyner, *The Prophetic Ministry*, Charlotte, NC: Morning Star Publications, 1997

Peter Lord, *Hearing God*, Grand Rapids, MI: Baker Book House, 1988

David Pytches, *Prophecy in the Local Church*, London: Hodder and Stoughton, 1993

James Ryle, *The Hippo in the Garden*, Guildford: Highland, 1992

Steve Samson, *You Can Hear the Voice of God*, Tonbridge: Sovereign World, 1993

Mark Stibbe, *Know Your Spiritual Gifts*, London: Hodder and Stoughton, 1997

Mark Stibbe, *Prophetic Evangelism*, Milton Keynes: Authentic, 2004

Notes

1   *New Bible Dictionary* (Second Edition), Leicester: IVP

2   Philip Greenslade, *Leadership: Reflections on Biblical Leadership Today*, Farnham: CWR, 2002

3   Francis Frangipane, *The Three Battlegrounds*, Tonbridge: Sovereign World, ch. 18

4   1963 letter from jail in Birmingham, Alabama

5   Philip Greenslade, *Leadership: Reflections on Biblical Leadership Today*, Farnham: CWR, 2002

6   Robert Brow, *Twentieth Century Church*, Bribe Island, Queensland: Victory Press, 1970

7   Mike Bickle, *Growing in the Prophetic*, Eastbourne: Kingsway Publications, 1995, pp.183–191

8   *Strong's Exhaustive Concordance* with Hebrew and Chaldee Dictionary (Reprint), Grand Rapids, MI: Baker Book House, 1977, entry 5197, p. 78

9   I am simply reporting what the Lord did to free one woman to let her personality shine through. Many faithful Christian women – especially among such groups as Brethren, Mennonites and Plain Quakers – see jeans (or any kind of trousers) on a woman as anti-biblical and wear their hair covered or tied back in a bun, or don high-necked, sober-coloured, loose-fitting long dresses for reasons of testimony and conviction. They believe that the Lord has spoken to them and is clearly leading them against their own personal preference into covering their heads and dressing in this way, as the lady in my story was dressed when first I saw her. I mean no disrespect here towards the way the Lord speaks to and deals with others. We have liberty of conscience on such matters (Romans 14:13–23).

10 Source of quote unknown, though sometimes attributed to Black Elk of the Oglala Sioux

11 Robert K. Greenleaf, "The Servant as Leader", original essay

written in 1970 and foundational to the now widely respected servant-leader life and business philosophy

12 Source unknown

13 "I like John Stott's blending of vision and action: 'The world can be won for Christ by evangelism and made more pleasing to Christ by social action. People of vision need to become people of action.' Vision is compounding a deep dissatisfaction of what is and a clear grasp of what could be. It is an understanding which leads to indignation over the status quo and a growing into an earnest quest for an alternative." Quotation taken from "Translating A.J. Gordon's Global Vision into Globalization: A Look Ahead",by R.Judson Carlberg in *Stillpoint* (the magazine of Gordon College), Fall 2005, pp. 14–15.

14 *Strong's Exhaustive Concordance* (Compact Edition), reprinted by Baker Book House, 1977, dictionary entry 2656, p.42

15 J.H. Thayer, *A Greek–English Lexicon* (Fourth Edition), reprinted by Baker Book House, 1977, p.539

16 Alec Motyer: *A Scenic Route Through the Old Testament*, Leicester: IVP, 1994, p.79

17 *See* Greg Haslam, *A Radical Encounter With God*, New Wine, 2007